THE MYTH OF RELIGIOUS NEUTRALITY

THE MYTH OF
RELIGIOUS NEUTRALITY

An Essay on the Hidden Role of
Religious Belief in Theories

Roy A. Clouser

UNIVERSITY OF NOTRE DAME PRESS

NOTRE DAME   LONDON

Library of Congress Cataloging-in-Publication Data

Clouser, Roy A., 1937–
    The myth of religious neutrality : an essay on the
hidden role of religious belief in theories / Roy A.
Clouser.
        p.   cm.
    Includes bibliographical references and index.
    ISBN 0-268-01390-X
    1. Religion.   2.   Theory (Philosophy)
3.   Religion—Philosophy   4.   Religion and
science—1946–   I.   Title.
BL48.C554   1991
200'.1—dc20   90-50928
                                                    CIP

This book is affectionately dedicated to
Herman Dooyeweerd (1894–1977)
and
my dear wife, Anita

CONTENTS

FOREWORD

This book offers a radical reinterpretation of the general relations between religion, science, and philosophy.

Despite the fact that the idea of those relations which is defended here is virtually unknown among professionals in these three areas, it is not historically new. It can trace its lineage through the thought of John Calvin and back to the Bible itself. However, it is an element of Calvin's thought that has not been preserved by the Protestant tradition, and is based on biblical teaching that has received short shrift by the vast majority of Jewish and Christian thinkers. Nevertheless, after undergoing a renaissance led by the Dutch Calvinists Groen Van Prinsterer and Abraham Kuyper in the nineteenth century, the idea was given an impressive development in the work of the twentieth-century philosophers Dirk Vollenhoven and Herman Dooyeweerd.

It is the thought of Dooyeweerd in particular that is reflected here, and is introduced in a way that will be especially valuable to those not already acquainted with its Dutch Calvinist background.

I am grateful to a number of people who have read the manuscript in part or whole and who made valuable suggestions for its improvement. These include Johan Vander Hoeven (Free University of Amsterdam), James `Ross (University of Pennsylvania), Grady Spires (Gordon College), Danie Strauss (University of the Orange Free State, Bloemfontein), Paul Helm (University of Liverpool), Hendrik Hart (Institute for Christian Studies, Toronto), Rev. Richard Russell (St. Thomas a Becket Church, Bath), Jonathan Gold (West Liberty State College), Martin Rice (University of Pittsburgh), James W. Skillen (Association for Public Justice, Washington, D.C.), and Carole Roos, my editor at Notre Dame.

Others were also of aid and comfort in their own special way: Dr. Charles Stephenson, Dale and Lorraine Fleming, the late Bea

xi

Shemeley, John and Audrey Van Dyk, Gil Hunter, Arnold Olt, and the late Peter Steen.

I also wish to express my thanks to several institutions for their support at various stages of the research and writing: to the University of Pennsylvania for a Harrison Fellowship, to the Free University of Amsterdam for two travel grants, and to the Institute for Advanced Christian Studies and the Andreas Foundation for writing grants.

But above all, I want to express my deepest gratitude to the two people whose help was of the greatest significance to this work. The first is the late Herman Dooyeweerd, who endured lengthy conferences with me at his home, two to three times a week, for a total of four months; the second is my dear wife, Anita, whose initial editing of the entire manuscript was invaluable. It is to them that this work is affectionately dedicated.

1
INTRODUCTION

To what extent does religious belief make a difference to the ways people understand and conduct their lives?

The popular answer is that it all depends on how religious a person is. It makes virtually no difference at all for an atheist, while a fanatic thinks and cares about little else. For the majority between these two extremes, religion deals mostly with a person's eternal destiny rather than with this present life, outside of providing moral guidance and comfort in the face of death. But most of the affairs of day-to-day life are indifferent to religious belief.

As a result of investigating religious belief and its influences for over thirty years, I have become convinced that these popular opinions are completely mistaken. Instead, I find that religious belief is the most influential of all beliefs, and the most powerful force in the world. Religious belief has the most decisive influence on everyone's understanding of the major issues of life across the entire spectrum of human experience. Moreover, it exercises this influence upon all people independently of their conscious acceptance or rejection of the religious traditions with which they are acquainted.

The enormous influence of religious beliefs remains, however, largely hidden from casual view; its relation to the rest of life is like that of the great geological plates of earth's surface to the continents and oceans. The movement of these plates is not apparent to a casual inspection of any particular landscape and can only be detected with great difficulty. Nevertheless, so vast are these plates, so stupendous their power, that their visible effects—mountain ranges, earthquakes, and volcanic eruptions—are but tiny surface blemishes compared with the force of the mighty plates themselves. Similarly, the great historic traditions of religious teaching, and the institutions devoted to their preservation, are merely the surface effects of religious belief which is a vaster and more pervasive force than all of them put together.

Among the reasons this influence is so often missed is that people are prone to two alluring mistakes about religious belief. One is to suppose that all the major religious traditions are basically like their own. The other is to suppose that the likenesses between religious traditions must lie in their most obvious and outstanding features. These two mistakes serve to keep hidden from view the true nature of religious belief, and thus most of its influence.

Our first task, then, will be to define the nature of religious belief by seeking features which the great religious traditions—and many lesser ones—have in common. The definition we arrive at will strike many people as surprising because it includes a number of beliefs not usually considered religious since they do not result in worship. For those under the spell of the two natural mistakes just mentioned, this definition may seem strange and suspicious. In fact, however, one of its greatest contributions lies in showing us why not all religious beliefs need have rituals or even ethical codes connected with them. Though surprising, this discovery is of enormous benefit as the first step toward exposing the vast array of unsuspected connections between the issues usually supposed to be religiously neutral and the religious beliefs which actually direct them.

In speaking of religious belief as the most pervasive of all beliefs I do not mean to suggest that we speak our native tongue or add a column of figures differently depending on our religion. Speaking and counting usually take place at a level of experience where our activities and our acquaintance with the world around us are remarkably the same for all people. But there is a deeper level of understanding which humans have always sought, the level at which the nature of our world and ourselves is interpreted and explained. In our culture, that level has long been thought to be attained through *theories*. It is by the theories of philosophy and the sciences that we try to explain all that we experience.

The central claim of this book is that all such theories cannot fail to be regulated by a religious belief of some kind.

To many readers this claim will be not merely surprising but outrageous. Scientific theories, especially, are supposed to be the most neutral and unbiased explanations of all. Such a claim may therefore tempt some readers to think that I cannot possibly mean it literally. So let me assure you that I am not overstating it now, only to water it down later. I will not, for example, argue that all theories have *unprovable* assumptions, call these assumptions "faith," and then conclude that religious faith in that way influences theories. That would be a huge waste of time. Everyone in philosophy and the sciences knows that theories have unprovable assumptions. But a belief is not religious just because it is unprovable.

Nor will I argue that theory making is influenced by the moral beliefs of the theorist, and then try to connect (or equate) religion with morality. There are notable instances of moral influences on theorizing, and some are cases in which the morality was directly derived from a religious tradition. But that is not at all the sort of thing intended by this claim. Nor will I be defending the oft-suggested view that philosophy and science are limited in what they can explain, so that religious beliefs fill in the gaps left over by theories. I am not claiming merely that theories in this way "leave room" for faith.

Rather, I will contend that one religious belief or another controls theory making in such a way that *the contents of the theories differ depending on the contents of the religious belief they presuppose.* In fact, so extensive is this religious influence that virtually all the major disagreements between competing theories in the sciences and in philosophy can ultimately be traced back to differences in their religious presuppositions.

This means that theories about math and physics, sociology and economics, art and ethics, politics and law can never be religiously neutral. They are all regulated by some religious belief. The effects of religious beliefs therefore extend far beyond providing the hope for life after death or influencing moral values and judgments. By controlling theory making, they produce important differences in the interpretation of issues that range over the whole of life.

This position is bound to provoke stiff resistance from many quarters. And doubtless one of the strongest objections will be directed against my claim that religious belief exercises its influence over *everyone,* for this is to claim that everyone really has some religious belief, despite the fact that many people say that they neither have nor want one. On this matter I must once more disagree with the prevailing popular opinion, which accepts that those who claim to have no religious belief really do not have any. After all, they should know whether or not they have one, shouldn't they? And isn't it just obvious that there are people who are totally nonreligious?

My answer is a firm "No." This popular view appears plausible only because of the two mistakes cited earlier. If religious belief must involve worship and creedal adherence, then certainly there are many people without it. However, once the definition of religious belief is made clear, and its involvement in theories exposed, it becomes quite plausible that people may have such a belief without knowing it and without ever engaging in worship. All the same, I do not attempt to prove that all people are innately religious. The project here is more modest, but still significant. What will be demonstrated is that no abstract explanatory theory can fail to presuppose a religious belief. This being the case, we may say that *it is only possible for a person to have no religious belief whatever if he or she does not believe any theory whatever!*

Let me briefly outline how I propose to defend such a seemingly hopeless cause.

After defining religious belief, we will take a hard look at what goes on in theory making, develop a definition of what a theory is, distinguish some major types of theories, and describe several components which are unavoidable for any theory whatever. We will review the more popular ideas of how religious belief and theories are thought to relate, and then clarify how religious belief in fact exercises its influence over theories. To demonstrate this influence at work, we will survey a casebook of illustrations which examines major theories in math, physics, and psychology. In each case we will find that the disagreements among the major competing theories in these fields are ultimately due to the differences among the religious beliefs presupposed in those theories.

The discovery of this relation between religious belief and theory making is not merely a matter of intellectual curiosity, but is of enormous importance. If theories differ according to the religious beliefs controlling them, then those of us who believe in God should have distinctive theories from those who do not share our biblical Faith. It is for this reason the book concludes with blueprints for constructing or reinterpreting theories so as to bring them under the control of belief in God. These include guidelines for a theory of reality, a theory of society, and a political theory, all of which consciously attempt to make the Judeo-Christian idea of God their controlling presupposition.

I want to make it clear, therefore, that the primary intent of this book is not to convert unbelievers or to refute atheism, agnosticism, or secular humanism. Insofar as such "isms" are mentioned at all, the references to them are always secondary to my main purpose. This book is addressed to those who believe in God. I write here as a Christian seeking to persuade my brothers and sisters in the religious family of those who serve the God of Abraham, Isaac, and Jacob that their faith mandates a distinct perspective for the interpretation of every aspect of life. And this distinct perspective extends to the construction and/or reinterpretation of philosophical and scientific theories, so that there is no area or issue of life which is neutral with respect to our faith.

I realize this is not a position which is held by the majority of Jews and Christians, despite the fact that the Bible writers themselves repeatedly teach that all knowledge depends on having the right God. The failure to grasp this fact has resulted in a long history of the Judeo-Christian community's unwitting acceptance of theories that are actually incompatible with its biblical faith. For example, the loss of this insight is responsible for much of the confusion over how to view the relation between science and biblical religion. The position defended here will make clear why it is not true that science and religion are by nature opposed to one another. Much of the supposed opposition of biblical religion and science has resulted from the fact that a great deal of theorizing— even by Jews or Christians—has been done under the undetected control of some nonbiblical religious belief.

The discussion begins at an introductory level. It assumes the reader to have no previous knowledge of philosophy, only a smattering of high school science, and to be basically confused about religion. As the book progresses, however, each succeeding chapter does assume what has been explained in previous chapters, so that it will not be possible to understand the position defended here if the chapters are read out of their order. Even at its most advanced level, however, the more technical points of argument are kept out of the text itself and are reserved for the notes. Remaining at a level accessible to the nonprofessional means that many points are left in need of more thorough analysis and argument. Although this is frustrating, it does allow the position as a whole to be conveyed. My hope is that the treatment afforded the major issues will be at least sufficient to make clear how they are interpreted, and the lines along which those interpretations can be defended.

Despite the limitations of starting at an introductory level, I hope this work will be sufficient to sensitize even the more sophisticated readers to the great influence of religious belief and to encourage those who believe in God to hold this position and work together to promote it.

PART 1
Religion

2

WHAT IS RELIGION?

1. The Problem

Defining 'religion' is notoriously difficult. The word is used in a large number of ways: it is applied to rituals, organizations, beliefs, doctrines, and feelings as well as to large-scale traditions such as Hinduism, Taoism, Judaism, Christianity, and Islam. Moreover, the very subject of religious belief is always emotionally charged. This sensitivity is natural since religion concerns people at the deepest level of their convictions, values, and feelings.

To help minimize these difficulties, let us keep two thoughts firmly in mind as we proceed. The first is that we are not now trying to establish which religions are true or false, right or wrong. We are trying to arrive at an understanding of what religion—any religion—*is.* The second thing to remember is that we will be focusing on one particular use of the term 'religion', and that is as it applies to *belief.* Our search for a definition of religion, then, will mean a search for what distinguishes a religious belief from a belief which is not religious. This is the key issue, for it is religious *beliefs* which prompt and guide the practices, rites, rituals, and attitudes we commonly call "religious."

What, then, is a religious belief? Consider the question this way. We all have literally thousands of beliefs about thousands of things. At this moment, for example, I believe myself to be the blood relative of certain other people; I believe $1 + 1 = 2$; I believe next Friday is payday, and I believe there was a civil war in England in the 1640s. While most people would probably agree that none of these are religious beliefs, the ancient Pythagoreans regarded $1 + 1 = 2$ as a religious belief! So we need to know what makes one belief religious and another not, and how it is that the same belief can be religious to one person and not to another.

9

As we proceed, we must also keep in mind what any definition must do if it is to avoid being arbitrary. A non-arbitrary definition must state the set of characteristics shared only by the things of the type being defined. Traditionally, the way of obtaining such definitions has been to inspect a number of things of the type to be defined and try to isolate just the combination of characteristics which are true of them and only them. This is a difficult thing to do even for objects we can inspect—like computers or chairs—but it is even tougher for abstractions and for ideas such as religious beliefs.

However, it is generally acknowledged that people can recognize various types of things prior to their being able to define them. We all know a lot of things are trees, for instance, long before we are capable of the difficult task of analyzing exactly the characteristics which are possessed by all trees, but only trees. So the process of defining may start out by examining a limited sampling of the things to be defined. In other words, we can start with items everyone agrees are trees or lilies or whatever, leaving out borderline and controversial cases.

It seems to me that it is relatively easy to make a "short list" which virtually everyone would concede to contain only religions. To begin with, surely Judaism, Christianity, and Islam, along with Hinduism, Buddhism,[1] and Taoism, can safely be placed on the list. Moreover, I can think of no good reason why anyone should doubt that belief in the ancient Greek Olympian gods, the Greek mystery cults, the beliefs and worship associated with the Roman pantheon, Egyptian polytheism, or Palestinian belief in and worship of Ba'al were also religions. Nor does it seem to me objectionable that teachings which have never generated a large following can still count as religions—the ancient Epicureans' beliefs and teachings about the gods, for example.

In fact, there seems to be a sizeable uncontroversial short list which further includes Druidism, the beliefs and worship centering on Isis and Mithra, Zoroastrianism, Shintoism, and a host of other candidates as well. What, after all, could be the reason for refusing to acknowledge that they are religions? They are (or were) all regarded as such by their adherents. And the adherents of at least the majority of them readily acknowledged others on the list to be alternative—or even competing—religions.

But despite the availability of an uncontroversial list of religious beliefs, it has proven exceedingly vexing to extract anything they, and only they, share in common. To illustrate this, let us now take a brief look at how some of the most widely accepted definitions fare when applied to the traditions on our short list. We will start with some currently popular ideas, and then look at a few of the most influential scholarly proposals.

One of the most popular ideas is that all religious beliefs include an ethical code of some sort, so that they all provide moral direction for life. Although this belief sounds very plausible, there are religions on the short list which do not include any ethical teaching at all. Ancient Epicureanism, for instance, seems to have made no connection between belief in the gods it acknowledged and moral duties to one's fellow humans. According to the Epicureans, the gods had no concern whatever for human affairs, so a person could be morally rotten for all the gods cared. Another example of this same lack is the Japanese Shinto religion. Moreover, some non-religious teachings and traditions such as the Boy Scout manual have included moral codes. This is enough to show that even if all religions did provide ethical teachings, that feature alone would not be sufficient to distinguish a religious belief from those which are not religious.

Not all religious beliefs inspire worship, either. The ancient Epicureans mentioned above are examples once again. According to them, the gods care nothing about the world, so the fact that gods exist is simply interesting to humans, but nothing personal. The Epicureans thought we could not help but admire the gods, just as we admire a starry night, but that it would make no more sense to direct praise or prayer to the gods than it would to the stars. Even today, there are forms of Hinduism and Buddhism in which there is no worship.

Possibly the most popular definition of all is that religion is belief in a Supreme Being. Many people seem to think this not only covers all religions, but they suspect that all religions worship the *same* Supreme Being under different names. But not all the traditions on our short list include belief in a Supreme Being. In Hinduism, for example, the divine (Brahman-Atman) is not considered "a being." It is instead the being-ness, or "being-itself" which is in all individual beings and which makes them possible.

For this same reason Brahman-Atman cannot strictly be called a god, since a god is always an individual and is personal. Buddhism goes even further. It denies that the divine is being-itself and insists it is nonbeing or Nothingness. So although these religions all believe in some divinity, they do not believe the divine is a Supreme Being—or even a being at all.

Surprisingly, some of the most widely accepted scholarly attempts to define religion do not fare much better than the popular ones. One of the most influential of these was that of Paul Tillich, who declared religious belief or faith to be identical with "ultimate concern."[2] This expression is supposed to bare the bones of all religions. Tillich contended that all people are ultimately concerned about something, and their state of being ultimately concerned about something is their religion.

But just what does it mean to be "ultimately concerned" with something? The most plausible way to understand the expression "ultimate concern" is to take it as referring to the state of being concerned about whatever is ultimate. This, to be sure, sounds like what we usually think of as religion, and there is reason to think it is close to what Tillich himself intended.[3] But even on this interpretation there is still the problem of how we are to define 'ultimate' so as to know which beliefs and concerns are about what is ultimate and are thus religious.

Tillich identifies the ultimate with "the holy" and "the divine,"[4] but of course that is not much help. (What do those terms mean?) However, he does add that what is *truly* ultimate—the only right object of ultimate concern—is "being-itself," or "the infinite."[5] Moreover, he makes it clear that whatever is infinite in his sense must be unlimited in such a way that there could be nothing else in addition to it. He thinks that if someone were to say that God is ultimate but also believe that God is one being and the universe another, then God would be limited by what he is not. In that case God would not be infinite, and thus not really ultimate. The result of this, Tillich says, is that anyone ultimately concerned with that sort of god (a god who is a being rather than being-itself) would be putting his or her faith in something which is not really ultimate and would therefore have false faith.[6]

By understanding 'ultimate' in this way, Tillich's definition of faith turns out to be too narrow. Rather than finding a common element to all religious beliefs, Tillich lapses into prescribing his version of what *true* religion is. Thus he fails to give a meaning to 'ultimate' which can allow for false as well as true religious belief. For if religious faith is being concerned about the ultimate in his sense, then anyone whose concern with anything which is not the infinite "being-itself" simply has no religious faith whatever. Tillich has therefore actually defined faith so that only his idea of true faith is faith at all. So whether his idea of *true* religion is right or wrong is beside the point just now, because it is a fact that there are religions which do not believe in anything that is ultimate in his sense.

Tillich was, of course, aware of this objection but he failed to realize that it is lethal to his definition. He tried to sidestep its significance by suggesting that those religions which are concerned with something which is not infinite intend their concern to be for the infinite but fall short. His sidestep amounts to saying that true religion is concern or belief which *succeeds* in being directed to the infinite, while false religion is concern which *intends* to be directed to the infinite and misses. But this just will not do. Clearly the biblical religions—Judaism, Christianity, and Islam—hold to the doctrine of creation found in Genesis. They do not therefore intend to believe in anything that is infinite in Tillich's sense. Instead, they deliberately put their faith in God, who is a personal being distinct from the universe. They hold that the universe depends on God for its existence because God brought it into being out of nothing, not because it is part of God. Thus, "ultimate concern," as Tillich defines it, is not a characteristic of these religions and so cannot be essential to the definition of all religious belief.

Another influential scholarly definition is this:

> Religion is the varied symbolic expression of, and appropriate response to, that which people deliberately affirm as being of unrestricted value for them.[7]

In other words, whatever is unrestrictedly valued is therefore regarded as divine, so that belief in it is a religious belief. The fact is, however, that although most religious traditions do value proper relation to the divine above all else, there are some that do not. The Epicureans mentioned earlier are an example. They believed in the gods without attaching any particular value to them, and most certainly did not value them unrestrictedly.

Finally, let us consider the proposal of William Tremmel who begins with the warning that he is not seeking an essential definition of religious belief. Instead, he says, he will construct a definition which combines a description of the functional elements of religion ("what religion *does*"), with a description of religious experience. Here is what Tremmel proposes:

   I. Religion is a complex form of human behavior whereby a person (or community of persons) is prepared intellectually and emotionally to deal with those aspects of human existence which are horrendous and nonmanipulable.

   II. Doing so from the conviction that there is at the center of human experience, and even of all reality, a being, or beings, or process (a divine Reality) in which and through which a person (or community of persons) can transcend the life-negating traumas of human existence, can overcome the sense of finitude.

   III. And doing so by the employment of various religious techniques: (a) a belief system (myths, doctrines, and theologies); (b) a ritual system (reverent behavior and dramatic performances); (c) a moral system (ethical doctrines and rules).

   IV. With all this (and especially in the conviction that there is a divine order basic to life) religion turns out to be not simply a method for dealing with religious problems (those horrendous, nonmanipulable circumstances of life), but also is itself an experience of great satisfaction and immense personal worth. Religion is not only something people "do" and "use"; it is also something that happens to them. It is an experience—a highly treasured experience, and even, at times, an experience of sheer ecstasy.[8]

While our primary concern here is with his characterization of religious belief rather than the description of the whole of religion, Tremmel ties the two together in such a way that they cannot be considered separately. The only thing he says about religious belief, other than saying it is the belief which motivates the practices he describes, is that it is belief in "a divine reality." And we are not told what 'divine' means. Thus we are left with having to make out the difference between religious and nonreligious belief solely by his description of the experience which gives rise to it and the practices it inspires. The result is that despite all the complexity of his description, it is still too narrow because it fails to apply to all religions.

Let us first consider Tremmel's characterization of religious experience. We are told that this is an experience of great personal worth and satisfaction—even ecstacy. The trouble with this description is that it could just as well apply to the experience of winning a sports event, receiving a standing ovation for performing a piece of music, or making love. As to the functional parts of the definition ("the way people behave"), it should be noticed that the "techniques" which people actually use to deal with what is "horrendous and nonmanipulable" also include psychotic withdrawal, drugs, and suicide. Consequently, this description is insufficient to distinguish religious techniques from techniques that are not religious unless psychosis and suicide count as religion.

Finally, I must also take issue with Tremmel's characterization of the divine as that which makes it possible for people to "transcend" all that is "life-negating," that is, everything that spoils our life, especially death. This is true of some religious beliefs, but certainly not all. In Judaism, Christianity and Islam, for example, God is said to offer believers forgiveness from the sin which now spoils this life, and the defeat of death by their resurrection from the dead to everlasting (sinless) life. But in the Hindu and Buddhist traditions something very different prevails. In many branches of these religions it is believed that individual, conscious life *must* include suffering, so that the only release from suffering is precisely to negate one's individual life and consciousness. In these traditions reincarnation is a curse, not a hope, and the goal of the pious is to cease being reborn by having their individual life and consciousness annihilated. In other words, according to the Hindu and Buddhist traditions, standing in right relation to the divine is the means by which the total negation of this life is accomplished rather than overcome.

Furthermore, it is objectionable that Tremmel characterizes the divine as that by which we overcome a sense of finitude. That is true of Hinduism and Buddhism. According to these traditions individuals who attain the right relation to the divine are absorbed into it so that their individuality is extinguished; thus not only their sense of finitude, but their actual finitude is utterly wiped out. But in biblical religion, there is no attempt to overcome human finitude or the sense of it. It is not finitude which separates humans from their creator, but sin. The final state of believers is guaranteed by the resurrection of the dead, which will be the restoration of their finite, conscious, individual lives in God's everlasting Kingdom.

For these reasons, Tremmel's characterizations of the divine are inadequate. They do not apply to all religions and are therefore too narrow to distinguish religion or to define religious belief.[9]

2. A Resolution

Out of what we have seen so far, one thing emerges clearly: all religious traditions seem to center around whatever they believe to be divine, but they disagree widely on how that is to be thought of. It is variously believed to be one supreme creator, two ever-opposing forces, a realm populated by many gods, being-itself, nothingness, etc. It is this great divergence that brought grief to the definitions just reviewed, and which has driven many thinkers to despair of ever capturing religious belief in a definition. Can we still hope to find something in common among such widely divergent ideas of the divine?

I want to propose that the way around this difficulty lies in the difference between the status of divinity, on the one hand, and what is believed to occupy that status, on the other. Let me explain this difference by using an analogy. If someone were to ask the question "Who is the president of the United States?" we could quite properly respond in either of two ways. One way would be to describe the person who presently holds the office of president. The other way would be to say that the president is the person who has the following duties and powers, and then to go on to describe the *office* of the presidency. The difference between the two ways of answering the question "Who is the president?" is like the difference between the two ways we can answer the question of the meaning of the term 'divine'. We may ask "What is divine?" meaning that we want a description of what it is that has the office or the status of being divine. Or we can take the question to ask for a definition of that *status* irrespective of who or what is believed to have it. My proposal, then, is that instead of trying to find something in common among all the differing ideas of who or what has the status of divinity, we shift the question to defining the status of divinity itself.

This distinction between the status of divinity and what occupies the status is not new; it had a wide acceptance among ancient pagan thinkers. They conceived the divine status as that on which all else depends, yet which does not depend on anything else for its own existence. For example, the ancient Pythagoreans believed the divine reality to be numbers because they believed all things are generated out of, and depend upon number combinations. Furthermore they thought that although all numbers are divine, the number one is the highest divinity because all other numbers depend on it while it does not depend on anything. Both the status of divinity and the description of the reality they believed to possess it are expressed in one of their prayers, a prayer to the number ten:

> Bless us, divine number, thou who generatest gods and men! O holy, holy tetraktys, thou that containest the root and source of eternally flowing creation! For divine number begins with the profound, the pure unity until it comes to the holy four; then it begets the mother of all, the all-encompassing, the all-bounding, the first born, the never swerving, the never tiring holy ten, the keyholder of all.[10]

Here the status of divinity is whatever "contains the root and source of . . . creation," while that which has this status is said to be numbers. (This is why the Pythagoreans thought $1 + 1 = 2$ was a religious belief.)

For Plato it was not numbers that are self-existent and thus divine, but realities he called "Forms." He says that these are "self-existent" (*Tim.* 50 ff; *Phil.* 53–54) and thus refers to them as divine; in at least one place he explicitly calls them "gods" (*Tim.* 37). Aristotle, too, is about as explicit as possible on what it means for something to be divine when he says:

> Therefore about that which can exist independently and is changeless, there is a science. . . . And if there is such a kind of thing in the world, here surely must be the divine, and this must be the first and most dominant principle. (*Metaphysics* 1064a34)

Notice that the divine is here characterized as whatever is able to exist independently from everything else, while its being the "first and most dominant principle" is later explicated to mean that all else depends on it.[11]

Since I am primarily addressing those who believe in God (as I said in the first chapter), it is apropos to call attention to the fact that the Scriptures accepted by Jews, Christians, and Muslims also support my definition of 'divine'. In Scripture, the fundamental teaching is that God is the creator.[12] This means he has a certain status relative to everything other than himself, namely he is the one on whom all else depends for existence while he does not depend on anything for his existence. Of course, God also has the status of being redeemer or savior, and of being the only one deserving of worship. But Scripture regards God's creatorship as fundamental; because he is creator, God can guarantee to redeem all of creation and restore believers to citizenship in his Kingdom; and because he is redeemer, humans owe him adoration and thanks. ("We love him because he first loved us.")

Since many believers tend to think of God primarily as the savior and object of worship, they suppose having a false god means believing in a substitute savior or object of worship. But this is not the way Bible writers themselves use the terms 'false gods' or 'idols'. They do not call something a false god only because those who believe in them call them gods, or even because they are worshiped (e.g., some writers refer to greed as idolatry). Rather, they call anything a god or an idol if it in *any* way replaces God. Viewed in this way, it should be obvious why anything (besides God) deserves to be called a God-surrogate if it is assigned the status of creator, and why any such belief deserves to be called a religious belief. From this point of view having a substitute creator is every bit as much a false religious belief as having a substitute savior.

This point is crucial for understanding the assumption of the Bible writers that all people are innately religious. For if being religious means only believing in something as savior or worshiping something, then it would be clearly false that all people are religious. But if it also means replacing God with something believed to be the nondependent reality on which all else depends, then it is not obvious whether people can really avoid every such belief.[13] (In later chapters I will be arguing that, at the least, no *theory* can avoid presupposing something to have the status of divinity.)

During the Middle Ages, Jewish, Christian, and Moslem theologians and philosophers tended to lose the distinction between the status of divinity and its occupant. Since God was accepted by all three religions to be the only divinity, the characteristics which ancient thinkers had seen as defining the status of divinity were thought of as attributes of God. The loss of the distinction obscured what was going on in other religions and thus blocked the way to defining religion itself. Among religious thinkers since the Middle Ages, one of the first to rediscover the distinction was Luther.[14] In our own time it has been re-recognized by a number of distinguished thinkers: William James, A. C. Bouquet, H. Dooyeweerd, and N. Kemp Smith, to name but a few.[15] However, it still has not received the acceptance it deserves.

Nevertheless, when we apply the distinction of the status of divinity to the traditions on our short list, it quickly becomes apparent that the meaning of the divine status is one thing they all agree upon! They all hold in common that *the divine is whatever does not depend on anything else for its existence,* so all that is not divine depends for its existence on the divine. This is true, for example, of the Tao in Taoism, of Yahweh in Judaism and Christianity (Allah in Islam), of Brahman-Atman in Hinduism, and of the Dharmakaya, Void, Nirvana, or Suchness in various branches of Buddhism. And it is also true of the divinities of all the other traditions mentioned on our short list. In fact, I have not yet found any religion, whether on or off the short list, which does not explicitly or implicitly share this same idea of the status of divinity. They all believe that the divine is whatever is "just there," and that all that is not divine depends on the divine in the sense that the divine can exist without the nondivine, but the nondivine cannot exist without the divine.

Thus it appears plausible to say that religious beliefs all have in common that they believe in something or other as the nondependent divinity on which all else depends. This is not to say, however, that in the teaching of every religion we will find the expressions "nondependent" or "self-existent" or their linguistic equivalents. It may well be that a particular body of belief will trace all things back to an original something, the status of which is never emphasized or even explained. But no matter how deemphasized or tentatively held, it is still regarded as divine according to this definition.

One preliminary objection to this is that perhaps everything is divine, so that there is no nondivine reality. There are, in fact, people who say they believe "all nature is god and all god is nature"; and there are others who think that everything is comprised only of matter/energy, which they regard as self-existent. Wouldn't these be religious beliefs according to our preliminary definition, but fail to be like most religions because they deny there is any nondivine reality?

The position that there is no nondivine reality may sound plausible at first hearing, but on careful reflection there are good reasons to doubt that anyone believes it literally. this is because it is patently obvious that most of the things we experience depend in many ways on other things, and thus are obviously not self-existent. A person who believes matter/energy to be self-existent would, indeed, be regarding it to be divine and would have a materialist religious belief. But even if the matter which makes up the objects of everyday experience is self-existent, the objects themselves—the individual combinations of matter—are not self-existent. They depend on the matter that constitutes them and on their relations to other objects, as is shown by the fact that they can be generated and destroyed by other things. Since such things are not themselves divine, there would still be a nondivine segment to reality and materialism would still have to include an idea of how the divine relates to the nondivine. Similarly for the case of the person who simply says all is divine without specifying the nature of divinity. The totality of all things may be regarded as divine, but surely many individual things within the totality are not. Their dependency on other things is obvious since they pass away before our eyes. There are religious traditions that may seem to avoid this point by their teaching that our ordinary experience is totally misleading or illusory: they say that things do not really depend on others or come into being and pass away, they only appear to do so. Hinduism, for example, claims that our ordinary experience is illusory and that only the divine is real. But this position is still forced to admit there is a difference between the illusory world we ordinarily experience and the divine (self-existent) reality. Even if what we ordinarily experience as nondivine is an illusion, the existence of the illusion still needs to depend on the divine.

A second preliminary objection to this definition is the discomfort it produces by being different from the ordinary ways we use the terms 'religious' and 'religious belief'. After all, on our definition it turns out that worship is not essential to religion and that some beliefs not usually thought of as religious are religious all the same. This is true, and no doubt some people will find this disturbing. In such a case, it will be helpful to keep in mind two things. One is that whenever we try to define a type of things precisely, the definition is liable to leave out certain features we regularly associate with things of that type. When we think of trees, for example, we usually think of their foliage. But that is not part of the definition of a tree; some trees have no leaves at all. Similarly, there may be features of a type we do not usually think are important but turn out to be defining characteristics. It surprises some people to learn that in botany lilies are classed with onions, for instance. So a precise definition may serve to refine our ordinary notions of things and ought not be rejected just because they differ from those notions.

The second point to be made about this objection is that in Western culture most people's ideas of religion are derived from the Judeo-Christian tradition. In one sense that is quite understandable. It is only reasonable that we think and speak of religious beliefs based on those we are familiar with. But it is not reasonable that we insist that all religious beliefs must be like those we are familiar with even when we are confronted with others which are quite different. This point is especially pertinent to the objection that the definitions defended here do not include worship as essential to religious belief. Many people have made such a strong association between religion and worship that they want to reject my definition of 'divine' for that reason alone. I will return to this point in more detail in the next section. For now I will simply point out that the definitions proposed here have been derived by extracting what is common to a sizeable number of religious beliefs. They are not simply arbitrary inventions intended to perform the magic trick of making irreligious people turn out to be religious after all. That accusation would be simply a play on words that should fool no one. People may indeed be irreligious in the popular sense, which is that they deny the prevailing religion of their time and place. They may further be irreligious in that they do not worship, hold nothing to be sacred, and deny any idea of salvation or life after death. But these denials alone will not show that they fail to regard anything as divine. To do that they would have to deny that anything whatever is nondependent, and that is a hard claim to make any sense of.[16] Short of this claim, there is a minimal sense in which a person has a religious belief no matter how otherwise irreligious his or her life may be. And to say that people are fundamentally religious beings in one sense of "religious" but can be irreligious in another sense is no stranger than saying that people are fundamentally moral beings, but often behave immorally.

With these preliminary objections out of the way, I will now offer a summary statement of what we have so far found to be true of all religious belief. It is this definition which, after further refinement, will be used throughout the remainder of the book.

> A religious belief is any belief in something or other
> as divine.

> 'Divine' means having the status of not depending
> on anything else.

It should be observed that there is nothing about this definition that requires there be only one divinity. In many religions there are two or more divinities. Moreover, where more than one divinity is believed in, a religion may think of the dependency of the nondivine on the divine as divided up in any of several different ways. For example, a religion could teach that one group of nondivine things depends on one divinity, while another group depends on another divinity. Or a religion could teach that a part of each and every nondivine thing depends on one divinity, while another part of each nondivine thing depends on another divinity. My point is only that the totality of what is not divine depends on (at least some part of) what is divine, no matter how the dependency arrangements are conceived. In fact, there have been some religions which believed there are certain divinities upon which little or nothing of our everyday world depends. But these "idle" divinities were still believed to be part of the realm of realities which was taken to be utterly self-sufficient, and so were part of the divine realm on which all the rest of reality depends.

The fact that there are many ways to conceive of the dependency of the nondivine on the divine explains how it is possible that in certain religions something may be accorded divine status but still not be esteemed or worshiped by its believers. Even though something is truly believed to be nondependent, if nothing very important to humans depends on it, or if it is thought to be the source of evil rather than good, it is a divinity people may fail to honor. In fact, if "divinity" is used as a term of honor, they may fail to refer to it as "divine" at all. This will not, however, change its self-existent status or the fact that belief in it is religious. Once again: what makes something divine is not whether it is personal and good, and what amounts to regarding something as divine is not whether it is loved and worshiped. It is believing something to be self-existent which is equivalent to regarding it as divine, even if it is also thought of as impersonal and is hated. Perhaps the most extreme example of this is the one mentioned in the New Testament: even demons believe in the existence of God though they fail to revere or serve him (James 2:19).

One of the first refinements our definition must now undergo is required by the distinction between the essential core of religious belief and those other beliefs (and practices) prompted by the core belief—the ones popularly thought of as "religion." While every religious tradition regards something(s) or other as divine, most of them also contain many other teachings in addition to their account of what is divine. These allied beliefs are also properly called "religious" beliefs because they directly concern the believer's relation to the divine. For example, while Hinduism teaches that Brahman-Atman is the nondependent reality on which all else depends, it also includes beliefs about Karma, reincarnation, and various ways of achieving unification with Brahman-Atman. Christianity, too, does not end its teaching with the doctrine that Yahweh the Creator does not depend on anything in any way, but includes beliefs about God's covenant with humans, the promise of a Messiah, God's incarnation in Jesus, and the resurrection of believers to eternal life.

I will call these additional teachings which occur in religious traditions "secondary beliefs" to distinguish them from the "core beliefs" about what is divine. But I must make it clear that this is not to say that the core beliefs and secondary beliefs can be separated. In most of the major world religions not only do the secondary beliefs presuppose the core belief, but the core belief is embedded in and conveyed through the secondary beliefs. (This is the reason it is the secondary beliefs which most people think of when they speak of religion, since these include teachings about individual salvation and moral duty as well as prescribe worship.)

The best general characterization of these beliefs is that they concern *how one comes to stand in proper relation to the divine,* however the divine is thought of. Therefore our definition must now be expanded this way:

> A belief is a religious belief provided that:
>
> (1) it is a belief in something(s) or other as divine, or
>
> (2) it is a belief concerning how humans come to stand in proper relation to the divine.

The beliefs defined in (2) are secondary in the sense that they depend for their content and importance on the core belief. Coming to stand in proper relation to the divine is believed to benefit humans by bringing about the full realization of their true nature. The guarantee of this benefit turns on the facts that humans depend on the divine for existence, and that nothing nondivine can overcome or defeat whatever is divine.

Of course, beliefs which are not themselves religious beliefs in either of the senses defined above may nevertheless be produced or altered by the influence of some religious belief. Take, for example, the belief of Jews and Christians that slavery is wrong. This conviction is not part of the Judeo-Christian idea of God, nor is it explicitly stated in the Torah, the Prophets, or the New Testament. But when Jews and Christians have examined the institution of slavery in the light of their core and secondary religious beliefs, they have almost universally come to reject it as incompatible with the social perspective engendered by their religion. (Such influence was often loose and indirect, of course, so that in some places it took a long time for this perspective to take effect.) My point here is simply to warn that when believers see such a connection between their religion and another belief, they frequently tend to overstate their case and identify the belief influenced by their religion as *part* of it. This actually happened during the antislavery movement in the United States. While the influence of religious on nonreligious belief is very significant, it is still crucial not to confuse the two; a belief is not itself a religious belief just because it is influenced by one.

3. Replies to Objections

We must now consider some important challenges to our definition. The first is whether this definition really fits with all the religions on our short list. Were Olympian gods of the ancient Greek pantheon believed to have nondependent existence? And what of any number of primitive religions such as that of the Melanesians who do not believe their gods to be absolutely self-existent?

Our definition is not shown too narrow by these examples for the reason that it is not necessary for a being to be divine in order to be considered a god. In many nonbiblical religions such separation is common. In the classical conception of the Olympian gods as found in the writings of Hesiod and Homer, for example, gods and goddesses were not thought to be divine as we have defined that term. Rather than being nondependent, the gods emerged from some primal, divine reality (Chaos or Okeanos) and are specific forms of that reality as much as humans are.[17] According to these accounts, then, it is Chaos or Okeanos which is actually self-existent, though in Greek religious practice neither was ever worshiped. Though both gods and humans were supposed to have arisen equally from a divine source of everything, there were still many significant differences between them. The most important of these was that the gods were supposed to be immortal and to have powers beyond those of any human. In these, and in other ways, the gods were more like the divine than humans were; they were personal beings in whom divine power was individualized, personified, and concentrated to a superhuman degree. Consequently they were the beings through whom humans could come to terms with the divine. The belief in these gods counts as religious on our definition, then, because it was a belief about how to stand in proper relation to the divine.

It is enlightening to compare these features of Greek thought and belief with the polytheism of divine Melanesians or the North American Indians. In these religions, too, there is an idea of a divine power or force which is distinct from any particular gods.[18] Among the Trobrianders it is called "Mana," while various American Indian tribes had different names for it such as "Wakan" or "Orenda." In these religions, as in those of ancient Greece, the divine itself is neither a god nor is worshiped,[19] but is a nondependent and self-operating power which pervades and causes certain things or features of the things which are not self-existent. The "Kami" in Japanese Shinto religion and "Numen" in ancient Roman religion are yet other names for this same idea. In these traditions individual gods are called divine only derivatively; they have more divine power than humans do, or share more characteristics with the divine than humans do, or are personifications of some characteristic of the divine. But strictly speaking they are not divine *per se* since they are not utterly self-existent. In each case, however, the beliefs about such gods are religious because they are ways of properly relating to the divine.

Rather than exposing a defect in our definition of religious belief, these religions show the need to distinguish two different meanings of the word 'god'. For the first of these I propose that the common noun (with a lower case "g") be understood to mean a being possessing more divine power than humans and/or sharing more characteristics in common with the divine than humans do.

For the second meaning I propose that the proper name "God" (with an upper case "G") be used for that which is solely and wholly divine according to our definition of that term. Thus the term 'God' as used by Jews and Christians is not synonymous with the term 'god' as it occurs in ancient Greek, Roman, Melanesian, American Indian, or Shinto religions.

One result of refining our definitions in these ways is that they are now able to settle the controversy as to whether Theravada Buddhism is really a religion. A number of scholars have doubted this because Buddha once remarked that he did not know or even care whether any gods existed, and because the Theravada tradition continues that same attitude. Nevertheless, on our definitions, Theravada Buddhism is confirmed as a religion despite the fact that some Theravada Buddhists themselves disavow that their belief is a religion. Surely none of them would say that the Nothingness from which all things come and into which they will all again be reabsorbed depends on anything whatever. Nor would they allow that the state of being absorbed into the Void (Nirvana) depends on anything else so that, once again, the Nothingness is divine. In addition, Theravada Buddhists would surely admit that they are engaged in their disciplines and meditations for the purpose of attaining the right relation to the divine, since that right relation is the state of Nirvana. Apparently, then, the Theravada disavowal is motivated by the popular Western belief that religion must include worship, while they do not worship.

The case of Theravada Buddhism is also instructive for the issue of whether it makes sense to say that a person may be an atheist but still have a religious belief. We have already seen that a number of beliefs not ordinarily thought to be religious turn out to be religious beliefs on our definition. I have already said why a person who believes, say, numbers or matter to have nondependent existence and to be what everything else depends on for existence has a religious belief every bit as much as a person who is devoted to a personal God or gods. The religious character of such a belief does not depend on whether the object of belief is like the God of the Bible in other ways, but only whether it has the status of nondependency. This means that many people may rightly call themselves atheists meaning that they do not believe there are any gods ('a-theist' means literally 'no-god'), but they will still have a religious belief if they regard anything whatever as the self-existent on which all else depends.

It is in this connection that, once again, the hurdle to be surmounted is the assumption that a truly religious belief would have to result in worship. The reason why worship is not an essential part, or even a necessary accompaniment, to religious belief is fairly simple. Worship is appropriate only when it is thought to aid the human condition by helping to put people in proper relation to the divine. Theravada Buddhists do not believe that worship provides such an aid, so they do not worship. Similarly, the materialist who regards physical matter as self-existent and all else as dependent on it will surely not be induced by that belief to pray to subatomic particles or sing hymns to force fields. Nor will a modern rationalist who regards, say, mathematical laws as self-existent be inclined to develop a liturgy of Quantitative Adoration for their worship. Nevertheless, these beliefs ascribe to matter or mathematical laws, respectively, the same nondependent status that a Jew or Christian accords to Yahweh, or a Hindu attributes to Brahman-Atman. Rather than having no religion at all these people simply have a different idea of what is divine, an idea in which worship is not appropriate.

Another variation of this objection is the claim that worship and other practices are the real key to understanding religion. Those who make this objection think that starting with belief as the key issue is mistaken because it amounts to "reducing" religion to something merely mental. In their view this is wrong because they think it rules out the possibility that religion may be studied by, say, a historian or sociologist.

The definitions proposed above are, as I see them, innocent of these charges. First of all, they do not reduce religion to something mental, if "reduce" means that religion is *restricted* to the mental. I do contend that it is only people and their beliefs which are religious in an unqualified sense, and that all other things which can be called religious are religious in the derivative sense of being involved in coming to stand in proper relation to the divine. But this does not mean there are no nonmental things, such as institutions and practices, which are related to religious core beliefs in that way. For this same reason, it is also not true that my definitions rule out historical, sociological, or other types of studies of religion. What the definitions do require, however, is that for these studies to succeed, they must depend upon first being able to recognize what religious core beliefs are and how historical events or social groups relate to them. For unless we are able to distinguish a religious from a nonreligious belief, and unless we can then discover the content of the religious belief held by the people participating in the practices or institutions we want to study, we could never be sure whether any particular practice or institution is religious.

To see why this is so, consider what happens if we try to get at the essence of religion by examining worship. On this view, any institution conducting worship would be a religious one, and any belief resulting in worship would be a religious belief. The primary problem, on such a view, would be how to recognize whether a certain human action is worship or not. For without knowing that the people involved believe what they are doing helps them attain proper relation to the divine, an on-looker could never tell whether any particular actions such as standing, sitting, kneeling, reading or chanting were or were not worship.

The same difficulty would attend an incredibly large number of other activities drawn from every quarter of life, since at one time or another all the following activities have been parts of worship as well as performed outside of worship: eating bread and wine, circumcising an infant, planting seeds, washing oneself with water, covering oneself with manure, burning down a house, killing an animal, killing a human, having sexual intercourse, burning incense, having one's head shaved, ringing bells, and setting off fireworks. It is only because of what is believed about the role of these actions in attaining proper relation to the divine that they become parts of worship. And it is only when an observer knows what the participants believe about their actions that he can tell whether they are acts of worship or not. Even an act of prayer cannot be distinguished from someone's talking to himself unless we know what the speaker *believes* about his speech act.

Of course, if we are observing others and cannot find out what they believe about those actions (perhaps because we do not speak their language), we are often able to guess that they are worshiping on the basis of the likeness between the actions we are observing and the actions of ourselves or others *which we already know to be worship.* And the actions we already know to be worship are those we know are believed to be required in order to stand in the right relation to the divine. So the fact that we can sometimes accurately guess that certain acts are worship is based on an analogy between them and other actions whose relation to a religious core belief is already known.

But perhaps it will be replied that worship can yet be successfully distinguished by observable characteristics alone, provided we take them in clusters rather than singly and pay attention to their connections to one another. For example, we might distinguish worship by the solemnity of its actions, the sequence of those actions and by their repetitive character. But this reply cannot work either. We need only think of other public rituals such as those which open sports events, comprise graduation exercises, surround elections, or accompany swearing-in ceremonies to see once again that it is what is believed about such rituals which alone makes them worship or not.

But while the objections to our definitions run into such difficulties, it is these definitions which make it possible to say precisely when a practice or institution qualifies as a specifically religious one. To see how they do this, however, it is important to keep in mind we are still speaking here of whether or not they are religious only in the secondary sense. (This is because our central thesis is that no theory, practice, or institution is neutral with respect to core beliefs.)

In the secondary sense, an institution or practice is religious if its primary purpose is to aid people to stand in the right relation to the divine. Thus a church, synagogue, or mosque would be specifically religious institutions. So would a camp-ground run for the religious improvement of those who attend. Likewise, prayer, fasting, sacrifice, or the celebration of a holy day would all count as specifically religious practices for the same reason. By contrast, a family, school, business, or government may be run differently owing to the influence of secondary religious beliefs without becoming a religious institution. A school which includes the study—even advocacy—of a particular religious belief is certainly under religious influence, as is a government which outlaws polygamy or a corporation which gives employees a certain holy day off. Such influences would not be sufficient to make those institutions count as specifically religious ones, however, since in each case the primary purpose of those institutions remain to educate, to govern, or to make a living, rather than to aid people to stand in right relation to the divine. In this way our definitions are able to serve as the interpretive key for historical and sociological studies of religion.

With these replies to criticisms, can we now say that our definitions of 'religious belief', 'divine', and 'god' have sufficient evidence to establish them as correct? I must confess to thinking that they do. I know of no religious tradition to which they do not apply, whether on our short list or not. Nor can I think of any clearly nonreligious belief or teaching which they would improperly class as religious. Therefore, I contend that the definition of religious belief at which we have now arrived is not arbitrary. Accordingly, I am not merely proposing that 'religious' be defined this way for my purposes here, leaving open the possibility that it could just as well be defined some other way if my purposes were different. Instead, I am defending this definition as having extracted the essential core of the status of divinity and having applied it successfully to a sizeable list of religious traditions. Therefore, I maintain this definition to be correct and applicable to all religions until and unless it can be shown to be faulty.

4. Some Auxiliary Definitions

Having now defined 'religious belief', 'divine', and 'god', the most important terms used in association with religious belief which are still left unclarified are 'faith' and 'trust'. In offering definitions for these terms, I will be assuming they both refer to types of belief and will take the position that a belief is an acquired disposition to regard its object as factual and to think, speak, act, or hold other beliefs in ways which suppose the statement of the belief to be true.

First, it is important to notice that in English the word 'belief' has a broader meaning than either 'trust' or 'faith'. It is quite ordinary for someone to say, for instance, that he believes his medical report will be bad or that she believes she is about to be fired. But it would not be ordinary usage for someone to say that he trusts his medical report will be bad or that she has faith she is about to be fired. What this shows is that not every act of belief is called "trust" or "faith." Rather we speak of trusting and having faith only when we regard what is believed as favorable to us. In addition, 'faith' and 'trust' are used of acts which manifest a personal reliance on what is believed, which is yet another characteristic that does not arise in connection with all acts of belief. For example I may believe there was an English civil war over three hundred years ago without personally relying on that belief in any way that makes a difference to me.

Now it might be objected at this point that given the way I have defined religious belief, some of them would not be cases of faith or trust since what they take to be divine is not seen as beneficial or results in no personal reliance. A materialist, for instance, might very well believe that matter/energy is divine, and as a consequence believe that there is no life after death. Wouldn't it be wrong, then, to suggest that the materialist is relying on that as something beneficial? My answer is that by regarding materialism as true, its adherents cannot help but see it as beneficial at least insofar as it liberates them from falsehood. It does not, to be sure, offer a hope of life after death as do many other religious beliefs, but the materialist will still have to see it as more beneficial to know an unpleasant truth than to believe a pleasant untruth. Moreover, the materialist definitely is *relying* on there being no God and (especially) no final judgment. And the same point applies equally to all other nonpersonal ideas of the divine: those who believe in them exercise personal reliance on them at least insofar as their ultimate destiny is concerned. Therefore, I find that faith and trust are indeed elements of all religious beliefs, even those which regard the divine as impersonal.

Of course, there are also nonreligious beliefs which we speak of as faith or as trust. We may have faith in a friend, or trust the weather report. But these are not religious for the reason that they are not cases of faith or trust in something as self-existent, nor are they beliefs about how to stand in right relation to that which is self-existent. In such cases the beneficial nature of the belief and the element of personal trust are split off from the belief's being about what is divine. It is this which accounts for the nonreligious senses of both terms.

Finally, there is at least one more trait typically possessed by religious trust which is not true of nonreligious trust. This is that religious trust takes its object to be *unconditionally* reliable. Nonreligious trust is always exercised with the reservation that its object is conditioned by circumstances which could affect its reliability. But religious faith is distinguished by taking its object to possess absolute trustworthiness. To rephrase Luther's point noted earlier: whatever our heart clings and entrusts itself to *as unconditionally trustworthy* is really our God. This cannot fail to be right, given our definition of 'divine', for nothing could be unconditionally trustworthy unless it were self-existent. Thus regarding anything as unconditionally reliable presupposes that it is divine in the sense proposed by our definition. (And this remains the case whether or not a believer's subjective *feelings* of confidence do or do not correspond to the unconditional status of the object of his or her trust. In any case of trust, it is as possible to feel less confidence as it is to feel more confidence than is warranted.)[20]

With this clarification behind us, we may now notice some finer shadings of meaning acquired by the religious sense of 'faith' and 'trust'. One of these is the difference between belief when it is followed by the word 'that', and belief when it is followed by the word 'in'. For example, we may have faith that our paycheck will be ready on payday, while we may trust in a friend to keep a secret. Similarly with specifically religious faith: we speak of both trusting that God will help us and of having faith in God. Granted that these two meanings are closely related, there still seems to be some difference between them.[21]

As I see it, faith or trust "in" something is the more basic expression, used to signify trust in its central meaning: openhearted acceptance of, and reliance on, what is believed. On the other hand, faith or trust "that" something is the case is an expression which is used with respect to belief which has undergone reflective judgment. It is faith whose content has been analyzed and given a conscious articulation; it takes the form of a statement of just what is being relied on. In the religious sphere, for example, "faith that" God will do such and such is often a reflective consequence of our "faith in" God as reliable. I do not mean to suggest, however, that faith or trust "in" is at odds with faith or trust "that." Since humans cannot help thinking about that which they trust, all trusting has an element of reflection—just as all thinking has an element of trust. So, too, religious "faith in" inevitably becomes also "faith that"; the two elements never exist in isolation. Nevertheless the two expressions are needed because they allow us to distinguish those two elements and to refer to them separately if we wish.

Closely associated with the difference between belief "in" and belief "that" is the difference between 'faith' or 'trust' when they are used to refer to the content of belief. It is 'faith' in the sense of the content of belief which occurs in such expressions as "the Catholic Faith," "the Jewish Faith," and so on. In this sense 'faith' is equivalent to 'creed'. This distinction between the act of belief and an elaborate statement of the content of a belief is important. We often need to be clear about whether we are talking about an act of trust or a statement of what is trusted. But once again it must be kept in mind that what is being distinguished here are components of all belief, components which never really exist in isolation.

Before ending this chapter of definitions, I want to dispel a possible misunderstanding which might arise from the way I spoke of people "regarding something as divine." I did say that whatever someone believes to be self-existent is thereby believed to be divine by that person. This way of speaking was not intended, however, to suggest that every idea of what is divine is equally right so that all faiths are true. Even though someone regards something as utterly nondependent it does not follow that it is; a person's faith may be ever so pious, fervent, and sincere, but still misplaced and false.

It is important to remember in this connection that what has been defined here is the status of divinity. That was the only thing I found all religious core beliefs to agree upon. Despite this agreement, they are still very far from agreeing upon what it is that has that status, or upon how the divine relates to whatever is not divine, or how humans come to stand in proper relation to the divine. Where there are incompatible ideas about these issues, the laws of logic guarantee that they cannot all be true. It cannot be true, for example, that only God (Yahweh) as revealed in Scripture is divine, but also true that it is Brahman-Atman that is divine. That could only be the case if "God" and "Brahman-Atman" were different names for the same reality, rather than for *different realities accorded the same status*. And since God is distinct from creation and Brahman-Atman is not, they cannot be the same reality. For the same reason, it cannot be true that the universe is entirely distinct from what it depends on (as in the case of God) but also true that it is part of what it depends on (as in the case of Brahman-Atman). That could only be the case if "distinct from" and "part of" were different expressions for the same relation. Thus it is not the case that the biblical God is the one all other religions are dimly aware of, but know less about or make mistakes about.[22]

In sum, logic requires that religious trust can be either well placed or misplaced as can nonreligious trust, since beliefs about the divine are—as are all other beliefs—either true or false but not both at once. It follows, therefore, that when two beliefs disagree about what is divine, one or both of them must be (at least partly) false.

In the next chapter we will use the definitions developed here to distinguish types of core beliefs which are basic to several of the world's major religious traditions. As that project proceeds it will become clear that although there are strong similarities among traditions of the same type, those which fall into different types are hopelessly incompatible. Far from being different paths up the same mountain, they do not agree on which mountain to climb.

3

Types of Religious Belief

Let us now turn to some of the major world religions of the present day and see how the definitions just developed can help us to understand them. We cannot, of course, work up a detailed comparison of even two such traditions, let alone five or six, without getting completely sidetracked from our main topic. But it will prove very enlightening if we look briefly at the prevailing ways the divine is now understood by some of the most influential of the world's religions. We will become more aware of the religious character of beliefs less familiar to us, which will put us in a better position to see how such beliefs influence theories.

1. The Basis for Typing Religions

Since we cannot deal in detail with each of the major world religions, I propose to deal with them in family groupings or types. Distinguishing these types is one of the first benefits to be reaped from the definitions in the last chapter. There we saw that the key to defining religious belief was to give up looking for anything in common among the differing ideas of what it is that is divine and to concentrate instead on the idea of the status of divinity. It now appears that we can gain further valuable insights if we continue the same approach. The specific ideas of exactly what is divine are extremely diverse and can be typed or grouped in many ways depending on what someone is looking for. In the past, for example, religions have been classified by how many gods they had, whether they advocated a strict or loose morality, and so on. But these ways of typing the major traditions are too narrow for our purpose and are largely arbitrary. So instead of looking at precisely how a religion describes whatever it believes to be divine, we will start with its idea of *how the nondivine depends on the divine* or a religion's "dependency arrangement."

Once we focus on this element of a religious belief, it becomes clear that there are three dependency arrangements which prevail in the world today. These are not the only ones possible; in my work in comparative religion I have been able to distinguish at least fourteen possible dependency arrangements. But the vast majority of the world's population now holds to one or another of only three. I will call these three the pagan, the biblical, and the pantheistic dependency ideas. 'Biblical', as I use it, is a blanket term for the traditions that believe in a transcendent creator: Judaism, Christianity, and Islam; while the term 'pantheist' includes Hinduism, Buddhism, and the more recent forms of Taoism. The pagan type of religions covers such a wide variety of specific traditions that I cannot represent it by simply naming a few of its more famous members, but we will shortly examine a few of its most influential representatives.

Before doing that, however, I want to make it clear that the term 'pagan' is not a derogatory term as I use it. It is not being used as, say, Christian missionaries used the term 'heathen' in the nineteenth century. It does not refer only to varieties of religious belief which are superstitious or irrational, or which are held only by people who are primitive. On the contrary, we will see that paganism can be quite sophisticated and that its sophisticated forms still exercise a tremendous influence in the world today.

2. The Pagan Type

The essential feature of the pagan dependency idea is that the divine is some part, aspect, force, or principle in the created universe. That is to say, it is a subdivision of reality taken as a whole. Put another way, the pagan dependency arrangement is that there is only one continuous reality, part of which is the divine segment on which all the rest depends. Perhaps the following schema will help to make this clear. If we use a solid line to represent the divine and a broken line to represent the nondivine, then our visual aid for the pagan dependency idea would look like Figure 1.

A wide variety of religious beliefs fall under this pagan type. Nature religions which worshiped a divine power in the earth, the sun, rivers, the sea, etc., are all faiths of this type. For example, one

Fig. 1

of the most commonly worshiped gods in the ancient world was the divinity which controlled storms. It was called Ba'al in the near East, Zeus in Greece, Jupiter in Rome. In addition, the beliefs in Mana, Numen, and Kami mentioned earlier also fall under this type, as do the ideas of divinity put forward by the Greek thinkers discussed in the last chapter. Although these traditions often disagreed in their idea of the divine, they all held it to have the same relation to what is nondivine. Thus Werner Jaeger's description of this relation in the thought of the Greek writer Hesiod applies quite well to all pagan belief.

When Hesiod's thought at last gives way to truly philosophical thinking, the Divine is sought within the world—not outside it as in Judeo-Christian theology that develops out of the book of Genesis.[1]

Here we need to recall the point made in the last chapter about religion not always resulting in worship. For as long as we think only of the forms of paganism which were expressed in ritual and worship, it will be nearly impossible to believe that paganism is a strong force in the world today. This is because paganism which results in worship—ritualistic paganism—has long been in decline in the face of advances by Hinduism, Buddhism, Christianity, and Islam, as well as from the pressures of modern science and technology. But pagan religious belief which is neither institutionalized nor conducts ritual worship has continued to flourish. Many modern thinkers in philosophy and the sciences maintain theories whose assumptions are as much pagan religious beliefs as those of their ancient Greek counterparts. The religious commune of the Pythagoreans died out long ago, and nobody *worships* numbers any more as they did; no one prays to the number ten, for example. But the belief that numbers or other elements of mathematics are parts of a realm of self-existent realities on which all else depends is far from dead. Indeed, it continues to dominate large segments of mathematical thinking to this day.[2] It would equally be a (non-ritual) pagan belief to regard matter and energy, rather than numbers, as the nondependent reality on which all else depends, for this, too, is a case of believing some aspect of the universe to be divine.

It would be instructive at this point to apply our definition of paganism to the theory of dialectical materialism proposed by Karl Marx. This is an especially interesting case since Marxism is a theory which is avowedly anti-religious. In its interpretation of everything from physics and biology to economics, history, and politics, Marxism professes to be opposed to all religions of whatever kind. In place of traditional religious teachings, Marx offers a philosophical theory. According to this theory, matter/energy is the basic reality, and within matter there is an innate law which drives things to change according to a process he calls "dialectical" development. This law has caused matter to organize in the forms which have developed over millions of years. Galaxies and solar systems, life in all its forms, human intelligence and society are all products of matter being organized by the law of dialectical development.

The Marxist conviction is that this dialectical law, when correctly understood, shows that free-market (capitalistic) economics is the cause of unjust and repressive governments and is doomed to pass away. This will take place as there develop governments willing to abolish private ownership, which is the root of all evil. Once communistic economic systems can be established, they will in turn bring about governments which are even more just, so that there will be ever greater happiness throughout all human society. The end result will be the eventual emergence of the final stage of history: a communistic society. In such a society the citizens not only will not practice private ownership, but will not even wish for it. Because of this, crime will disappear and so will the need for any government at all. Society will be free of the alienation of one group from another since there will no longer be classes with adversarial interests. There will no longer be any alienation from nature, or from the means of producing the necessities of life. People will be happy and good and will live in peace.

It should be clear, however, that although Marx was indeed an atheist, his theories all presuppose the self-existence of matter; physical matter, along with its innate law of dialectical development, is "just there."[3] Matter depends on nothing whatever, and all of reality is either identical with or depends on matter. For this reason, despite its protests to the contrary, Marx's theory is based on a religious belief. And, what is more to the point, this religious belief is a typically pagan one since it takes something about the creation to be the self-existent segment of reality on which all else depends. We are entitled to this conclusion because our definitions show not only that a belief can be religious without involving worship, but that it can be religious whether or not its subscribers admit it. I mention this again because it is especially true of non-ritual paganism that their advocates often deny their beliefs to be religious at all, but refer to them as "secular" or "nonsectarian," which is intended to mean that they are religiously neutral. As soon as we compare these beliefs with our definition of 'divine', we see that much of what is passed off as "humanist" or "secular" is in fact an alternative religious belief.

The examples of Pythagoreanism and materialism were cases of paganism in which there was only one divinity. However, the most popular pagan belief throughout history has been a sub-type which is called "dualism" to indicate its conviction that there are two divinities rather than one. According to this sub-type, it is the interaction between the two divinities (or two groups of divinities) which produces all of reality that is nondivine. The form-matter belief of the Greeks is an example of such dualism, as are the Chinese Yin-Yang doctrine and Persian Zoroastrianism. Figure 2 shows the previously offered schema altered to reflect this difference.

Fig. 2

Usually in religions which believe there are two divine realities, one of the divinities is regarded as the source of what is good in the world while the other as the source of what is evil. The most influential version of dualistic paganism, that of ancient Greece, is a case in point. It saw the two divinities as: (1) Matter, an original stuff of which all things are made, and (2) Form, the principle of orderliness which makes the stuff into the intelligible world we experience. Some Greek thinkers understood this divine orderliness as being logical in nature, while others saw it as mathematical. Applied to the idea of human nature, this dualistic faith taught that humans, too, are combinations of form and matter. The human body is constituted of matter, which generates feeling and passion. By contrast, the human mind was an embodiment of form because of its ability to reason logically and mathematically. On this outlook, all that is good, beautiful, and true is generated or known by the mind's exercising rational thought and attempting to impose order in life. All that is evil and disordered is brought about by the bodily impulses of irrational feeling and passion. Human life is therefore a struggle between an emotional nature and a rational nature, between one's body and one's mind.

From the basic duality of its two divinities, this version of paganism sees not only human nature but all of reality as permeated by corresponding pairs of oppositions: good vs. evil, rational vs. irrational, change vs. stability, order vs. disorder, beauty vs. ugliness, etc. This outlook still enjoys great popularity in our culture today. But no matter how comfortable many nonpagans have come to feel about it, this dualistic picture of things is in conflict with both the biblical and the pantheistic types of religious belief.

3. The Pantheistic Type

The chief examples of contemporary religions advocating the pantheistic dependency arrangement are Hinduism and Buddhism. This arrangement may best be seen as the inverse of the one held by paganism. Instead of locating the divine as a subdivision of all reality, the pantheistic belief is that the nondivine is a subdivision of the divine. This, however, creates an obstacle to drawing a schema to illustrate this arrangement. Since the divine is regarded as infinite and all-encompassing, the circle representing divinity would have to be infinitely large. So I will simply stipulate that the finite circle in Figure 3 stands for an infinite one.

This schema shows that pantheistic religions share with pagan religions the conviction that there is only one continuous reality. The two disagree, however, over whether there is more to reality than what is divine (pagan), or whether the divine is co-extensive

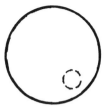

Fig. 3

with reality so that the nondivine is a subdivision of the divine
(pantheistic). Given this difference, we may say that from the pagan standpoint there is a clear-cut distinction between what is divine and what is not, but on the pantheistic standpoint this
distinction is a tricky issue. For if the nondivine is *in its entirety*
part of the divine, how can there be anything at all that is not divine? And if there is not, just what distinction is being drawn? The
answer given by the pantheistic traditions is to say that, yes, the
divine is the very essence and being of all things, but that individual things and events of our universe do not appear to be divine as
we ordinarily experience them. They further insist that the divine
reality beneath the surface appearance is not easily discovered. So
the distinction made in the pantheistic traditions is not between a
portion of reality which is divine and a portion which is not, but
is between the divinity of all reality and *the illusory appearance
that there are realities which are not divine.* Because the difference between the illusion of everyday experience and the divine
reality which lies behind it is so great, the Scriptures and disciplines of the pantheistic traditions do not simply teach this doctrine but are aimed at inducing a mystical experience of it. Only by
mystical experience can a person overcome the veil of illusion, see
behind the world of mere appearance, and become aware of the
divine reality which is hidden by it. This divine reality is called
Brahman-Atman in Hinduism; Dharmakaya, the Void, Suchness,
Nothing, Nirvana (and other terms) in Buddhism; the Tao in
Taoism.

Here it should be stressed that the sense in which the Hindu and
Buddhist traditions hold that the world is unreal as it is known by
ordinary experience and reason is an *extreme* sense. They do not
mean merely that the everyday world is real but less important

than the divine which it conceals; they mean that *everything about it is unreal.* According to them, mystical experience shows the divine not only to be the true nature of all things, but in fact to be the *only* reality so that the divine is really all there is! Even the most commonplace features of the everyday world are illusory.[4] For example, according to these traditions there really are no distinct individual objects, nor real differences of qualities—even including the difference between good the evil! At bottom all things are one; there is only the divine.

This doctrine usually appears strange and unpalatable to Westerners who often point out that it leads to logical contradictions. In answer to such criticisms, these traditions warn that without the necessary mystical experience, people will always fail to understand or to believe in the (hidden) identity of all things with the divine. Logical criticism, they say, fails to recognize that logical thinking is also part of the everyday world of illusion. As such, logical thinking is part of the deception that prevents people from discovering the divine unity of all reality. According to the pantheistic dependency arrangement, therefore, the divine is not only never to be thought of as any one part or aspect of the everyday world; since logic is ruled out, it cannot be conceptualized at all. So it should be clear why, since the Hindu and Buddhist traditions regard ordinary experience and logical reasoning as parts of the illusory world, they both insist on mystical experience as the only means for discovering the truth about the divine.

Differences between the pagan and pantheistic dependency arrangements result in important disagreements between them. Take, for example, their different interpretations of human nature. According to the most influential version of paganism which I sketched earlier, what is wrong with people is their failure to recognize human reason as governed by the same divine principles that give order to all reality and to overcome the impulses of emotions by making rationality the highest value in their personal lives and in society. By contrast, the pantheistic traditions insist that what is wrong with people is their attachment to the illusory world as it is encountered in ordinary experience and understood by reason. Since no distinct part or feature of the universe is divine on the pantheistic standpoint, the proper purpose of life is to discover the true (divine) reality by rejecting and escaping the illusory world of ordinary experience. The highest value is precisely to reject everyday reality in favor of the mystical experience which alone discloses the hidden divine unity of all reality. So on the pantheistic view, what is wrong with people is that they succumb to the temptation to see the everyday world as either real and partly divine (the pagan view) or as real but not divine at all (the biblical view).

This theme of world-rejection is carried out by the more extreme sects in their explicit teaching that people's duties in life do not include changing the world. Rather they are to change their perception of the world so as to reject it and withdraw from it. This can only be accomplished by intensifying the mystical experience to the point where one's (illusory) self is annihilated by being reabsorbed into the divine "as a drop of water is absorbed into the ocean."

4. The Biblical Type

In contrast to both the pagan and the pantheistic dependency ideas, biblical faith *denies that there is one continuous reality.* The Hebrew idea of creation, which is basic also to Christianity and Islam, is that Yahweh (or Allah) the Creator is distinct from the universe which he brought into existence out of nothing. According to this dependency arrangement, the divine is not part of the universe nor is the universe part of the divine; there is a fundamental discontinuity between the creator and all else which is his creation. The basic difference has been well expressed by Will Herberg, using the expression 'Greco-Oriental' to cover both the pagan and pantheistic dependency ideas, and the term 'Hebraic' to refer to the biblical idea:

> Hebraic and Greco-Oriental religion, as religion, agrees in affirming some Absolute Reality as Ultimate, but differ fundamentally in what they say about this reality. To Greco-Oriental thought, whether mystical or philosophic, the ultimate reality is some primal unpersonal force ... some ineffable, immutable, impassive divine substance that pervades the universe or rather is the universe insofar as the latter is at all real....
>
> Nothing could be further from normative Hebraic religion.... As against the Greco-Oriental conception of *immanence,* of divinity permeating all things and constituting their reality, Hebraic religion affirms God as a transcendent person, who has indeed created the

universe but who cannot without blasphemy be identified with it. Where Greco-Oriental religion sees a continuity between God and the universe, Hebraic religion insists on discontinuity.[5]

As a consequence, the biblical traditions neither exalt some part of creation to divine status nor demean its reality as illusory. The universe is real because it has been created by God, and it is important because it is the arena in which humans are to live in fellowship and service to God. But at the same time, there is nothing about it which is not dependent on God. Every thing, event, and state of affairs; every part and property, fact and facet, law and norm—in short, everything other than God himself—has been brought into being by God who is the only divinity there is. Figure 4 represents this biblical dependency arrangement.

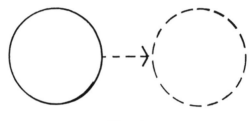

Fig. 4

It is because of this dependency arrangement that the idea of revelation is so important in the biblical traditions. God is not something people can discover by searching the universe or by means of a mystical experience in the pantheistic sense. Instead, the biblical traditions are all anchored on the belief that God has created within the world an intelligible revelation of his relations to the universe, especially his relations to humans. This body of teaching is the authoritative guide for all knowledge of God and the most important truths about humans. It includes the teaching of the core belief that only God is divine, as well as teaching the contents of God's covenant of redemption which are the secondary beliefs necessary for humans to stand in proper relation to him. By becoming subscribers to this covenant, or treaty of salvation, people become members of his Kingdom and receive eternal life.

In biblical religion, religious experience has an indispensable role in the person's belief in God, but that experience is never a "mystical" experience in the pantheistic sense. The experience of God is never direct experience of the Divine Being, but is always mediated through creation. Still less does this experience lead to union with the Being of God. The promised destiny of believers is not to be absorbed into God's Being since in the biblical religions humans are distinct beings from God and always will be. Rather, it is individuals, as members of the corporate body of God's people, who are the objects of God's love and forgiveness. And it is as individuals that they will be granted everlasting life in God's Kingdom.

In short, the difference between the being of the creator and that of any creature cannot be bridged: God is not the creation and the creation is not God. This does not, of course, mean that God cannot enter into creation and act in it; it does not mean he cannot be present with his people, or that he cannot communicate with them. It simply means that his presence and communication are always to and through some part of creation he uses for that purpose. His communication does not set aside normal human faculties: he designed humans so that their capacities to experience and know would be able to receive his revelation as well as his world. Even when the biblical prophets had unusual experiences in connection with receiving revelation from God, that revelation was never something which abandoned ordinary human experience and reason altogether or showed the world to be merely illusion. On the biblical view the world does not conceal the divine, as is supposed by pantheism but was formed so as to reveal God. (The reason people fail to recognize God's revelation in nature and his word is called "sin" by Bible writers. We will return to that point presently.) Thus, while there is always that about God which is beyond human comprehension in biblical religion, humans are able to know truth from and about God because he has done two things: first, he has structured the universe so that if it is rightly interpreted it points beyond itself to its transcendent, divine Origin; second, he has accommodated himself to human experience and reason and communicated this accommodation of himself throughout history, including bringing about a written record of this communication in Scripture.

For these reasons, the experience of God is mediated through his revelation and is never an achievement of unaided human effort, as it often is in the pantheistic traditions. Thus the role of biblical prophet is not that of a Hindu Swami or a Buddhist Zen Master. In Hinduism or Buddhism the Masters are experts who by their own initiative have found the formula for experiencing the divine. By contrast, a biblical prophet is a deputy chosen by God to deliver his message; he is not an expert who discovered religious truth, but a messenger to whom God revealed religious truth (in fact, the prophets often complained that they did not understand the message they were given). Moreover, the religious experience itself is never the norm or standard of belief in biblical religions, instead it is the experience of recognizing God's word as the norm and standard of belief. In other words, the experience is not the ultimate religious authority, God's self-revelation in his word is. And this is the reverse of the pantheistic idea of mystical religious experience, where the experience itself is the ultimate religious authority.

Corresponding to these differences about religious experience and revelation there is yet another difference which is important. On the pantheistic outlook, a person must pursue the achievement of mystical experience through most of a lifetime or through many lifetimes. Only when this is achieved will a person see the truth of the unity of all things, and thus attain the salvation of release from the curse of endless rebirths by being absorbed into the divine unity. But on the biblical view, the provisions of the covenant guarantee that directing one's faith and love to God already assures the believer of salvation. It is a gift from God at the outset and not an achievement earned en route. The assurance of salvation is thus an integral ingredient of being a Jew, Christian, or Moslem and does not come only after, and as a product of, a lifetime of struggle.

Of course, there is a struggle connected with serving God in our daily life. There is effort and sometimes agony in trying to respond as we should to the love God freely offers. And there is a deepening of faith in God and love toward others which can only come about with prayer and work, which are often accompanied by pain. Nevertheless, it is not the believer's ultimate destiny which is at stake in the daily struggles to serve God. For according to the Scripture, any person who believes the truth of God's revelation and loves God has already received the promise of God's redemption and the gift of everlasting life. It is not something he or she must spend a lifetime struggling to deserve, and hoping desperately to achieve before dying.

To continue the contrast, we should notice that the biblical standpoint also has a distinctive view of human nature which is even more antagonistic to the pagan and pantheistic views than those were to one another. In contrast to the most popular pagan view, the biblical teaching about what is wrong with people is not that they have a body, feelings, and emotions. According to Bible writers, people's minds, bodies, emotions, thoughts, etc., may be good or evil depending on whether they are used in the service of God. Once again, Herberg puts the point well:

> However familiar and plausible [the] dualistic view may seem to many religious people today, it is nevertheless utterly contrary to the Hebraic outlook. In authentic Hebraism, man is not a compound of two "substances" but a dynamic unity.... The body, its impulses and passions, are not evil; as parts of God's creation, they are innocent and, when properly ordered, positively good. Nor, on the other hand, is the human spirit the "false divinity" of the Greeks. Spirit is the source of both good and evil, for the spirit is will, freedom, decision.[6]

In this connection it is important to notice that the biblical conception of sin is not primarily that of moral wrongdoing. While immoral acts are, indeed, called sins and are condemned, the central idea of what is wrong with people is religious. That is, "sin" is the name for the condition of human nature which causes people to fail to recognize God's revelation, and also to fail to love and serve God with their whole being. On the biblical view, then, sin is only secondarily a matter of immoral intentions and behavior. It is first of all a matter of not directing one's faith and loving service to the creator, and instead regarding something God has created as divine. As one Rabbi put it long ago:

> God's anger is revealed from heaven against all the ungodliness and wickedness of men who resist the truth.... Who changed the truth about God into a lie and worshiped and served what God created rather than the Creator. (Rom. 1:18)[7]

It is interesting to compare this quote from Paul with the contrast between pagan and biblical religion which was drawn by a pagan thinker, Alfred North Whitehead. Whitehead quotes from the Bible the question, "Canst thou by searching find out God?" (Job 11:7). Recognizing that the text expects a negative answer, Whitehead makes the witty observation that this attitude is "good Hebrew but it is bad Greek"; that is, it is biblical but not pagan. He then adds the jibe that the biblical position is that of "thicker intellects" who "gloried in the notion that the foundations of the world were laid amid impenetrable fog."[8] Elsewhere Whitehead returns to this same point, this time rejecting both the biblical and the pantheistic standpoints in favor of the version of paganism which sees human reason as akin to the divine order of the world. He says:

> What is the status of the enduring stability in the order of nature? There is the summary answer, which refers nature to some greater reality standing behind it. This reality occurs in the history of thought under many names, the Absolute, Brahma, the Order of Heaven, God.... My point is that any summary conclusion jumping from ... such an order of nature to the easy assumption that there is an ultimate reality ... constitutes the great refusal of rationality to assert its rights. We have to search whether nature does not in its very being show itself as self-explanatory.[9]

These lucid contrasts of pagan and biblical belief, stated on behalf of the pagan standpoint, comport well with both the comparison by Paul and the schemas I have offered. They show that the central differences between the dependency ideas are clearly recognized by pagans as well as by Jews and Christians. And they serve to confirm my claim that pagan belief—at least in its nonritual versions—is alive and well in Western thought and culture.

The contrasts just drawn between the three types of dependency ideas merely scratch the surface with respect to comparing a few of their most outstanding features. Nevertheless, they may be sufficient to provide a better grasp of three points which will be helpful in all that follows: (1) that beliefs may differ widely over just what is divine and over how the divine relates to what is not divine; (2) that the types of these beliefs reviewed here are irreconcilable; and (3) that it is easy to fail to recognize that a belief is religious when it comes from an alien and unfamiliar tradition, especially when it has no worship attached to it.

Having sketched a broad contrast among these types of religious beliefs, we will now turn to the question of what a theory is and distinguish some major types of them. Only by doing that will we be in a position to answer the questions of whether religious belief unavoidably plays a role in theory making, and just what that role is.

PART II
Theories

4
WHAT IS A THEORY?

1. Introduction

Why should we be concerned about the relation of religious belief to theories? Surely there is more to the interpretation of life than what is afforded by theories. After all, aren't theories highly technical creatures which are understood only by scientists and philosophers and which contribute little to the understanding most people have of themselves and the world around them?

While some theories are very technical and understood only by experts, many others are not. The idea that all theories are beyond the average person comes from associating the word 'theory' with the latest advances in physics, chemistry, or astronomy. However, we should remember that there are also influential theories about political rights, human happiness, morality, the understanding of art, the rearing of children, effective medical treatment, and public education, to name a few. Many of these theories are within the ken of the average person; indeed, it seems unlikely there is anyone who does not adopt some theory on at least one of these topics. The truth is that the average person is highly influenced by theories.

Another reason we should be concerned about the relation of religious belief to theories has to do with the authority theories are claimed to have. A widely held belief is that once theories are formulated, tested, and accepted by experts, they become the most authoritative standard for judging the truth of whatever they are about. This implies, of course, that if one's values or religious belief is opposed by a widely accepted theory, one would be perverse to reject the theory and keep the belief. In the last century and a half this conclusion has been drawn repeatedly by advocates of Darwinian biology, Freudian psychology, and Marxist politics, to mention only the most obvious examples.

51

Can those of us who believe in God accept that theories are the final arbiters of truth? Are they really neutral with respect to religious belief, and so able to command the overriding allegiance that is commonly ascribed to them? And what about the popular view that although theories are authoritative in one realm of life, faith is authoritative in another? Is that a satisfactory way for a believer to understand their relation? To answer these questions, we must first get some grasp of what a theory is.

2. What Is a Theory?

The very soul of a theory is its hypotheses, and a hypothesis is a guess that is proposed in order to explain something.

Of course the fact that all hypotheses are guesses does not mean that all guesses are hypotheses since not all guesses are intended to explain something. At times we guess in order to win a prize, make a joke, etc. In what follows, we will be concerned with only the guesses which are made for the purpose of explaining something and which are therefore the very special guesses we call "hypotheses."

In what follows I will use the terms 'hypothesis' and 'theory' interchangeably to indicate either a single explanatory guess or a set of closely related explanatory guesses. However, there is another way in which 'theory' is often loosely used which I cannot adopt. This is the practice now common among many scientists and philosophers of using the term 'theory' for any sort of explanation whatever, whether it employs hypotheses or not. For them, the term 'theory' simply means any account, interpretation, or aid to understanding.

This is confusing and unacceptable because it obscures what is essential to theories in contrast to other ways of explaining. For example, it leaves in the dark the difference between a theory and a myth. In a myth, the forces of nature are personified so that their relations are explained as we would explain relations among people. It was this type of explanation which the ancient Greek philosophers replaced with hypotheses which were then debated by producing arguments and evidences. Since we no longer make myths as explanations it may not seem important to preserve the difference between them and theories. However there are still other ways of explaining things rather than by theory making. For example, the directions for how to get to my office or instructions as to how to operate a helicopter offer explanations which do not propose any hypotheses and would not deserve to be called theories. Therefore I will use the term 'theory' to indicate only the explanations that do offer hypotheses and then try to justify those hypotheses with argument and evidence.

Given the definition of 'theory' as an explanatory guess, it should be obvious that the business of making them is not exclusive to scientists and philosophers. A detective may make a theory about the case she is working on; a motorist may devise one about a strange noise coming from his car's engine; and an office worker may propose a hypothesis as to why the boss is so grouchy today. Since all of these guesses are made in order to explain something, they are theories every bit as much as are the proposals of atomic theory or Freudian psychology. Moreover, both sorts of theories—the commonsense guesses as well as those of scientists and philosophers—are prompted by the same frustration: they are made when we cannot directly *discover* the answer to some question. When that happens, we guess at an answer.

However, there are important differences between the way theories are made by scientists and philosophers and the commonsense way theories are made around the house or office. Two such differences which have received almost universal recognition are: (1) theories in science and philosophy are more *abstract* than those of common sense, and (2) the methods of evaluating theories offered in science and philosophy are much more complex and sophisticated.[1] This greater sophistication is partly a result of the abstract nature of these theories, but is also prompted by the fact that such theories often disagree with each other. The testing methods are therefore geared not only to evaluate a theory itself, but to weigh it against its competitors.

In the remainder of this chapter, we will take a look at some differences between highly abstract and commonsense theories. This is necessary because despite wide acknowledgment of these differences they are rarely accorded their full importance.[2] They not only figure prominently in the evaluation of theories, but in gaining a proper view of how theories relate to religious belief. So we first need an account of abstraction, after which we will look at some differences between scientific and philosophical theories and distinguish between types of hypotheses that occur in both science and philosophy. We will then end with a short account of some guidelines for evaluating each type.

3. Abstraction

Everyone seems to agree that scientific and philosophical theories are highly abstract, so there are two things to account for: what is meant by abstraction, and what is meant by its being "high." An obvious starting point is to consider the literal meaning of the term 'abstraction'. To abstract means to extract, or remove something (mentally) from some wider context. This activity is virtually the same as focusing our attention, something we do frequently every day. For example, if we are trying to find a book that has a green cover, we may search the shelf by looking at all the books with green covers. In order to do that, we must first have mentally singled out the color green from all the other colors and from all the other qualities or properties a book may have. This level of abstraction is so common that we ordinarily pay no attention to it. We regularly perform such actions as avoiding something because it smells bad, judging something too large for a container, or preferring a course of action because it is fair. Commonplace as such actions are, they all require that we have first singled out odor, size, or fairness from among all the other properties exhibited by whatever it is that smells bad, is too large, or is fairer. In such cases the "extraction" of a property in our thought is not done so strongly as to isolate it from the thing or event that displays it. In other words, this level of abstraction does not focus on a thing's odor or size or whatnot to such a degree that it disrupts the continuity of those properties from all the other features of the things. Thus the property singled out is still experienced as a characteristic of the thing that exhibits it. I will call this the lower level of abstraction.

By contrast, we are capable of intensifying the focus of our attention to such a degree that we actually isolate a property from something, and focus our attention on the property itself. This type of abstraction I will call "high" abstraction. Since everyone agrees this is what distinguishes scientific and philosophical theories it is an important point, so I want to illustrate it in greater detail. Take the case of someone who has just bought a new car and is showing it to a group of friends. One of the friends says that she loves the color of the car, another comments that the car is beautiful, while still others ask how expensive it was and how much it weighs. All of these remarks show that the speakers have abstracted (at a low level) different properties of the car: its color, beauty, cost, and weight. But none of these properties has been isolated; they are still conceived as properties of the car.

If, however, someone were to focus on the property of weight itself, apart from the car (or any other particular object), he would conceive of weight in a highly abstract way. Other properties such as velocity, mass, and density could also be isolated. In this way highly abstract thinking can supply us with a whole new realm of concepts over and above those which are available without it. This adds a new dimension to theorizing by making it possible for hypotheses to be guesses of (or about) highly abstracted properties, functions, relations, etc., *in addition to* being of (or about) the things and events which have those properties, functions, etc. In this way, high abstraction can be used to explain both other abstractions and the things and events we continue to experience in the unbroken connectedness of all their properties.

Consider a simple example of how this can happen. By isolating properties in the focus of our attention, we create the possibility of asking about their relations, and patterns of connections among relations, all of which are also conceived in isolation from the things in which they occur.[3] For theories, the most important of the relations that can be discovered are laws. In the case of the properties of our present example, these would include

$$momentum = mass \times velocity$$

or

$$density = \frac{mass}{volume}.$$

Other examples would be the laws of motion or of thermodynamics, or Einstein's famous $E = MC^2$. Thus high abstraction makes it possible for us to ask questions about isolated properties and to answer those questions by isolating relations among them, especially laws. Neither the questions nor the answers could be conceived without high abstraction. Furthermore, producing arguments and evidence for (or against) the truth of such theories also involves high abstraction; in fact, these are often more sophisticated and ingenious than the hypotheses themselves.

The theories of science and philosophy therefore differ from commonsense theories by employing high abstraction in any one (or combination) of at least three ways: (1) in asking the question(s) the theory is proposed to answer, (2) in inventing the hypotheses proposed as answers to questions, or (3) in evaluating the truth of the hypotheses proposed.[4] From now on I will be dealing only with theories that employ high abstraction, so I will not continue to draw this distinction. The term 'theories' will always refer to the highly abstract type, and the term 'abstraction' will always refer to *high* abstraction rather than the mere singling out of an element of experience without isolating it.

4. Aspects of Experience

In addition to the three ways just listed, high abstraction plays yet another role in theory making. We not only abstract individual properties and patterns, we also abstract *kinds* of them. Take the properties we were just considering: weight, mass, momentum, and density. We can see that they all fall within the kind *physical.* Distinguishing this large-scale, overarching kind is as much an abstraction from the things and events we experience as are the individual properties and laws that fall under it. Once distinguished, it forms a distinct domain or field of inquiry and research that includes numerous subdivisions corresponding to the various branches of physics.

The same is true for many other kinds of properties which have been abstracted and made into areas of study. For example, *biological* properties are the field of study of biology, *spatial* properties and laws the field of study of geometry. Likewise, theories in *economics* or *ethics* have resulted from isolating those kinds of properties and laws and constructing theories in those fields. Over the past twenty-six centuries, many other kinds have been isolated and become distinct fields of investigation and theory making. A rough approximation of the kinds of properties which have been isolated for study include at least those on the following list (the members and order of which will be discussed in more detail later):

fiduciary
ethical
justitial

aesthetic
economic
social
linguistic
historical
logical
sensory
biological
physical
kinematic
spatial
quantitative

I will call these kinds of properties and laws "aspects" of our experience, and I am going to refer to the disciplines devoted to their study as "sciences." The term 'aspect' will serve to emphasize that the kinds are exhibited by, and extracted from, the objects of our pre-abstractive experience. The term 'science' is already used for any specific discipline in which theories are constructed.

This list should not be understood as a dogmatic pronouncement about all genuine aspects—many thinkers would offer a somewhat different list. Rather it is intended as a description of, not a theory about, what people experience. As such, it will help us understand theories by starting off with a working list of various kinds of properties and laws which have become distinct fields of study for theorizing, and for this purpose it is not necessary that we arrive at the one true list. Further, when I use such expressions as "aspects of things," or "aspects of the world," or "aspects of our experience," these expressions must be understood to refer to aspects in the same way the list does. They refer to what appear to be aspects from the standpoint of describing what we experience aside from any theorizing. They do not imply that our ordinary experience could not be mistaken, or that a theory could not show that things are different from the way they appear.

Although many sciences are devoted to an entire aspect or subdivision of it, and even take their name from it, there are others which stake out their field and take their name from a particular class of *things* they want to investigate. Entymology, paleontology, and botany are examples.[5] But such sciences do not count against the role of "aspects" in theorizing, for even when a science names its field by a particular type of things it still cannot study every aspect of those things. It is always some specific aspect(s) of insects, or fossils, or plants which they investigate. They need not be *confined* to only one aspect. For example, cultural anthropology deals with several aspects of ancient cultures and includes theories about how certain data relate *across* aspects. But whether or not a science thinks of its field as a particular aspect or as a certain range of things, in every case its aspectual delimitations remain the crucial factor: at every point a theory must make clear the kind(s) of properties it is dealing with and the kind(s) of laws it is using to explain its data.

Having made this emphasis on the role of abstraction in isolating aspects, I now freely admit that many people working in the sciences would say, if asked, that they are unaware of abstracting entire aspects. I think this is true, but that it fails to count against the necessity and importance of such abstraction. The reason someone may be unaware of abstracting an entire aspect is that this act is usually done so automatically it is not noticed by the thinker who does it—something like the way we are often unaware of moving our eyes while we read. In both cases there is a sub-event taking place within a larger act *for the sake of* that larger act. We move our eyes in order to read, and our attention is fixed upon our intended purpose rather than the eye movement done in order to accomplish that purpose. In the same way, and for the same reason, the activity of high abstraction can go unnoticed because it is done for the sake of investigating and theorizing about the properties and laws that fall within it. So it is not surprising that someone engaged in a science may notice the role abstraction plays in the conceptualization of specific properties or relations, but not notice its role in isolating entire aspects. The role is so basic that it can go unnoticed.

I will now offer some examples to illustrate how the abstraction of aspects is involved in the sciences. To appreciate the point of these examples, one must keep in mind that abstracting an aspect does not result in the thinker's experience or thought being emptied of everything but the aspect which is abstracted. What these examples will be showing, then, is how isolating an entire aspect is *added* to our experience and is an addition that is indispensable for the enterprise of scientific theorizing.

For the first illustration, take the case of a biologist looking at microbes through a microscope. As she experiences them, the microbes appear to have spatial size and shape, sensory color, and physical mass, etc. It may also be significant what quantity of them exist in a certain area. But these properties are all understood from the standpoint of her abstractive focus on the *biological* aspect of the microbes. It is that focus which guides and directs her thinking. Even though the size, mass, color, and number of the microbes are not themselves biological properties, they are all important insofar as they contribute to her understanding their biological life-processes. It is the focus on the biological aspect which guides the sorts of questions she will pose and the explanatory guesses she may make.

To see that this point applies equally to other sciences, consider a case in which a thinker's focus is guided by the isolation of the economical aspect. The economist may even be concerned with the same set of microbes the biologist was examining. But rather than being concerned with them as data to be covered by a biological explanation, he will instead be offering an economic explanation of them—an explanation whose explanatory principles include the law of supply and demand and the law of diminishing returns. The microbes will be covered by the economist's explanation because of their economic properties and laws, even if those economic properties might change were the microbes dead rather than alive.

These are illustrations of a role played by abstraction in theory making that is often not sufficiently acknowledged. Without the abstraction of entire aspects, it would not be possible to specify the kind of properties being investigated or the kind of laws being used to explain whatever a theory is seeking to explain. For these reasons—and others we will shortly discover—the abstraction of aspects is essential to theorizing. No matter exactly what list of aspects a thinker begins to theorize with, theorizing necessarily presupposes some list or other.

5. Types of Theories

First let us consider the difference between scientific and philosophical theories. Both are highly abstract, of course, but whereas scientists stake out one or more specific aspects as their domain, philosophers seem to lack such a "home ground." In fact, scanning the list of aspects given earlier could tempt one to suspect that since there are sciences devoted to every aspect, there is nothing left for philosophy to be *about*. This suspicion might be strengthened by the subjects philosophers write about. For example, there are scores of works devoted to the philosophy of mathematics, the philosophy of history, philosophy of law, and so on. This makes it appear that philosophy lacks its own domain, and so intrudes on everyone else's. Nevertheless, I am happy to report that philosophy does have a territory of its own, and once that territory is properly understood the difference between a scientific theory in an aspect and a philosophical theory about it becomes clear.

Earlier we noticed that some sciences theorize across aspects as well as within them. Noticing this allows us to see the possibility of developing a general theory; a theory not restricted to specific aspects, but giving an account of how all aspects interconnect. This is just what distinguishes philosophy from the sciences devoted to one or more specific aspects. Philosophy aims at an all-encompassing overview; it offers theories which seek to explain the general connection of all the aspects and *therefore of all the sciences*. While philosophers have occasionally disagreed with this definition and tried to argue that philosophy should have a less ambitious goal, these arguments are themselves testimony to the fact that from the beginning philosophical theories have tried to develop this sort of overview. The twentieth-century philosopher, Gilbert Ryle, expressed the point this way:

> The kind of thinking which advances biology is not the kind of thinking which settles the claims and counterclaims between biology and physics. These inter-theory questions are not internal to those theories. They are not biological or physical questions. They are philosophical questions.[6]

The famous psychologist, Jean Piaget, also recognized this distinctive feature of philosophy when he said that

> going over the bounds of one's own discipline implies a synthesis, and that discipline specializing in synthesis ... is no other than philosophy itself.[7]

The two sorts of theories invented by philosophers to "synthesize" or connect all the aspects of reality into an overview are a general theory of reality and a general theory of knowledge. The technical terms for these theories are, respectively, 'ontology' (also nicknamed "metaphysics") and 'epistemology'. It is the development of ontologies and epistemologies which distinguish philosophical theorizing and are its distinctive "home ground." When a philosopher theorizes about math, physics, logic, or ethics, it is not simply an intrusion into the domain of a science because it is done by bringing the results of a general theory of reality or knowledge to the study of those specific aspects. For this same reason, whenever scientists become involved with issues that require a view on how their specific aspect relates to all the others, they have crossed the border from science into philosophy. This observation is not intended as derogatory; there is nothing wrong with theories within a specific aspect relating to a wider perspective. In fact, I will argue later that it is impossible to make theories within a particular aspect that do not assume (even if unconsciously) some answer to the question of how that aspect relates to all the others. The difference is therefore one of emphasis: while scientific theories must at least *assume* some answer to the question of a general overview, that overview may remain a background assumption which is never consciously raised, questioned, or defended. But whereas a scientist may merely assume an overview, the philosopher *specializes* in it; philosophers make it the first order of business to justify the overview they invent or adopt, and all their other theories are developed in accordance with what is required by their theories of reality and knowledge.

But just what is meant by a "general theory of reality"? It is a theory that tries to discover the *essential nature* of reality. Its aim may be stated as trying to find what *kinds* of things there are. But saying it this way must not be mistaken for asking what *types* of things exist. Types of things would be an enormous list that would include: shoes, mountains, animals, clouds, people, etc. So the question here is not what types of things there are, but what is the basic nature of them all. Traditionally, such theories have tried to answer this question by proposing some one or more of the aspects accepted by a thinker as the basic nature of everything. For example, some theories have proposed that all things are basically physical, others that everything has a nature that combines physical with logical properties and laws, still others that everything is essentially mathematical, or sensory, etc.

The same is true of a general theory of knowledge. This is a theory that tries to account for what is essential to all knowledge, not just a specific kind of knowledge, such as mathematical knowledge, aesthetical knowledge, or ethical knowledge. Instead it tries to answer such questions as: "What is knowledge itself?" "How do we get knowledge?" and "What is truth?" To answer these questions, a theory has to account for the general connection of all the different aspectual kinds of knowledge. And as was the case with traditional theories of reality, traditional theories of knowledge have also taken the approach of proposing one or two aspectual kinds of knowing as the key to all the rest. Some theories have held knowledge to be essentially mathematical, for example, while others have said it is sensory, or logical, or historical.

It should be clear, then, that the business of philosophy involves explaining the general connection of the domains of all sciences in a way similar to the way a science tries to explain the relations of the data within an aspect.

The second distinction we can make concerning theories is between two types of hypotheses, each of which occurs in both science and philosophy. I will call the first of these an "entity hypothesis." The term 'entity' is used here because it is the widest and most indefinite term we have in English to refer to any sort of reality: things, events, states of affairs, relations, properties, laws, and anything else one wants to speak of. An entity hypothesis, then, is one which proposes some new entity as the solution to a question or puzzlement. This type of hypothesis assumes the explanation is some underlying, hidden reality. It then makes proposals as to the sorts of entities—things, laws, properties, functions, etc.—which comprise that underlying reality. In this way the gaps in our knowledge of what we experience are filled by educated guesses about entities we do not experience. It is as though we have been given a jigsaw puzzle to put together but cannot seem to make the pieces fit. To resolve the difficulty we guess that there is a missing piece which, were it of such and such a shape, would go into a particular spot and enable all the other pieces to fit in a way as to form the correct configuration. Most of the theories that are well known to the public are entity theories. Atomic theory and the Big Bang theory in physics, the theory of biological evolution, and Freud's psychological theory of an id, ego, and superego are all examples of theories proposing entities we do not experience in order to explain features of things we do experience.

Whenever some new entity is proposed, thinkers in that field are concerned to evaluate the theory; that is, they want to find out whether the entity is real. But since the entities proposed by theories usually cannot be directly experienced, they can be checked only indirectly.[8] The briefest way to summarize such indirect evaluation is to say that a theory is assessed by how well it explains what it was invented to explain, and whether it explains better than any competitors it may have. The standard evaluation checklist includes such items as the theory's logical consistency, how thoroughly it explains its data, and also how broadly its hypotheses can be applied. This last step is often the most persuasive. When a hypothesis that was offered to explain one puzzle is unexpectedly found to solve a number of others as well, it is hard not to believe that the entities it proposes are real.

Many entity hypotheses are also evaluated by experimentation. But as there are several common misunderstandings about the role of experiments, I want to take time to dispel two of the most common of them. The first is the notion that unless there is an experiment to test a theory, that theory cannot really count as scientific. The truth is, however, that experiments, although desirable, are often not possible and a theory is not discarded just because no experiment can be constructed. The second misunderstanding is that if an experiment is successful, then the theory has been proven beyond doubt and should henceforth count as indubitable truth. This mistake is often combined with yet another, namely, that experimental proof distinguishes scientific theories from those of philosophy. According to this compound error, scientific theories can be proven by experiment but philosophical theories are unprovable.

While it is true that there are philosophical theories which have opposed one another for thousands of years, and that most scientific theories have a much shorter life-span, this is not because one is always provable and the other never is. The fact of the matter is that *experiments can never prove any theory true beyond all doubt.* They perform a different service.

In order to understand why experiments cannot prove a theory true, we must first understand two simple logical rules. The first says that if it is true that "If A then B," and A is true, then B must be true. For example, A could mean "It is raining" and B could mean "The sidewalk is getting wet." In that case, "If A then B" would mean "If it is raining then the sidewalk is getting wet." Now the rule says that if that is true, and if it is raining, then the sidewalk is getting wet. Written as a formula the rule looks like this:

1. If A then B
2. <u> A   </u>
3. Therefore B

The crucial thing about this rule is that while it works from left to right, it does not work from right to left. We are not entitled to say:

4. If A then B
5. <u>   B </u>
6. Therefore A

For even if the sidewalk is getting wet, that will not tell us that it is raining. Other things could cause the sidewalk to get wet besides rain. But to claim that a successful experiment has proven a theory is to make the mistake represented in 4, 5, and 6 above. The argument would run:

7. If the theory is correct then the
   experiment succeeds.
8. <u>The experiment succeeds.   </u>
9. Therefore the theory is correct.

Thus the notion that a successful experiment can prove a theory true is based on a logical mistake. There is, however, another logical rule that does go from right to left. It runs like this:

10. If A then B
11. <u>   not B   </u>
12. Therefore not A

Applied to our sample argument, this would mean that if it is true that rain will wet the sidewalk, and if it is true that the sidewalk is not wet, then it is also true that it is not raining. When the value of an experiment is understood in this way, we can get a logically valid argument that looks like this:

13. If the theory is correct then
    the experiment succeeds.
14. <u>The experiment does not succeed.</u>
15. Therefore the theory is (at least
    partly) false.

Here we have the true value of experiments for theories. They cannot prove a theory true, but they can prove that it is false. Of course, even this value is subject to limitations: showing a theory to be partly false will not, all by itself, show exactly which part of it is wrong. And it is always possible that the experiment was not properly conducted or that it was not properly conceived in the first place. The real role of experiments in theory making, then, is that when a theory survives a number of (well-planned and well-executed) experimental attempts to prove it false, theorists in that field begin to feel more and more confident about it. The theory is then said to be "confirmed." But no set of successful experiments can ever extend the confirmation of a theory to the point where it can be said to be proven beyond all doubt.

Why is it, then, that refutation by experiment seems to happen often in the sciences but not in philosophy? The answer is that there is another type of theory besides entity theories, a type not usually able to be checked by experiment. And although entity theories and theories of this other type occur in both science and philosophy, the most famous theories in science are entity theories while the most famous philosophical theories are of this other type. This type does not begin by proposing the existence of some unexperienced reality, but explains its data in another way. Think again of our analogy of a jigsaw puzzle. If the data to be explained are represented by the pieces of the puzzle, then this second type of theory seeks to explain by viewing them from a certain *perspective* as to their mutual juxtaposition and relations rather than proposing the existence of a missing piece. In other words, this approach regards the pieces present as sufficient for solving the puzzle provided they are arranged in the right way. This type of theory I will call a "perspectival hypothesis."

An example of a perspectival hypothesis is the Marxist interpretation of history. According to this theory, the key factor in understanding history is always the *economic*. This means that the economic factor is seen as decisive in explaining the course of history and other possible explanatory factors such as religious beliefs, racial hatred, political rivalry, or the personal influence of powerful individuals are always controlled by the economics of the situation, rather than the other way around.

It is important to distinguish perspectival from entity theories for several reasons. First it allows us to recognize that the theories which are central to philosophy—the theories of reality and knowledge—are clearly perspectival. We already noticed that this is connected to the prevailing assumption in Western philosophy about how to construct such theories. The assumption is that the way to arrive at the essential nature of reality or knowledge is to select one or two aspects (from whatever list of them the thinker starts with) as identifying that essential nature. In other words, the assumption is that the basic nature of reality or knowledge is to be found by assigning a priority to one or two aspects over the rest. And it is clear that no priority assignment could be defended without an account of the mutual relations of all the aspects.

Second, it allows us to notice that the program of establishing a perspective by making an aspectual priority assignment may be carried out in two ways. The more popular version admits that reality has many genuine aspects, but argues that the one or two the theory has selected are what make possible the existence of all the others. In other words, it argues that its selection, call it aspect *X*, could exist apart from the other aspects but the others could not exist apart from *X*. Consequently, theories employing this approach may be seen as arguing that their selected one or more aspects characterizes the *basic* nature of reality. In the second version a theory argues that the aspect it has selected is the only genuine aspect; that all the (alleged) others can be shown to collapse into the one it has selected. This second version, then, is one in which a theory argues it has found the exclusive nature of reality or knowledge. In chapter 10, we will examine in more detail both of these versions of the prevailing Western assumption about how to construct theories of reality. At that time we will see why they unavoidably presuppose some religious belief.

Finally, recognizing the distinctiveness of perspectival theories is important because it allows us to notice how theories of reality pervade the concepts and theories of the sciences devoted to a particular aspect and are not confined only to philosophy. In fact, the argument to be made later will be that it is through theories of reality that the influence of religious belief is conveyed to scientific theories: scientific theories necessarily presuppose an overview of reality, while overviews of reality necessarily presuppose some religious belief. Religious belief, we will see, regulates overviews of reality directly, and through the mediation of such overviews regulates scientific theories indirectly.

In my classes I have found resistance to the idea that scientific theories cannot avoid presupposing a view of the essential nature of reality. People who are comfortable conceding that theories of reality unavoidably presuppose a religious belief often balk at extending the point to science. So although the more detailed defense of this claim will wait until the Casebook chapters (in which it will be illustrated for theories in math, physics, and psychology), some preliminary explanation seems called for here. Why is it that some perspectival overview of the essential nature of reality is unavoidably presupposed in the making and interpreting of entity theories constructed *within* a specific aspect?

There are, I believe, several ways in which assumptions about the nature of reality come into science, but perhaps the easiest to see is this: whatever aspects are assumed to be the basic (or exclusive) nature of reality are reflected in the nature assigned to the entities a scientific theory proposes. A proposed entity cannot simply be named. It is not enough for a theory to say, for example, "There are atoms." We need to know what *kind* of thing an atom is. How its nature is conceived will figure prominently in the ways it is supposed to explain whatever it is being proposed to explain.[9] But assigning a basic (or exclusive) nature to an atom or any other proposed entity cannot help but reflect the thinker's view of the basic or exclusive nature of all reality. It would make no sense for a theory to propose the existence of entities with natures at odds with the nature of as much of reality as they are intended to explain. For instance, suppose atoms are thought to have a basically physical nature; that is, it is their physical properties and laws which make possible all other properties and laws that may be true of them. But what is true for the atoms themselves would have to be assumed true of whatever they explain. That is, whatever they explain would also have to be assumed to be made possible by the physical properties and laws of atoms. So if atoms are taken to explain any data that are nonphysical, those nonphysical data would have to be regarded as made possible by the physical properties and laws of atoms. To deny this and yet insist that atoms nevertheless *explain* the data would make no sense. As we will see in chapter 8, this example is not merely hypothetical. There have been wide disagreements about the nature of atoms in the history of physics, and these disagreements have led to varying conceptions of how to do physics and what it can explain.[10]

This does not mean that a scientist proposing, defending, or adopting an entity hypothesis need have been influenced by any particular philosopher. It is not that overviews of the nature of reality *as elaborated in philosophical theories* necessarily exert a regulatory influence on theories in science. It is the *issue* of the nature of reality that cannot be avoided, whether or not what a scientist presupposes about it has ever been elaborated as a theory in the history of philosophy or whether the scientist is even conscious of the issue. As we will see in the Casebook, it is the differing views scientists take on this issue which account for the major disagreements that exist within the sciences despite the clearcut steps they use for evaluating their entity hypotheses.

5. Criteria for Judging Theories

The methods for confirming entity theories tend to be more precise and definite than those for perspectival theories. The thoroughness of explanation of entity theories can be checked because there are logical and mathematical ways to tell whether other known facts are implied when an entity proposal is added to the initial data a theory is dealing with. This often leads to predictions which can be checked by experiments. The breadth of application is easier to determine for an entity theory. It can be obvious whether a proposed entity, when plugged into a gap in another theory, yields confirmable results. Many theorists also evaluate an entity theory according to how many new entities it needs to propose. Their rule is that if two rival theories explain things equally well, the one with fewer hypotheses is to be preferred. In these ways, entity hypotheses can be evaluated, improved, or disproved.

By contrast, these standard procedures for judging entity hypotheses do not seem to work for perspectival hypotheses. Since proposing a perspectival slant on interpreting data is not a matter of adding proposed entities to initial conditions and seeing if they entail specific results, perspectival theories do not take the logical (deductive) format that entity theories do. And when rival perspectives are compared for thoroughness, whichever one looks true—or more nearly true—to a person will naturally seem to explain things better.[11] The fact that an alternative perspective may give a more detailed explanation will not make it look more likely true, but only make it seem false in greater detail. Moreover, the breadth of any perspective is (at least potentially) universal; all reality can be viewed from the standpoint of its quantity, or spatiality, physicality, sensory qualities, etc. Furthermore, since a perspective is not a proposal of an additional entity to fill a gap in the data to be explained, it is almost never possible to show that it logically or mathematically implies predictions which can be tested by experiment. Finally, it makes no sense to check two perspectives to see which proposes fewer entities, since neither proposes any.

Instead of following the criteria for entity theories, the judgment of a perspective seems to take the form of seeing whether certain data can have *any plausible account at all* on its standpoint. For example, it seemed clear that older forms of materialism could not give any plausible account of concepts. But modern materialists can point to the capabilities of computers and claim that human concept formation is essentially the same process. Whether that can be successfully defended or not, it is clear that materialism now has some sort of account of conceptual thought whereas previously it had none. Similarly, most of the arguments among perspectives have been challenges as to whether perspective *X* could produce any account of certain data, and then debating the plausibility of the accounts given from that perspective. This method is clearly looser than the ways entity theories are judged, and yields less definite results. They are less definite because even if it can be shown that existing accounts of certain data from a particular perspective do not work, that will not show that no plausible account could ever be given from that point of view. So the debates go on century after century.

It is possible, however, to offer additional guidelines which can be useful in evaluating perspectival hypotheses. Each of these guidelines will be the statement of a type of incoherency to be avoided by any theory, perspectival or otherwise. But although these guidelines apply to entity theories in addition to the usual tests described above, they will be presented here mainly with their application to perspectival theories in mind.

The first of these is the test of logical consistency. This test applies, of course, to our everyday speech and thought as well as to theories and simply means that we cannot be right if we assert (or assume) the truth of two beliefs that are logically contradictory or contrary. For example, we cannot be right if we believe both that our missing socks are in the bureau drawer and that they are not in the bureau drawer, or if we believe that all humans are mortal and no humans are mortal. Obviously, a theory cannot be right if one part of it says there are *x*'s and another part denies there are *x*'s.

Straightforward logical inconsistency between statements of a theory is only one sort of incoherence, however. A theory might also include a claim which, while not inconsistent with another statement of the theory, is in some way incompatible with its own truth. So our second rule is that a theory must not make any claim that would either: (1) cancel the possibility of its own truth, or (2) cancel the possibility of our knowing its truth. If a claim does either of these two things, it becomes incoherent when applied to itself. Following Alvin Plantinga, I will call any such claim "self-referentially incoherent."

As an example of the first of the two varieties of this incoherency, take the claim sometimes made by Taoists that nothing can be said of the Tao. Taken without qualification (which is probably not the way it is intended), this is self-referentially incoherent since to say "Nothing can be said of the Tao" is to say something of the Tao. Thus the statement applied to itself cancels its own truth. As an example of the second variety of self-referential incoherency, take the claim once made by Freud that every belief is a product of the believer's unconscious emotional needs. If this claim were true, it would have to be true of itself since it is a belief of Freud. It therefore requires itself to be the product of Freud's unconscious emotional needs. This would not necessarily make the claim false, as the incoherency does in its first variety, but it would mean that Freud could not claim to know it is true. The most it would allow him would be to admit that he could not help but believe it. And since the truth of this claim would require that everyone believes whatever they believe for exactly the same reason, there would be no way left for Freud or anyone else to discover whether any belief is true—including the belief that all beliefs are the product of unconscious emotional needs.

These two criteria—logical consistency and self-referential coherency—are alike in being rules for the preservation of coherence among beliefs which occur within a theory. In that respect they differ from the next two criteria which concern the compatibility between beliefs occurring in a theory and factors which lie outside the scope of the theory proper. The first of these says that a theory must not be incompatible with any belief we have to assume for either: (1) the theory to be true, or (2) for us to know that it is true. I will call a theory which violates this rule "self-assumptively incoherent."

As an example of (1) consider the claim made by some philosophers that all things are exclusively physical. This has been explained by its advocates to mean that nothing has any property or is governed by any law that is not a physical property or a physical law. But the very sentence expressing this claim, the sentence "All things are exclusively physical," must be assumed to have a sensory sound or appearance, and to possess a linguistic meaning. These are not physical properties, but unless the sentence had them it would not be a sentence; were it nothing but physical sounds or marks it would not linguistically signify any meaning whatever and thus could not express any claim—just as a rock or a cloud or an ocean fails to signify any meaning or express any claim. Moreover, to assert this exclusivist materialism is the same as claiming it is true, which is another nonphysical property, and assumes that for any assertion to be true its denial would have to be false—which is a relation guaranteed by logical laws. (Indeed, any theory which denies the existence of logical laws is instantly and irredeemable self-assumptively incoherent since that very denial is proposed as true in a way that is assumed to logically exclude its being false.) What this shows is that the claim "All things are exclusively physical" must itself be assumed to have nonphysical properties and be governed by nonphysical laws or it could neither be understood nor be true. Thus, no matter how clever the supporting arguments for this claim may be, the claim itself is incompatible with assumptions that are required for it to be true. It is therefore incoherent.[12]

As an example of (2), take Friedrich Nietzsche's proposal that maybe there are no things with properties at all. Perhaps, he said, we only experience the world that way because of the way our brains happen to have evolved. But this proposal is based on an inference from the theory of evolution, which cannot be true if there are not things with properties. Biological evolution is precisely a theory concerning the processes whereby living things attained an increasing complexity of biological properties. Thus Nietzsche's proposal is incompatible with the assumption that evolutionary theory is true, while at the same time that assumption is the reason he gives for the truth of his proposal.

The fact that the previous examples of self-assumptive incoherency had all to do with theories that deny a genuine plurality of aspects is no accident. Although such theories are not the only ones to violate this criterion, most of the violations are by theories of this type. The criterion is thus our first defense for regarding the appearance of a plurality of aspects as genuine: any attempt to deny there are any aspects at all or to reduce them to only one genuine aspect will always be self-assumptively incoherent.

The second guideline that lies outside the explicit content of theories is even more external than the first. The first is external only in the sense that it concerns assumptions required by a theory which may not be explicitly stated or acknowledged in the theory itself. But our final criterion stands outside theories altogether and concerns the conditions which make possible the very theory-making process itself. It is this: a theory must be compatible with any state or activity of the thinker without which it could not be produced.[13] As with the previous criteria, this guideline can also be violated in either a strong or a weak sense. The strong sense, once again, is when a theory could not be true because of its violation of the criterion, while the weaker sense is that a theory could not be known to be true because of its violation. I will call any theory which violates this criterion "self-performatively incoherent."

In order to start with as simple an illustration of this rule as possible, take the trivial case of someone saying that no one can speak, or that there is no such thing as language. Since one has to speak in order to say it cannot be done, and since one has to speak in a language in order to say there are none, these claims violate the criterion in the strong sense, and could not possibly be true. To illustrate the weak version of the criterion, take the case in which I am asked to determine the temperature of water in a glass with a thermometer. The fact is, once I put the thermometer into the water I cannot coherently claim to know what the temperature was prior to my performing that act. The act itself has changed— or could have changed—the temperature of the water. So the very activity necessary to discovering what I wanted to know prevents my ever being able to know it. Thus to claim that "The water in the glass *was* twenty degrees C." is to ignore the fact that the action by which this information was obtained prevents our knowing the claim is true.

A more serious example of this incoherency is the one noticed by Descartes. In reflecting on what can and cannot be reasonably doubted, Descartes saw that one thing that could not reasonably be doubted was his own existence. This was because he had to exist in order to doubt. He even had to exist in order to think or say "I do not exist." Thus his state of existing and his acts of thinking or speaking were all incompatible with the claim "I do not exist."

He therefore concluded that "I do not exist" had to be false, in which case he could not reasonably doubt the truth of "I exist" whenever he thought of it.

This example is important because it highlights the way this criterion can yield significant results by comparing a theory's claims to conditions that stand outside the theory itself, and which are not even beliefs. Like the previous criterion, the demand for self-performative coherency does not set aside logical laws or distinctions. Nevertheless, it gives us a way to test theories which goes beyond mere logical consistencies. It reminds us that a theory may avoid violating any logical rules and even remain compatible with its own assumptions, but still be seriously flawed. Notice that there is nothing logically self-contradictory about the sentence "I do not exist," nor is the truth of "I exist" required by logical rules alone. All the same, Descartes saw that the first could not be true and the second could not be false in some more-than-logical sense. That sense we have here identified.

This test of whether a theory is self-performatively coherent is one we will find particularly illuminating when we examine theories of reality in more detail in chapter 10. There we will look at the traditional strategies for defending such perspectival theories and find that they have always tried to justify their candidate for the basic nature of reality by showing them to be self-existent. The application of our test will show, however, that *any theoretical attempt to justify a claim about what is self-existent is incompatible with the activity of high abstraction* as that was described earlier. We will find all such attempts to be unavoidably self-performatively incoherent in the weaker sense. We will therefore conclude that no theoretical justification for any claim about what is self-existent is possible, since all attempts to do so are at odds with the very activity of abstraction that is necessary for the conceptualization of those claims. On this ground we will maintain all beliefs about what is self-existent to be equally unjustifiable faiths.

But before this position can be defended it is necessary to clarify it further. This is the task of the next two chapters. Chapter 5 will contrast our position with its major competitors concerning the relation of faith to theories. Then chapter 6 will give a more detailed account of what is meant by saying some religious belief always "controls" any theory of reality. With these clarifications behind us, we will then be prepared for the Casebook chapters.

5

Theories and Religion:
The Alternatives

In this chapter I will give a brief sketch of the major positions which have been taken on the general relation of religious belief to theory making in the history of Western thought. To the best of my knowledge only three ideas other than the one I defend here have ever been proposed.

1. Religious Irrationalism

The title I have given to this first alternative view should not be taken to mean that religious belief is in some sense substandard or disreputable when rationally assessed. It is not a judgment on the worthiness of religious belief but a view as to how, in general, such belief relates to reason. Taken in this way the irrationalist view can be stated quite simply: the two have nothing to do with one another so that neither is capable of passing judgment on the other.

On this view, the reasoning that goes on in scientific and philosophical theory making is unable to say anything about the truth or falsity of any religious belief. I will refer to the sort of reasoning this view sees as walled off from religious belief as "theoretical" reasoning. Those who hold this view reject the notion that religious belief can be proven or disproven, or even that a theory can explain why people who have a religious belief have it. On this view, a person's faith is an inexplicable fact, suspended in mid-air, with no strong connections to anything else—with the possible exception of morals.

This position was neatly put to me on my very first day in graduate school. A tutor in the philosophy department asked me why I had come to the university and what my main interest was. When I replied that I was entering the philosophy of religion program, he winced in disappointment and remarked, "Here at Harvard we teach philosophy and we teach religion. It's up to you if you see any connection." In fact, the way he put the point was mild in comparison with the way other thinkers have stated it. Some have held that religious belief and theoretical reasoning are so mutually inimical that the very attempt to give reasons for a faith destroys it. For example, Soren Kierkegaard said of those who want to explain or justify their faith in a rational way:

> Would it not be better to stop with faith, and is it not revolting that everybody wants to go further?... Would it not be better that they should stand still at faith, and that he who stands should take heed lest he fall? For the movements of faith must constantly be made by virtue of the absurd....[1]

By calling faith "absurd," Kierkegaard means (among other things) that it is not rationally justifiable. But he also means that theoretical reason and faith are mutually exclusive:

> Therefore it is certain and true that he who first invented the notion of defending Christianity... is de facto Judas number two....[2]

And again, at greater length:

> Suppose a man wishes to acquire faith; let the comedy begin. He wishes to have faith but he wishes also to safeguard himself by means of an objective inquiry.... What happens?... It becomes probable, it becomes increasingly probable, it becomes extremely and emphatically probable. Now he is ready to believe it, and he ventures to claim for himself that he does not believe as shoemakers and tailors and simple folk believe, but only after long deliberation... and lo, now it has become precisely impossible to believe it. Anything that... is something he can almost *know*... it is impossible to *believe*. For the absurd is the object of faith, and the only object that can be believed.[3]

Another thinker who took this line was Friedrich Schleiermacher, a nineteenth-century German theologian. For Schleiermacher, religious belief was isolated from reason because religion is strictly a matter of feeling. So he defined religion as the "sum of all higher feelings," and drew the consequences this way:

> Wherefore it follows that ideas and principles are all foreign to religion.... If ideas and principles are to be anything, they must belong to knowledge which is a different department of life from religion.[4]

Like Kierkegaard, Schleiermacher sees faith and knowledge as mutually exclusive. But while Schleiermacher thinks that reason cannot intrude into the realm of faith even if it wants to, Kierkegaard thinks that such intrusions are possible but are always destructive of faith.

There are, of course, other variations of this position beside the two just cited, but all have in common the theme of disparaging the role of reason for religious belief; they maintain that at best it can do no good, and at worst can do great harm. A diagram may help make this position clear.

Religious Belief is:	**Theoretical Reason** is:
1. optional	1. religiously neutral and autonomous
2. isolated from theoretical reason	2. final court of appeal in its realm

There are two features of this position I want to call attention to before going on to look at the other positions. The first, indicated by the first item on the left side of the diagram, is that while every normal person has reason, faith is considered an option which may or may not be exercised.

The second feature is that although this position limits the scope of reason, it does not disparage reason altogether or advocate that we stop thinking. It is willing to go along with the highest estimation of the competency of theoretical reason in matters having to do with the rational side of life. It accepts that reason is the final court of appeal in these matters and that it is—in principle—neutral with respect to any outside influence and autonomous (self-governing). Rather than disparaging reason altogether, irrationalism simply maintains that there is a nonrational side to life which provides a niche for religious belief into which theoretical reason cannot (or ought not) intrude. It therefore surrenders any hope of obtaining rational support for faith, but at the same time gains immunity from any rational critique of faith. In return, the irrationalist likewise grants theoretical reason immunity from being censored by faith. On this view the two are so walled off from one another that there cannot be a direct conflict between an article of faith and a theory of science or philosophy.

2. Religious Rationalism

Over against the irrationalist position, there is another which I call "religious rationalism." On this position, *all* beliefs are to come before the judgment seat of rational inquiry, religious belief included. As the philosopher A. N. Whitehead once put it, "The appeal to reason is to the ultimate judge, universal and yet individual to each, to which all authority must bow."[5] On this position no other consideration—no amount of faith, hope, feeling, etc.—is to be allowed as a competing authority to the verdict of reason.

Thus, rationalism agrees with irrationalism about the neutrality of reason, but denies the same limits to reason's scope. It holds reason to be autonomous in the sense that it is not, in principle, under any influence other than its own rules. This does not mean that people are always neutral and unbiased when they evaluate beliefs or construct theories, of course. But however successful or unsuccessful people may be in preventing extraneous influence from coloring their judgment, the rules of rational thinking by which we make and evaluate theories are themselves neutral, and would lead to unbiased conclusions if only people could keep from letting other influences interfere.

In some older versions of rationalism, reason was not only supposed to be neutral and the final court of appeal, it was also often thought to be competent to judge every issue whatever. Those who held this view did not mean that they actually possessed an explanation of everything, only that everything is in principle rationally decidable or knowable. This conviction was based on the belief that the orderliness which underlies the whole of reality is the same kind of orderliness that makes human rationality possible.

From the beginning, however, many rationalists hedged about this last point. Some doubted whether reality is completely open to rational explanation, and others doubted that human reason has the power—even in principle—to decide every question. Today there are few, if any, who would subscribe to this point. But all religious rationalists deny that it is legitimate to hold any beliefs reason cannot decide. Instead of allowing for a legitimate niche for beliefs not rationally decidable, they demand that belief be suspended on such issues. At the same time, however, they insist that religious belief is one of the issues theoretical reason can decide. Diagrammatically, the position that religious belief depends upon the verdict of theoretical reason looks this way:

Religious Belief is:
1. a theory or conclusion of reason
2. optional

Theoretical Reason is:
1. neutral respecting all matters
2. final court of appeal in all matters
3. able to decide all matters (?)

Being a rationalist about the relation of theoretical reasoning to religious belief does not, however, assure agreement as to what reason's verdict on religious belief will be. One of the great champions of this position was Plato, who concluded that reason shows religious belief to be true by proving there are gods. By being rational, he says,

> we are assured that there are two things which lead men to believe in the gods. . . . One is the argument about the soul . . . that it is the eldest and most divine of all things . . . the other was an argument from the order of the motion of the stars and of all things under the domination of the mind which ordered the universe. (*Laws* XII, 966)

But the same rationalist position was also held by the twentieth-century thinker, Bertrand Russell, who arrived at quite a different conclusion:

> So far as scientific evidence goes, the universe has crawled by slow stages to a somewhat pitiful result on this earth and is going to crawl by still more pitiful stages to a condition of universal death. If this is to be taken as evidence of purpose, I can only say that the purpose is one that does not appeal to me. I see no reason, therefore, to believe in any sort of God, however vague and however attenuated.[6]

Among those who hold the rationalist position, there has been a definite trend over the last three centuries away from Plato's conclusion and toward Russell's. As a result, many thinkers now take it for granted that reason has refuted religious belief and replaced it with the theories of science and philosophy.

Before going to the next alternative view, it is worth noting that both rationalism and irrationalism agree that not everyone has a religious belief. For both, it's a matter of choice whether someone has faith or not. The rationalist opposes the irrationalist only by insisting that the decision is to be made by the same rational procedures that go into evaluating theories.

3. The Radically Biblical Position

The rationalist position was the dominant influence in the culture of the ancient world when the rise and spread of Christianity introduced belief in another authority onto the world scene. The biblical religions, Judaism and Christianity, denied that reason is the final authority or that theory making is the only or best way to all truth. They taught instead that while reason is important, its highest function is to enable humans to understand the revelation of God and to serve him on the basis of what he has revealed. Accordingly, most Jewish and Christian thinkers rejected the rationalist position. Even those who tried to remain as close to rationalism as possible had to deal in some way with relating reason to the word of God as another, distinct, authority.

Today most Jews and Christians relate the authority of reason to the authority of God's word by carving out two distinct realms, one for each authority, and saying that the authority of revelation from God is confined almost entirely to matters of faith and morals. Because this view is so widespread, most believers are quite surprised to learn that both the Jewish and Christian Scriptures extend the authority of God's word to the whole of life, including reason itself. That is to say, the Scriptures themselves teach that what God has revealed about himself is somehow the key to *all* knowledge and truth! Because this teaching is so seldom acknowledged, I want to take a moment to show that it is in fact found both in the Psalms and Prophets, and in the New Testament.

The prophet Jeremiah, in deploring the inroads of pagan religion among his countrymen, says that by rejecting the word of the Lord there is no wisdom left in them (Jer. 8:9). And in the Proverbs the remark is repeatedly made that the foundation (or key part) of wisdom and knowledge is the fear of the Lord (Prov. 1:7; 9:10; 15:33). The same point is made again in the Psalms (111:10) and in the book of Job (28:28).

The New Testament repeats these claims. When Jesus accused some of the religious authorities of his day of misinterpreting the Scripture, he added that by distorting the meaning of God's word they had "taken away the key to knowledge" (Luke 11:52). And Paul, in teaching that Jesus was the Messiah and thus the completion of God's revelation, added that "in him are hid all the treasures of wisdom and *knowledge*" (Col. 2:3). Elsewhere he comes back to this point twice: once to say that the consequences of religious enlightenment extend not only to morals ("all that is good") but also to *all truth* (Eph. 5:8, 9), and again to say that anyone turning from pagan religion to the true God becomes a new person for whom the whole of life is changed (2 Cor. 5:17). Nor are these isolated comments that are able to be dismissed as some sort of poetic exaggeration. In Ephesians 4:17–18, and again in Romans 12:1, the turning of one's heart to the true God is said to renew one's *mind* and *understanding.*

The striking thing about all the remarks just quoted is that they do not speak only of our knowledge *of God* being dependent on our belief in him, but of *all* knowledge and wisdom of whatever sort. I emphasize this because most people have a tendency to read these passages as though they say that the fear of the Lord is the foundation of *religious* knowledge, or that religious enlightenment extends to all that is true *about God.* But the fact is that they make a very radical claim—the claim that somehow *all* knowledge depends upon religious truth. Because the views that carve out distinct realms for faith and knowledge are so influential, many sincere Jews and Christians find this teaching extreme. For this reason, I call this viewpoint the 'radically biblical' position. Diagrammatically, it is the inverse of the rationalist position since it reverses the controlling role:

Theoretical Reason is:

1. not neutral because controlled
   by religious belief
2. not final court of appeal
3. not able to decide all matters

―――――――――― ↑ ――――――――――

Religious Belief

1. guides and directs the use of
   reason in all of life

Sometimes it is objected that many of the texts I have cited speak of "wisdom" rather than "knowledge." The suggestion is that these biblical passages mean only to convey the much more modest point that it is being practically or morally wise that depends upon believing in the one true God rather than a false divinity. This, however, is quite mistaken. The term 'wisdom' was used in the ancient world for what we now call scientific knowledge as well as for practical and moral insight. The ancient thinkers who worked in mathematics, physics, astronomy, and the like were called "wise men" or some equivalent term, and the word 'philosopher' means "lover of wisdom." So in the ancient world having either practical or theoretical knowledge qualified a person as "wise." In addition, several of the quoted sections specifically say that all "knowledge" or "truth" depends on having the true God.

The radically biblical position differs from the rationalist and irrationalist with respect to whether faith is optional. Rather than speaking of religious belief as something a person may choose to have, the Bible writers regarded everyone as having some faith or other. According to them, what is wrong with people is not that they lack faith, but that they have faith in the wrong divinity. On this position, then, faith is a natural function of humans which, like reason, can be exercised rightly or wrongly, but cannot be dispensed with altogether.

It is fair to ask whether on this position it is wrong-headed for believers to try to justify their belief in God rationally. I think the biblical position is that it is neither possible nor desirable to give a theoretical justification of faith in God which would convince an unbeliever, but I would hasten to add that this does not rule out critically reflecting on one's faith in order to better understand its teachings, or to compare them with the teachings of other faiths. Nor does it mean that rational discussion with unbelievers is totally useless for it can clarify biblical teachings for unbelievers as well as for ourselves. The position of the Bible writers is only that we ought not to expect that unbelievers will become believers by rational persuasion alone, nor ought we to think that we must have some sort of rational justification of our faith in order for it to be intellectually respectable.

Despite the rejection of theoretical justification as a necessary basis for belief in God, the radically biblical position is not a kind of fideism which asks for blind adherence. Rather it holds that our belief in God does not depend on rational justification because it is grounded in the *experience* of his revelation in both nature and his word, which experience is the result of the grace of God overcoming the effects of sin on the human heart and mind.[7]

Belief in God is therefore neither blind nor is it walled off from rational understanding. On the contrary, it is religious belief that controls and directs the way people interpret the whole range of their experience, so that all truth does indeed depend on having the right God. Moreover, these two teachings—the religious control of theoretical thinking and the denial of the need to justify faith—are importantly connected. If faith controls and directs reason, it would logically follow that all theoretical attempts to prove or discredit belief in God would amount to circular reasoning. In other words, our attempting to give a convincing proof of God to unbelievers is futile because our faith sets the limits for what looks true to us, just as their religious belief does for them.

Now it is this radically biblical position I will be defending in all that follows. I will maintain that the exercise of theoretical reason is always regulated and directed by some religious belief so that reason is never autonomous nor theorizing religiously neutral. On this view, faith is not a faculty of the mind separate from the faculty of reason, but an integral part of reason; reason is essentially faith-oriented. But to distinguish this view adequately, it must also be contrasted with the most popular view, a view which insists that faith and reason are separate faculties of the mind and which, therefore, carves out distinct realms for the authority of reason and the authority of faith. Nevertheless, this final alternative does not simply wall off faith and reason as irrationalism does, but relates the two in a much more complex way.

4. Religious Scholasticism

The radically biblical position has not been held by most Jews or Christians. Long before the rise of Christianity, there were strong differences of opinion among Jews concerning the proper attitude to take toward the relation of their faith to the rest of life, particularly toward the dominant pagan, rationalist culture of the Greco-Roman world. Some Jews utterly rejected that culture as incompatible with what it meant to be a Jew, while the majority thought that most of the ancient culture could be acceptable. On the majority view, all that is needed to be truly Jewish is to maintain the worship of the true God and the rituals and moral standards of the Law of Moses over against pagan polytheism and loose morality. In other words, the second of these two opinions saw most of life and culture as religiously neutral, so that being distinctively Jewish was restricted to faith and morals.

The same issue faced early Christians as well, and there arose the same differences of opinion among Christians that had divided Jews. Some thought that an unbridgeable chasm separated the entire Judeo-Christian tradition from the ancient world culture. They saw the effects of their faith on the rest of life as all-encompassing. One of them, Tertullian, referring to the biblical outlook as that of "Jerusalem" and the dominant culture as the outlook of "Athens," asked, "What has Jerusalem to do with Athens?" But the majority thought their opposition need not be nearly so radical. They held that the culture of their day was not so much wrong as incomplete. They regarded science, philosophy, art, law, etc., as neutral with respect to religious belief. (After all, doesn't 1 + 1 = 2 for a pagan as well as for those who believe in God?) So they adopted the attitude that, except for their belief in God and the need to correct pagan morals by biblical standards, Christians could accept the culture of their day without compunction. In short, they took the position that there is no radical opposition between biblical religion and any particular culture, since most of life is religiously neutral. Thus they adopted the view that the proper understanding of most aspects of one's culture do not differ depending on what one's religion is. They took biblical texts such as the ones quoted earlier to mean that only religious wisdom and knowledge depend on having the true God.

This interpretation came to dominate the thinking of most theologians in the first few centuries after the rise and spread of Christianity. Because it was eventually developed brilliantly in the work of a number of theologians and philosophers who were professors, it later came to be called the position of the "school men" or "scholastics," and still later was simply called "scholasticism." One elaboration of this view by Thomas Aquinas in the thirteenth century was so extensively worked out, and subsequently so influential, that many historians and philosophers today use the term 'scholasticism' as a name only for Thomas's theories or theories very like his. I am not referring to a particular group of theories or style of theorizing in my use of "scholasticism" and still less to theories which are heavily Aristotelian as Thomas's were. Instead I am using the term for the strategy of understanding the relation of religious belief to reason by dividing beliefs into two classes: beliefs which are the deliverance of reason, and beliefs which are the deliverances of revelation accepted on faith.

This position sought to avoid a head-on collision between the all-encompassing claim pagan rationalism made for reason and the equally all-encompassing biblical claim that right faith is necessary to knowledge by an ingenious compromise which limited the scope of each. The compromise was to say that although everything other than God is creation, creation is to be divided hierarchically; it has a lower level and an upper level, each of which is discovered in a different way. The lower level, called "nature," is open to all people through experience and reason, and reason is the neutral and final authority in the realm of nature. But most of the upper level, called the realm of "super-nature" or the realm of "grace," can be known only by revelation from God which must be accepted on faith. Such revealed truths include facts about God that are unprovable by reason, the nature of the human soul, angels, and information about life after death. These truths are therefore not open to all people but only those to whom God's grace has given the gift of faith. For without faith to accept revelation, reason is relatively helpless to discover truth about the supernatural realm. (I say "relatively helpless" because most scholastic thinkers held that reason unaided by revelation could prove that God exists and that humans have a soul, but nothing more. It cannot show how humans come to stand in proper relation to God.) In this way, each all-encompassing claim is in one sense discarded and in another sense retained: reason and faith are seen as two distinct faculties of humans, each of which is the final authority in its own realm.

But whereas the irrationalist position walls off the rational side of life from that of faith, scholasticism sees the relation of faith and reason to involve two-way interaction. Perhaps the best way to think of this interaction is to say that on this position faith and reason each have duties toward one another; each has its own proper domain, but each also affects the other. For example, reason not only discovers truth about nature and proves the existence of supernature, but also systematizes revealed doctrines and checks theories of reason for their compatibility with these doctrines. This is the task of theology. In case a theory of philosophy or science is found to be irreconcilably in contradiction with revealed truth, that theory is to be discarded as false. The duty of faith toward reason is thus to supply an external check on whether reason has fallen into error; it is seen as an advantage for reason to have such infallible truths by which to test its hypotheses. In the final analysis, therefore, the authority of revelation taken on faith is superior to that of reason alone.

So the dominant issue for scholastic thinkers has always been how to interpret the relation between the realms of nature and grace. For although the main distinctions of the general scholastic scheme seem sharp and clear, in practice they generated endless messy debates over just how to apply them in particular cases. Diagrammatically, scholasticism's main distinctions can be represented this way:

Realm of Supernature or Grace	Faith accepts revelation as the supreme authority concerning God and the soul and related matters
Natural Realm	1. Reason is neutral and final authority concerning nature; 2. Reason harmonizes religion with the theories of science and philosophy; 3. Reason proves the existence of the supernatural and systematizes revealed doctrines.

Despite the disagreement over the details of how faith and reason interact in specific cases, wide consensus emerged among scholastic thinkers on a number of main points. First of all, while all humans are naturally rational beings not all exercise faith. The faculty of faith comes to a person as a gift from God which is an addition to what a human is naturally. The great champion of scholasticism, Thomas Aquinas, put the point this way:

> Nobody receives grace of himself howsoever he prepares himself, even though he does all that lies in his power ... for grace surpasses all human effort ... if it be God's will to touch the heart then grace will infallibly follow. (*Summa theologica* Ia-IIae, q. 112, a. 3)

This addition of faith does not displace a person's reason, as we saw, but supplements it. As Aquinas says:

> The gifts of Grace are added to us in order to enhance the gifts of nature, not to take them away. The native light of reason is not obliterated by the light of faith.... The principles of reason are the foundations of philosophy [and science], the principles of faith are the foundation of Christian Theology. The truths of philosophy ... cannot

be contrary to the truths of faith. . . . Nature is the prelude to grace. It is the abuse of science and philosophy which provoke statements against faith. . . .[8]

Thus the guidance that faith offers to reason is a largely negative and external check on what reason may accept. It is not seen as an internally motivating influence. Were the influence of truths learned by faith internal to the operation of reason, reason would no longer be religiously neutral and autonomous. And were it not neutral, there would be no religiously neutral theories for the interpretation of nature that could be held in common with people who lack faith. In that case, the difference between what can be learned by faith and what can be known by reason would be wiped out. What is more, if reason were not neutral it could not offer compelling proof that there is a supernatural realm. But, says scholasticism, reason can indeed provide rational evidence that there is a supernatural realm by proving the existence of God and the human soul, which it does in a neutral and unbiased way. Thus reason points to a realm that needs to be revealed by God if we are to know more about it.

This last point might appear to blur the boundary between nature and grace just a bit, so Aquinas explained it to mean that certain items available to reason were revealed by God anyway so that those of weaker intellect would be sure not to miss them. But since they are knowable by reason alone, these items are not—strictly speaking—articles of faith. He says:

That God exists, and other such Theological truths which can be known by natural reason are not articles of faith, but preambles to the Creed: faith presupposes reason as grace presupposes nature. . . . (*Summa theologica* Ia, q. 2, a. 2, ad 1)

Because scholasticism leaves such a wide latitude for both faith and reason while still admitting a strong interaction between them, many believers find it difficult to see how the radically biblical view differs—let alone why it does. After all, doesn't Scripture regard people as rational beings as well as beings who have faith? And doesn't it imply that reason can discover some truth about God on its own hook?

The first part of our objection to scholasticism has already been given. It is that Scripture views all truth as somehow tied to having the right God. This is a stronger position than scholasticism's view that no specific theory or finding of reason may contradict any specific doctrine of theology. No matter how detailed the application of the scholastic program, it remains an external and largely negative check on the deliverances of reason. The fact is that most of these deliverances will turn out religiously neutral on the scholastic view, since the majority of them neither contradict revealed doctrine nor are entailed by it. But the biblical remarks about all truth being religiously conditioned would require the role of religious belief to be internal as well as external, positive as well as negative. On this view, reason has no "hook" of its own on which to operate. So despite scholasticism's insistence that the authority of faith is superior to that of reason and that revealed truth about supernature is more important than rational truth about nature, its position is still too weak concerning the role of religious belief in reason.

Our second objection finds it in opposition to the scriptural view of humans as naturally religious beings. Genesis teaches that humans were created for fellowship with God, and Bible writers always address their reader as though they already believe in God or some God surrogate. This is why the Psalms say that anyone who insists there is nothing divine is a fool; it is because the whole while they assert that they in fact regard something as divine. So the radically biblical position cannot agree that the function of faith is a "donum superadditum"—an addition to the nature of a believer that was not there before. The gift of God's grace is not the addition of a function previously missing, but the redirecting and repairing of a malfunctioning faith. As Calvin puts it, we are made so that we would naturally have "both confidence in him, and a desire of cleaving to him, did not the depravity of the human mind lead it away from the proper course of investigation" (*Institutes,* 1, 2, 3).

Furthermore the radically biblical position denies that creation is a hierarchy divided into two realms, each of which is known by a different human faculty. Both God and creation are known by the same faculty, namely, reason which is by its very nature faith directed. This is not to suggest, of course, that there is nothing distinctive about the ways we know creation and the ways we know God. Since God is not a part of creation, he must reveal himself if we are to know him. In addition, there is the effect of sin on human reason. As we have already seen, the biblical idea of sin is more a religious than a moral matter primarily having to do with putting one's faith in a false divinity rather than God, and only secondarily concerning moral wrongdoing. As such, sin is a condition of humans in which their reason is misdirected by a malfunctioning faith, so that faith must be restored to proper working order if reason is ever to recognize God's revelation for what it is. As Scripture tells us, nature—seen rightly—would display its dependent creatureliness (Ps. 19:1). But reason misdirected by false faith does not correctly read nature's display. It instead represses what would otherwise be obvious, and regards something other than God as divine (Rom. 1:18–24). This can only be remedied by the restoration of faith to its proper working order, so that God's word is seen for what it is and makes possible the correct interpretation of nature. As Calvin once remarked, the Scriptures are the spectacles through which the book of nature can be properly read.

5. The Conflict of These Alternatives

The scholastic outlook sketched above had permeated the whole of European thought by the fifth century and was eventually adopted by virtually every leading Jewish, Christian, and (later on) Moslem thinker. Corresponding to the division of what can be known into natural and supernatural realms, this outlook saw all of life as known by faith or reason, as sacred or secular, as matters of the soul or the body, and so on. On this outlook, therefore, life was neither completely unified nor highly diversified. Everything had to be understood as two-sided: it was either a matter of the supernatural in which faith is the supreme authority, the destiny of one's soul is at stake, and the church is the representative institution on earth; or it was a matter of nature in which reason is the supreme authority, one's bodily welfare is at stake, and the state is the chief representative institution.

Among thinkers who believe in God, scholasticism is still by far the most popular position in the world today. Its subscribers in religious studies, philosophy, science, art, and literature still outnumber any one of the other three positions, but it no longer has the almost total adherence that it did between roughly A.D. 500–1500 What is more important, it is no longer the leading outlook of Western culture. This loss of leadership came about in the sixteenth century when scholasticism was simultaneously challenged by two movements. One of these advocated the autonomy and neutrality of reason in all matters and wished to dispense with reason being limited by faith. The other rejected limiting faith to the supernatural and argued that reason is intrinsically guided by faith.

The revival of the rationalistic position was the result of the gradual rediscovery of the accomplishments of the ancient world. The scholars involved in this rediscovery began to regard ancient culture as superior to their own and in time began to refer to the era between the fall of Rome and themselves as a "middle age," that is, an in-between period between the last great culture and the one they hoped to usher in. They saw themselves as the defenders of reason, revivers of rationalism who would bring back the glory of the ancient world by restoring the supreme command of reason. Nineteenth-century historians who agreed with them began to call their movement a "Renaissance," a rebirth of the freedom of reason in order to rebuild the greatness of Western civilization.

From what did they think reason needed to be freed? They said it should be free from every restriction whatsoever, but clearly they were thinking especially of the restrictions imposed by faith according to the scholastic partition. They called for a new outlook which did not set limits beforehand to what reason could or could not accept, and which did not constantly point to a realm of supernature as more important than the natural world. They confidently predicted that if their outlook were given free rein, they could begin to create paradise here and now instead of simply hoping for it after death.

At the same time that this Renaissance movement was gaining momentum, another movement arose to challenge the scholastic establishment. This movement, called the Reformation, was unlike the Renaissance in that it came from within the church. Although the flavor of this movement differed somewhat depending on its leaders in various localities, one of the clear thrusts of the movement was an attempt to revive the radically biblical position. The Reformers—Luther, Calvin, and their associates—saw the word of God as permeating and transforming the whole of life, not merely as an external constraint or check on reason but as its internal driving motivation. Most of their efforts were understandably aimed at reformulating theology and reorganizing the church, but the fundamental conviction behind their reforms was the rejection of the scholastic partition of nature and grace.

In the course of his work, Luther reverted to a scholastic view on a number of issues, but Calvin carried forward the anti-scholastic strain of Luther's thought. In commenting on the supposed religious neutrality of reason in the study of nature, Calvin said:

> It is vain for any to reason ... on the workmanship of the world, except those who ... have learned to submit the whole of their intellectual wisdom (as Paul expresses it) to the foolishness of the cross. ... the invisible kingdom of Christ fills all things and his spiritual grace is diffused through all.[9]

Throughout his writings, Calvin takes the view that human reason is not neutral because it is affected by sin, where sin is understood to be a religious matter with definite, deleterious effects on human reason. As he sees it, false religious belief cannot help but distort reason across the board, not just in theology and ethics. By the same token, when Scripture reveals the true God it not only reveals the proper object of faith but restores the proper perspective for the operation of reason. To be sure, Calvin does not spell out exactly *how* belief in God does this, any more than the Bible writers do, but that will be the task of the succeeding chapters of this book. I will offer a specific interpretation of this claim in chapter 6, and show its accuracy for theories in math, physics, and psychology in chapters 7, 8, and 9. Then in chapter 10, I will spell out the consequences this has for theorizing on the basis of belief in God, and contrast them to the scholastic program in detail.

These two new movements of Renaissance and Reformation came into head-on conflict with the entrenched scholasticism and with one another by the mid-sixteenth century. One of the first casualties of this conflict was the radically biblical element of the Reformation movement. Though many of the doctrinal reforms of Luther and Calvin were preserved in branches of Protestantism, the radically biblical element of their teaching was not. In fact, the immediate successors to the leadership of the Reformation movement (Phillip Melancthon and Theodore Beza, respectively) abandoned the idea that all knowledge is conditioned by religious belief and returned to the scholastic position. So even though Protestant and Catholic theologians continued to disagree over specifics such as the doctrine of the church, the interpretation of the sacraments, and (later on) papal infallibility, their general view of the relation of faith and reason was largely the same. Their main difference over faith and reason was only that Catholic thinkers harmonized their faith with theories about the natural realm derived from Aristotle (due to the influence of Thomas Aquinas), while Protestant thinkers felt free to harmonize their faith with whatever theories about nature were currently fashionable. The result has been a virtual parade of Protestant scholastic accommodations such as with Cartesian dualism, phenomenalism, Kantian idealism, Hegelian monism, romanticism, Marxism, existentialism, etc. Meanwhile the radically biblical position, though it survived in the work of a few individual thinkers and some small theological traditions, was marginalized by most of Protestant thought.

The crucial point here is that both camps of mainstream Christian thought, along with most Jewish thinkers, had lost all appreciation of the religious control of the whole of life. Theories were thought to be religiously neutral rather than presupposing either God or a false divinity. Consequently, almost no theistic thinkers saw that harmonizing their faith with a theory is impossible unless that theory already presupposes their faith. Instead of recognizing that if a theory does not presuppose belief in God it inevitably presupposed belief in some other divinity, they assumed theology was free to work out a peace treaty between their faith and whatever theory sounded most plausible. The radically biblical objection to this is, of course, that any supposed harmony of a theory with faith in God is mere illusion so long as the theory presupposes another, incompatible, religious belief.

Perhaps the main reason for the demise of the radically biblical position was that around the time of the Reformation, and in the century and a half just after it, there was a series of remarkable cultural achievements that seemed to be utterly neutral with respect to religious belief. These included the revival of algebra, the development of analytic geometry and the calculus, the invention of the microscope and telescope, the discovery of the laws of motion and gravitation, and the beginnings of comprehensive theories covering such fields as mechanics, optics, and astronomy.

The fact that most of these accomplishments were brought about by people who advocated the Renaissance position (or at least joined its spirit) did more than just induce the Reform movement to surrender its radically biblical element. Ultimately, it resulted in the triumph of the revival of rationalism—first under the title "Humanism," and later called "Enlightenment." This position won the intellectual and cultural leadership of the Western world and has remained in that position into the twentieth century. Currently there are signs that it is now being challenged by various versions of irrationalism—some religious, most not.

In fact, in the last century and a half, the radically biblical position has been more and more eschewed by the Protestant tradition owing to the specific interpretation of it which has been advocated by the largest single group of its adherents, that is, the interpretation taken by fundamentalists. Fundamentalists have retained the idea that religious faith guides the whole of life, theories included. They, too, see the guidance of faith as a matter of positive and internal direction, rather than merely a matter of forbidding theories to contradict theological doctrines. But the fundamentalist understanding of how faith exercises its influence is so implausible that it brings the entire radically biblical position into disrepute.

So now that I have said that the scholastics hold a numerical plurality, that the rationalists are in the driver's seat, and that the irrationalists are coming on as challengers, what can possibly be said in defense of the radically biblical position? At least twice in history it has surfaced only to be given up by its own would-be champions. And most of its present adherents are fundamentalists. So why bring it up again? The simple answer is that the radically biblical position does not have to be given a fundamentalist interpretation of how faith regulates reason. Rather we will defend an alternative interpretation which shows how the role of high abstraction in theorizing makes the control of any theory by some religious belief inevitable. As we examine some representative theories in the Casebook chapters, we will see that each of them is affected *in its essentials* by some religious belief, not just slightly altered around the edges. So the defense of the radically biblical position will take the form of demonstrating how theories are controlled by a religious belief, and of showing why that is unavoidable. In this way, the radically biblical position, unlike the others, does not merely tell us how we *should* relate religious belief to theory making; it purports to describe what everyone is really doing whether they admit it or not.

But before presenting the case for this position, we must clear up just what is meant by the terms 'control' or 'direct' or 'regulate' as they have been used to express how we see the general relation of religious belief to theories. Therefore, the next chapter will criticize the fundamentalist idea of religious control and present the idea of control which will be defended as the proper interpretation of the biblical teaching about faith and reason.

6

THE IDEA OF RELIGIOUS CONTROL

1. The Mistake of Fundamentalism

The term 'fundamentalist' is used in a variety of ways and is applied to many different doctrines and attitudes. For my purpose here I am concerned only with how fundamentalism sees the relation of religious belief to theories. On this score the fundamentalist attitude has been essentially the same whether it occurs in Judaism, Christianity, or Islam. In each of these traditions the fundamentalist party has held to two points which distinguish it. The first is an assumption even more deeply characteristic than the widespread idea that it takes a literal interpretation of Scripture. This deeper characteristic I call the "encyclopedic assumption." It is the view that sacred Scripture contains inspired and thus infallible statements about virtually every conceivable subject matter. The assumption is usually understood to extend to the inferences and suggestions that can be drawn from Scripture as well. Unlike scholasticism, fundamentalism does not merely see revelation as limiting what reason may accept by forbidding it to contradict theology. Instead, Scripture is seen as *able to provide at least some truths for almost every sort of theory-making enterprise.*

Fundamentalism therefore advocates that theorizing begin by seeing what Scripture has to say on whatever subject is to be investigated and the theory be built around the scriptural teaching. Thus the crucial point here is not whether the fundamentalist interprets Scripture literally[1] (there is an important sense in which fundamentalists do not interpret it literally enough), but that it expects the guidance of Scripture to take the form of offering infallible information about virtually every subject matter. So while all Jews, Christians, and Muslims expect some sort of guidance for theorizing from Scripture, the fundamentalist idea of that guidance goes well beyond the scholastic ideas of it held by the majority of

94

thinkers in each of these traditions. Whereas the scholastic view is that a theory about, say, geology is acceptable provided it does not contradict any revealed doctrine of the faith, the fundamentalist expects revelation to contain specific geological truths.

As an illustration of the encyclopedic assumption in operation, consider the work of Richard Kirwan, the father of British mineralogy. Keenly interested in the newly rising science of geology, Kirwan issued a major publication in that field titled *Geological Essays*. Throughout all his theories in these essays, Kirwan assumes that the flood of Noah, recorded in Genesis, must be the main geological event in the history of the planet earth. Since the Bible does not give as much information about the flood as the encyclopedic assumption leads him to expect, Kirwan suggests that the text we now possess must be an abridged version and that the original Genesis must have contained far more geological information! He further assumes that the six days of creation spoken of in the biblical account are the basic guidelines for doing geology. Then, having "found" geological evidence that the history of the earth falls into six stages, Kirwan argues:

> Here then we have seen seven or eight geological facts, related by Moses on the one part, and on the other, deduced solely from the most exact and best verified geological observations, yet agreeing with each other not only in substance, but in order of their succession. On whichever of these we bestow our confidence, its agreement with the other demonstrates the truth of the other. But if we bestow our confidence on neither, then their agreement must be accounted for. If we attempt this, we shall find the improbability that both accounts are false, infinite; consequently, one must be true, and, then, so must also the other.[2]

Passing by the faulty logic of this argument, I want to concentrate on the way it expresses the encyclopedic assumption. It is obvious that what is expressed here is not the scholastic view of an interaction between truths of nature and truths of supernature. And even more obviously, there is no complete isolation of faith from theoretical reason as the irrationalist maintains. Instead, religion is seen as impinging on everything, and its impingement is supposed to be that the revelation of God contains truths which are key facts for the construction of geological theories.

At the same time, geology and other sciences can be expected to confirm the Scriptures according to Kirwan. The way they are expected to do this brings us to the second major characteristic of the fundamentalist position, which is the tendency to understand the providence of God as *intervening* in the natural order, rather than as *upholding* the natural order. The term 'providence' is the theological name for the teaching that God's power sustains in existence everything other than himself. In the biblical writings, this is viewed in the broadest way possible. It is by God's providence that the sun rises and sets, the seasons change, the rain falls "on the just and the unjust," and the laws of nature continue to regulate the universe. Of course, Bible writers also speak of times when God himself acted in creation to reveal himself and to perform events which were out of the ordinary. Such revelatory or miraculous events are not merely part of God's providence, but are his own acts in addition to his providence. But neither God's providence nor his special acts in connection with revealing his covenant are matters of his *intervening into a natural order that would just be there anyway.* From the biblical point of view, there is nothing that would just "be there" if God had not created it and continued to sustain it. So while God does act in creation, he does not literally "intervene" in it, since nothing is independent of him. (Even God's miracles do not set aside the natural order he sustains, but are the products of his power within that order.)

But the fundamentalist viewpoint tends to confuse the special acts of God with his providentially sustaining all things. It wants to find gaps within the providential order of things (or in our explanation of the natural order) which require that only God could be their cause, in the same way God is the direct cause of miracles and his own saving acts in history. These gaps are therefore viewed as the way science can confirm the truth of Scripture, since they represent items that supposedly can be explained only by a special act of God. In this way, the fundamentalist position sees God's providential involvement with the order of creation as more than its planner, creator, and sustainer; it actually sees God as the last step in many of the series of natural causes investigated by science. And it fails to see that this would make God *part* of creation!

Let me rephrase the same point this way: whereas you or I might look out the window and remark "it's raining," a biblical prophet would have said something like "the Lord is sending rain on the earth." Both remarks would have reported the same fact, though the second contains an additional reminder that it is by God's plan and providence that all the natural forces coincided to cause the rain when it occurred. But the fundamentalist understands the prophet's remark to suggest that there is some particular feature of the conditions that produce rainfall which, if scientifically investigated, could not be explained without appeal to God. And that is just what is wrong. There is nothing in the biblical teachings which suggest that the way God sustains and controls the world is such that if we investigate its processes we will find features of them which have no natural explanation. The biblical view is not that rain and other natural events are all partly miraculous, but that no things, events, or laws of nature would exist at all unless God sustained them.

God's creativity and providence are the ultimate reasons why there are such things as winds, clouds, and water, and why there are the laws which guarantee their orderliness. But it is the created order which explains created events in the sense that science looks for explanations. A scientific explanation of rain does not include why space, time, matter/energy, and all the laws that govern creation exist at all. While God is the creator of the causal order which allows us to explain rainfall, he is not himself one of its causes alongside all the other causes—not even its first cause. (Strictly speaking, God is not the cause of the universe, but the creator of all the kinds of causality in the universe.)[3]

This is not to deny that the Scriptures teach that the created universe somehow reveals its creator. But contrary to the fundamentalist, Scripture does not suggest that creation witnesses to its maker by requiring that we import him to explain how things work. Scripture sees creation as revealing its maker by exhibiting itself to be dependent, rather than self-existent either in part or in whole. Viewed from the standpoint of the teaching of Scripture itself, then, it is a serious mistake to confuse God's providence with those occasions on which he acted and reacted with humans in the course of revealing and carrying out the provisions of his covenant in human history.

But there is another, even more seriously mistaken side to this fundamentalist notion of how science confirms biblical teaching. This is the strong element of rationalism implicit in this position. Expecting religious teaching to be proven or confirmed by the theories of philosophy or science is to treat religious belief as though it were itself a theory, or at least to be evaluated as theories are. This tendency can be seen in the controversy fundamentalists have with the current theories of geology and biology in which they claim to derive a competing "Scientific Creationist" theory from the Bible. But the revealed truths of Scripture are not *theories* or hypotheses we put forward to be accepted because they can fill explanatory gaps better than competing hypotheses. Rather, we believe them because the grace of God has removed the effects of sin on our minds so that we directly see the biblical message to be the truth from and about God. For this reason, the fundamentalist "gap idea" is as unbiblical an idea of how to defend revealed truth as the encyclopedic assumption is of how to interpret it. In fact, these two fundamentalist views offer each other mutual encouragement. Once Scripture is viewed as giving truths for every science, it would be natural to argue that when those truths are used by a science they deliver more successful explanations than any alternative hypothesis. It is then an easy step to regard such success as confirming the truth of Scripture.

To avoid such misunderstandings, it is necessary to keep in mind that the purpose of the biblical writings was to record the activities of God's establishing his covenant with humans. When the Bible writers speak of natural events, historical events, political events, etc., they always do so in order to proclaim, interpret, or illustrate something about God's covenant. The biblical writings are always—first and foremost—a book of *religion.* It is simply a colossal error to suppose that because an event is religiously important, such as the importance of the flood to the covenant with Noah, that it must therefore also be of key importance to geology or any other science.

To illustrate what I mean by understanding Scripture as dealing with its subject matter from a *religious* point of view, consider for a moment the famous account of the creation of the world in Genesis. A host of fundamentalists have taken it to provide basic guidelines for astronomy, biology, and paleontology, as well as geology. They have supposed that the "days" of God's creativity mentioned in Genesis must be distinct eras or stages in the history of the planet, or that when God is said to have created forms of life to reproduce "after their own kind" that this is some sort of basic principle for doing biology. But a close look at the text itself shows a quite different purpose, one which discourages the fundamentalist interpretation.

In the Genesis account, the days of creation are as follows: Day 1, God separates light from darkness; Day 2, God separates sea from atmosphere; Day 3, God separates land from sea and creates plant life; Day 4, God creates sun, moon, and stars, Day 5, God creates sea life and birds; Day 6, God creates animals and humans. The stress in this account is on the way everything depends on God. There are no other competing forces on an equal footing with God. Instead, it is he who brings into existence everything other than himself. So the emphasis of the text is on the creative activity of God: "And God said, 'Let there be. . . . .' " There is virtually nothing said about what we would have seen take place had we been there to observe the early stages of the universe. All the text says about the consequences of God's creative decrees is, "And it was so."

Another important thing to notice about the text is the literary layout of these "Days" of creation. By "layout" I mean the way Days 4, 5, and 6 correspond to Days 1, 2, and 3. Day 1 separates light from darkness, while Day 4 introduces the sun, moon, and stars; Day 2 separates sea from atmosphere, while Day 5 speaks of the creation of sea life and birds: and Day 3 sees the appearance of dry land while Day 6 records the creation of animals and humans. The following diagram may help convey this point.

Day 1	Day 2	Day 3
light	sea	land
darkness	atmosphere	plants
Day 4	Day 5	Day 6
sun	sea life	animals
moon	birds	humans
stars		

My contention is that there is a match-up here that is not just a coincidence. But if the match-up is intentional, it shows that the "Days" were not intended to give the chronological order in which things appeared in creation. Instead, they comprise a way of expressing the "why" of God's creating rather than its "how"; that is, they are intended to convey an order of *purpose*.[4] The basic difference between light and darkness, for example, is introduced as the planned background for the existence of the sun, moon and stars. And the differentiation of dry land from sea and the creation of plants are the pre-planned conditions for the support of animal life and humans. Viewed in this way, it becomes ridiculous to argue—as fundamentalists have done—over whether the "Days" of creation are twenty-four hour periods or geological eras. How can there be twenty-four hour periods prior to the creation of the sun, moon, and stars? And what can be the justification for saying the Days are geological periods if they are not intended to give a chronological history of the universe at all? Such interpretations stem from the encyclopedic assumption, and this assumption seriously fails to grasp the thoroughly religious character of the account.

This religious character of Scripture cannot help but be obscured whenever Genesis is read as supplying answers to scientific questions. For though there is nothing wrong in our asking such questions or in investigating the creation scientifically, those are not the concerns of the Genesis account. The fundamentalist program errs by imposing its own questions and concerns on the Genesis text, rather than reading it in terms of its own questions and concerns.

Perhaps one of the things which led fundamentalists to adopt the encyclopedic assumption is that Scripture does occasionally contain specific truths which any believer would have to include in certain theories. There are teachings about the norms of ethics and justice in Scripture and also applications of these norms to concrete cases. Such specific teachings can flatly contradict certain theories about ethics or justice and thus provide guidance to a believer working in those areas. For example, some theories claim that humans are not ethically responsible for what they choose or do, and others deny there are any ethical norms for human life at all. Clearly, these theories are logically incompatible with scriptural teachings, and are thus ruled out for anyone who accepts the authority of Scripture. (Though here it must be kept in mind that Scripture does not try to give a complete code of ethics or justice, let alone a *theory* of them.) But recognizing that there are specific teachings in Scripture which can directly impinge on theories is a long way from establishing that to be the general model for the way revealed truth should be seen as relating to theories.[5] The existence of such teachings do not, therefore, warrant the encyclopedic assumption. Fundamentalism is guilty of a hasty generalization here, and its constant search for such specific truths at every turn merely helps to conceal the essentially *religious* focus of the biblical writings.

However, despite my rejection of the fundamentalist notion of how religious belief generally extends its influence to theories, I fully agree with the fundamentalist about the *scope* of that influence. On that issue, I agree that the irrationalist and scholastic positions do not adequately take into account the important claims Scripture makes about *all* our knowledge being somehow dependent on having knowledge of God. But if we reject the fundamentalist's understanding of how religious belief influences theories, what alternative interpretation is left for the radically biblical position? My answer to this is that our religious core-belief, our faith in God as the sole divinity, exercises its most profound and pervasive influence by acting as a *presupposition* to the making of theories in philosophy and the sciences.

2. Presupposition

Perhaps the best way to explain what a presupposition is and how it can influence other beliefs is to give an example, such as the following illustration of an informal debate. George states that although he does not enjoy paying taxes any more than anyone else, it still seems clear to him that the government is not doing enough about poverty. He adds that since our country is enormously rich compared to the way most of the world lives, there is no excuse for allowing any of its citizens to lack the basic necessities of life when that can be prevented. Janet replies that the government gives away too much already. She adds that the very existence of a welfare handout only encourages people to depend on it. The government ought to be encouraging people to earn their own way.

George then retorts that most people find it humiliating to accept welfare help; they would much prefer to be independent. But, he adds, even if a minority did prefer taking charity, that should not deter the government from doing what it ought to do, which is to supply the poor with the help they desperately need. Janet says the government has no right to confiscate part of the pay of those who work each week in order to deliver it to those who do not. She fears that the outcome of George's view is that the government will end up regulating the economy totally in order to care for everyone totally. George protests that he is not advocating complete government control of the economy or of people's lives. He adds that his ideas could be carried out for the cost of just one aircraft carrier and Janet responds that the money would be better spent on the defense of everyone than on supporting a group of parasites.

Let us assume that neither George nor Janet is any more harsh or uncaring than the other and neither is more burdened by taxes than the other. Why, then, do they tend to see the whole issue in such utterly opposite ways? One major factor behind their disagreement is that each has *presupposed* a different idea of the proper role and limits of government. This issue is never explicitly brought up by either George or Janet, but remains an assumption which guides and regulates all they say.

Both George and Janet assumed that government, properly understood, *owes* its citizens certain things—protection from foreign invasion, for instance. And both assumed that there are limits to the authority of government so that there are some things it should not do—such as confiscate everything in order to dole out all the needs of life to each citizen. But they disagreed on the government's powers and obligations in the area of economics. George assumes that government has an obligation to supply basic subsistence to citizens who cannot or will not achieve it for themselves. Janet, on the other hand, assumes that the proper role of government does not extend to support of the needy. Each thinks the debate is on government spending for welfare and neither realizes that the disagreement turns on the more basic issue of the proper role of government. This example illustrates the first feature that I want to stress about presuppositions: they are beliefs which can exercise an influence over other beliefs, even when remaining unconscious.[6]

A second feature of the way presuppositions influence people is that even when they are held unconsciously, they direct or regulate the way people think. The thinking of George and Janet was driven in different directions by their opposing presuppositions about government. The longer they argued the further apart they got, because their assumptions led them to see each new point or each new proposal of the other as further off the mark. The more each applies the consequences of his or her own presupposition to the points brought up by the other, the more they followed distinct directions of thought which carried them further and further from one another's viewpoint. For instance, they both agreed that a welfare program can lead people to become dependent on it, so that there is the risk of discouraging people's initiative. George found that risk acceptable because he assumed that some form of public assistance is a duty of government. For him the risk would have to be much greater to excuse government from a duty. Janet thought that same risk unacceptable because of her assumption that such assistance is not one of the duties proper to government at all. To her the same risk appears ridiculous when the whole program is above and beyond the call of governmental duty in the first place. So even if they could both agree on exactly what the statistics of that risk are, it would make no difference to their positions on the issue: to Janet the risk would be a good reason against government assistance, while to George, it would not look like a good objection.

This sort of disagreement is a common occurrence. We have all seen situations where intelligent people confronted with the same facts interpret them quite differently. Where one person sees a certain interpretation as quite plausible, another sees it as outrageous, while still another sees it as possible but not likely, and so on. And often the right sort of probing and discussing can expose presuppositions of conflicting perspectives which are the real core of the disagreements.

The worst difficulties in the way of discovering someone else's presuppositions are of two types. One of these is that of cases involving deception; the other type arises in cases where we try to recognize presuppositions held by people in a very different culture from our own. This is because the key element in recognizing someone's presuppositions is the ability to imagine ourselves in the place of the other person. Where we can do that with reasonable accuracy, we can often infer another's belief. But both deception and wide cultural disparity make putting ourself in the other's place very difficult indeed.

However, it is easier to discover what is being presupposed by a particular abstract theory than it is to discover what is being presupposed by beliefs which are not part of theories. In the context of scientific or philosophical theory making, people are generally quite earnest about what they are doing, quite anxious to be as clear as possible, and have nothing to gain by proposing or defending a theory they do not believe. Thus, the possibility of deception rarely interferes in the world of theory making. Of course, the obstacle of cultural difference remains and can perhaps only be overcome by experiencing and appreciating the other culture. But at least one of the two major difficulties with recognizing presuppositions is reduced to a minimum when we are dealing with highly abstract theories.

These features of presuppositions are important because it is by acting as presuppositions that religious beliefs exercise their most important influence on scientific and philosophical theorizing. This point therefore sharply distinguishes the radically biblical position from all the other positions concerning the relation of religion to theory making, including the position of the fundamentalist. The radically biblical view does not seek to find statements in Scripture on every sort of subject matter to establish religious influence. What we want to say is that the influence of religious beliefs is much more a matter of a presupposed perspective guiding the direction of theorizing than of Scripture supplying specific truths for theories.

Before proceeding to defend this position, it is necessary to be more specific about precisely what a presupposition is. Just how is this concept to be defined?[7]

One point cannot be overemphasized: a presupposition is a belief. This is why, strictly speaking, it is not beliefs or the sentences which express them that presuppose; it is people who presuppose. It is people who presuppose the truth of one belief by holding another belief. Thus a presupposition is a belief-in-relation to some other belief;[8] it is a belief anyone would have to hold in order to believe another of which it is the presupposition, even though it is not deduced from the other. So saying that a sentence has a presupposition is a shortened (but misleading) way of saying that any person who holds the belief the sentence expresses would also have to accept its presupposition(s).[9] For example, suppose someone knocks at my door and asks if John is home. I reply, "John will be back in half an hour." My answer presupposed the belief "John is not here now." Notice that my answer does not explicitly *say* that John is not home, nor can that fact be logically deduced from it. But it does presuppose it. If I spoke that sentence knowing all the while that John was home, I could justly be accused of deception.

This understanding of presupposition has been rejected by some critics who contend that, when applied to sentences, it does not adequately distinguish between what a sentence presupposes and what is logically deducible from it. For example, they say that while it seems clear that "John will return in half an hour" presupposes "John is not here now," it is unclear whether it can be said to presuppose "John exists." Of course it seems to presuppose "John exists," but the problem is that "John exists" can also be logically deducible from "John will return in half an hour" (depending on exactly how we logically formulate it). And surely, they say, there is something peculiar about the same sentence both presupposing and logically entailing the same belief. What is peculiar about this is that in order to presuppose something we must *already* know it, while we learn what it logically entails only *after* we draw an inference from it. So the problem is how can "John exists" be at the same time believed in advance of, and also be a consequence of "John is not here now"?

In my opinion this is not a problem at all, and the mistake of the criticism lies in ignoring the point made earlier about people, not sentences, doing the act of presupposing. The same point applies equally to the act of drawing logical consequences. Sentences do not yield logical consequences all by themselves; people must draw those consequences. And therein lies the way around this supposed difficulty. For in normal speech—unless we are talking to ourselves—there are at least two people involved: a speaker and a hearer. And there is nothing strange about the fact that the speaker of "John will be back in half an hour" can presuppose "John exists" at the same time its hearer learns that fact as a logical inference. Since two different people are involved, there is no paradox at all. We are not forced to the absurd conclusion that the information already known by the speaker is also subsequently acquired by the speaker's drawing an inference from what he himself said. Since the speaker already knew the information, he simply drew no inference. On the other hand, a hearer who did not know whether John existed could learn it by inferring it from "John will return in half an hour."

To summarize, we have found that a presupposition has the following characteristics:

First: it is a belief standing in a certain relation to another belief. The relation involved is that the presupposition is an informational requirement for holding the other belief. This means that no one could coherently hold the belief while denying any of its presuppositions, even though its presuppositions are not known by being logically inferred from the other belief.

Second: a presupposition need not be conscious to exercise its influence on other beliefs of the one who believes it. As a consequence, people may profess ignorance of—or even deny—a particular presupposition despite the fact that certain of their other beliefs show they unconsciously assume it. (People can, and do, hold incompatible beliefs.)

Third: in everyday affairs, beliefs and the sentences expressing them can have so many different presuppositions that it is often hard to tell what someone is presupposing. This difficulty is especially compounded by both wide cultural disparity and the possibility that someone may deliberately attempt to mislead others about what he or she is presupposing. Where deception is not a factor, however, people frequently do succeed in discerning what others are presupposing by imagining themselves in similar circumstances. The second of these difficulties is reduced considerably in the context of theory making, however.

In addition to these summarized characteristics, I also want to point out that some beliefs which act as presuppositions do not, in turn, have either premises or presuppositions of their own because they are acquired by direct experience. I will call these "basic presuppositions." In what follows, I will take the position that religious core beliefs not only influence theories by acting as presuppositions, but also that they are *basic* presuppositions.

The radically biblical position is therefore in sharp contrast to the alternative views of the general relation of religious belief to theories. Those views all focused on the logical compatibility of specific religious beliefs to specific claims of theories. We admit that revealed beliefs can, indeed, act as "control beliefs" when related to theories in that way.[10] Moreover, such relations are more direct and easier to see than those by which religious beliefs function as basic presuppositions to theory construction. But those contacts are also piecemeal and occasional and are severely limited in their scope. For that reason they fall short of being adequate to the biblical claims that having the right God is somehow basic to all knowledge. So our position dissents from the traditional scholasticism as well as from fundamentalism by concentrating on the way religious core beliefs act as guiding presuppositions to theorizing. Because this influence is all-pervasive, it will be defended as the proper model for the most general way religious belief relates to theories on the ground that it alone can do justice to the biblical claims that having the right God is basic to all truth.

PART 3
A Casebook

7

THEORIES IN MATHEMATICS

1. Introduction

It is a very old idea in Western culture that if any sort of knowledge is neutral, certain, and the same for all people, it is mathematics. And, to be sure, there is an element of truth to that opinion. There is a level at which the truth of, say, simple arithmetic is obvious. In the light of our account of theories we can say that this is because the quantitative aspect of experience can be abstracted, which allows quantitative properties to be represented by numerals and relations among them to be noticed and formulated. In this way many mathematical truths and techniques can be discovered without the need to formulate any theories.

Nevertheless, there are questions about mathematics which cannot be answered by abstraction and discovery, but require the proposing of hypotheses. Two such questions are: (1) what do mathematical symbols represent? and (2) how can we know mathematical truths to be exceptionless? It is about such issues as these that mathematicians (and philosophers) make theories, and these theories are quite controversial. In fact, the disagreements over these theories are among the widest and sharpest which have arisen in the course of Western theory making.

What I intend to show in this chapter is that the theories that arise in math differ according to the content of the religious belief that controls them, and are not exceptions to the central claim of this book. Moreover, this religious control is exercised through the mediation of a view about the essential nature of reality. That is, the hypotheses of math will be shown to presupposes a perspectival overview of all the aspects of reality, which in turn presuppose some aspect(s) as divine. In this way, I will be arguing that the vaunted neutrality of mathematical knowledge, and the universal agreement concerning it, is not true of the theories by which mathematics itself is explained.

Let us consider a bit further the two questions posed above. Take the second question as to how we can know that mathematical truths are exceptionless. We can directly observe, of course, that $1 + 1$ *often* equals 2. That is not itself a theory. But when we see the truth expressed by $1 + 1 = 2$, we never suppose that it is simply a description of what we have seen so far. Everyone who recognizes its truth is led, without further reflection, to suppose it is a universal truth—a truth that does not change with time or place. But how we can know that $1 + 1 = 2$ is true *always and everywhere?* No one can observe even one thing at all times, let alone everything for all time. But if this knowledge does not come from observation, then how do we get it? To answer this requires a theory.

This is not the only puzzling question about the formula which requires a hypothesis to answer. Consider the first question about what our numerals stand for. The marks printed on this page such as "1", "2", "+", or "=" are not themselves numbers, but numerals and other symbols, which are said to stand for numbers and the relations among them. But what exactly is a number?

When children first learn arithmetic, they often suppose the numerals stand for things and events of their everyday experience. It is easy for them to get that impression because the problems given in elementary textbooks usually mention such examples as 3 bales of hay, 6 pairs of shoes, and so on. But it soon becomes apparent that although numerals can be applied to the objects of ordinary experience, those objects are not what the numerals *stand* for. If numerals stood for things, it would be impossible to subtract 8 from 5, or divide 16 into 4. But although we cannot take 8 items from a pile which contains only 5, we can subtract 8 from 5 and get -3. But if the symbols do not stand for experienced objects what do they stand for? Both mathematicians and philosophers have proposed many theories to answer this question.

2. The Number-World Theory

One very famous hypothesis in answer to this question is that the numerals and other markings of mathematics stand for real entities in another world or dimension of reality. These entities are never observable, nor are they locatable in space. We cannot look out the window and see a thing which is the number 2 in the backyard even though we can see things to which the number can be applied. According to the theory, the world of mathematical entities is not only real, it is *more real* than the things which are observable and exist in space and time. It is more real in two senses: the entities that populate it are eternal and can never change or pass away, and its laws are changeless and govern what is possible and impossible in the observable universe. Versions of this theory were held in ancient times by Pythagoras and Plato, and different versions of it are still very popular among mathematicians to this day.

The great mathematician, G. W. Leibniz (who invented the calculus) also held a version of this theory. Leibniz once said that the formula $1 + 1 = 2$ is, like all truths of mathematics, an

> eternal and necessary truth which would not be affected even if the whole [observable] world were destroyed and there were no one to count and no objects to be counted.[1]

Clearly, this is an entity theory since it proposes that there is a (hypothetical) realm of mathematical realities in addition to the world of our experience. For Leibniz, these entities are unobservable, eternal, and changeless, and their laws guaranteed the truths expressed by mathematical formulas. In this way, he saw the number-world theory as able to answer our first question as well as the second.

However, this proposal about the existence of such entities presupposes a perspectival hypothesis about how the quantitative (mathematical) aspect of experience relates to all the others. For Leibniz's entity theory to be true, it would have to be the case that the quantitative aspect of experience relates to the other aspects by being utterly independent of them, and of the objects possessing them. At the same time all the objects in the observable universe, and their (other) aspects, are made possible by the eternal realities represented in mathematics.[2]

Of course, strictly from the standpoint of our experience, the quantitative aspect is but one among a multiplicity of aspects which we can isolate by the process of abstraction. But having isolated and studied that aspect, Leibniz adopted the perspective that this aspect is basic to all the others. Thus, he had no trouble believing the entity theory that says mathematics does not merely deal with the quantitative aspect of the things we experience, but is the reflection in our experience and thought of a realm of unobservable, independent entities which make observable things possible.

3. The Theory of J. S. Mill

Let us contrast the number-world theory of what numerals symbolize with the theory of John Stuart Mill. Mill's theory was that they symbolize sensory perceptions. He thought it farfetched to say that our knowledge could exceed the observations from which it arises. What we experience, said Mill, are our own sensations, and all our knowledge is of them. We employ numbers in order to speak and calculate about the sights, tastes, touches, smells, and sounds we experience.

Mill defended this view of math by arguing that not only the quantitative aspect but all aspects of our pretheoretical experience are actually identical with the sensory aspect. Mill's theory was that the nature of all reality is sensory, period; all we can know is *exclusively* sensory in nature. Thus, in Mill's theory, the fact that there seem to be many aspects which differ from the sensory is a mistake, and the commonsense experience in which things appear this way is misleading. The things we experience, he held, are nothing more than bundles of sensations. (His own expression was that a thing is "the permanent possibility of sensation.") This committed him to a theory in which all knowledge, including math, must be derived from sensation.

Obviously, then, Mill disagreed with Leibniz's theory about a realm of eternal numbers and laws which is not sensorily perceivable. He held instead that $1 + 1 = 2$ and other mathematical formulae are generalizations about our sensations, that is, they represent nothing more than our sights, tastes, touches, smells, sounds, and feelings. The formula about $1 + 1$ is a way of saying that we find in our perception that whenever we have experienced one sensation and another sensation we have experienced two sensations.[3] This view requires, as Mill admitted, that we do not know that $1 + 1$ *must* equal 2, or that it always does. We are at best entitled to believe that $1 + 1$ will *probably* make 2 in the future because it has so often made 2 in the past! It also means that what the numerals symbolize can exist only if there are objects to count and people to count them. And for the same reasons, it means we have no grounds for supposing that anything about math is eternal or changeless.

Here we can see that just as in the case of the number-world theory, a philosophical perspective is presupposed by Mill's theory about what numerals symbolize. His theory is controlled by the perspective that says the nature of reality is exclusively sensory. So Mill holds that what appear to be different aspects to pretheoretical experience are actually identical with the sensory aspect.

4. The Theory of Russell

Yet another theory to answer the question of what the numerals symbolize is the one espoused by Bertrand Russell. Unlike Mill, Russell could not accept the proposal that the symbols of math refer to sensory perceptions since that would remove the necessity and exceptionless character of mathematical truths. But like Mill, he rejected the theory of an unseen eternal realm of mathematical entities. He hastened to add, however, that by rejecting that theory he did not mean that $1 + 1 = 2$ is false:

> I do not mean that statements apparently about points or instances or numbers or any of the other entities [of math] . . . are false, but only that they need interpretation which shows their linguistic form is misleading, and that, when rightly analyzed, the pseudo-entities in question are not found to be mentioned in them.[4]

Russell went further than simply rejecting the theory of a realm of independent mathematical entities. Like Mill, he also denied that there is a distinctively quantitative aspect to our experience at all. But unlike Mill, Russell proposed that all of mathematics collapses to *logic,* rather than sensation. Math, says Russell, is nothing other than a short-cut way of doing logic.[5] So the entity hypothesis Russell defends is that what the numerals stand for are *logical classes,* rather than Plato's and Leibniz's eternal numbers or Mill's sensory perceptions. Thus Russell's entity hypothesis also presupposes a philosophical perspective about how all the aspects relate. According to this overview, the aspect studied by math is one which collapses to the logical aspect. As a consequence, he views all of math as either identical with, or derivative from, logic.

Russell, like Leibniz before him, thinks that this hypothesis about what mathematical symbols stand for also answers the question about the exceptionlessness of mathematical truth. But for him it is logical laws which are eternal, changeless, and make possible the world of everyday experience. The laws of logic thus make both mathematics and all the rest of reality possible. He puts it this way:

> Philosophers have commonly held that the laws of logic, which underlie mathematics, are laws of thought, laws regulating the operation of our minds. By this opinion the true dignity of reason is very greatly lowered: it ceases to be an investigation into the very heart and immutable essence of all things actual and possible, becoming, instead, an inquiry into something more or less human and subject to our limitations. . . . But mathematics takes us . . . from what is human, into the region of absolute [logical] necessity to which not only the actual world, but every possible world, must conform. . . .[6]

Clearly, then, Russell's entity theory concerning what mathematical symbols represent and how we can know mathematical truth to be exceptionless presupposes a view of how all the aspects interrelate. In his theory the logical aspect—at least so far as its laws are concerned—enjoys an independence from the others which the others do not have from the logical. Once again, from the standpoint of how it is experienced, the logical is but one of many aspects. But having once abstracted it, Russell regarded it as more than merely an aspect of our experience. Instead, as he said, he saw it as the very "heart and immutable essence of all things." So Russell's philosophical perspective was that the ultimate nature of all things is (at least partly) *logical,* and that (at least most of) the other aspects of things depend upon logical order to make them possible.

5. The Theory of Dewey

Finally, in contrast to the theories above, John Dewey gives very different answers to our questions. In reply to the question as to what mathematical symbols stand for, Dewey says, "Nothing." And in answer to how we can know the truths they express to be exceptionless, Dewey replies that the formulas are not true.

According to Dewey, humans are to be understood as essentially biological beings struggling to survive in a certain environment. All living beings do the same, of course, but humans cope with their environment by trying to alter it to suit themselves, rather than adjust themselves to it. They manage to do this because they have been endowed by evolution with a superior intelligence, and the way they utilize this intelligence is to make instruments or *tools*. This idea of a tool is much broader in Dewey's thought than the way we normally think of tools. For Dewey, all human cultural products are tools, even such things as values and institutions. Likewise, an idea, a language, a theory, or a concept is a tool.

On his view, the very questions the other theories have been trying to answer are wrongly posed. The symbols of math do not *stand* for anything any more than any other tool stands for anything. Like all other tools, they merely do certain jobs. Just as it would be inappropriate to ask what a hammer stands for, but appropriate to ask what it can do, the apparatus of mathematics does not stand for something else. The same point holds for the question of the truth of math. Just as it is inappropriate to ask whether a hammer is true or false, it is equally inappropriate to ask that of mathematical formulas. $1 + 1 = 2$ is neither true nor false, says Dewey, though it performs certain tasks well. It is the success of math in accomplishing certain tasks that we refer to when we say that mathematical formulae are *true*. Dewey puts it this way:

> If ideas, meanings, conceptions, notions, theories, systems are instrumental to an active reorganization of the ... environment ... if they succeed in their office, they are reliable, sound, good, true.... That which guides us truly is true—demonstrated capacity for such guidance is precisely what is meant by truth.[7]

In other words, to say that something is true is to say no more than that it works. And Dewey means this quite literally. Notice he does not say that whether something works is the *test* of whether it is true, but rather that it is what it *means* to be true.

Dewey does recognize that mathematics is a highly refined and enormously useful tool and that it outstrips most other conceptual tools in precision and usefulness. But he argues that it has reached this stage of development by a long history of experimental trial and error, which most mathematicians now ignore. He says that since it now appears so sure and certain, math is often accorded the status given it by Plato and Leibniz: a body of self-contained truths independent of the rest of reality. But this, Dewey says, is a mistake:

> Such a deductive science as mathematics represents the perfecting of method. That a method to those concerned with it should present itself as an end on its own account is no more surprising than that there should be a distinct business for making any tool.[8]

And again,

Mathematics is often cited as an example of purely normative think-ing dependent upon [absolute rules] and [other-worldly] material. . . . The present-day mathematical logician may present the structure of mathematics as if it had sprung from the brain of a Zeus whose anat-omy is that of pure logic. But . . . [math has] a history in which matter and methods have been constantly selected and worked over on the basis of [experiential] success and failure.[9]

To summarize: on Dewey's theory, math itself is neither true nor false in the traditional sense, but just works. Its symbols and for-mulae do not stand for unseen eternal realities, sensory percep-tions, or logical classes, because they do not stand for anything at all. Their meaning is their use. They guide us in "reorganizing our environment." Where they do that successfully we call them true, but that is a misleading way of saying that we are successful when guided by them.

This theory, often called instrumentalism, is another case of a theory within a science being guided and controlled by a view of the nature of reality—a presupposition about how all the aspects of experience relate. From the outset, Dewey's view of math and all other human conceptual activities is governed by a *biological* perspective. For Dewey, humans are to be viewed primarily as liv-ing organisms struggling for survival. This perspective leads him to take the instrumentalist interpretation of truth and, conse-quently, the instrumentalist view of math. For him, the truths of mathematics are, like all other "truths," tools of biological survival. And if the truths of math are all tools of our making there is then no reason to believe they show us the heart and essence of reality, or give us absolute certainty. Rather, they are all the products of human invention which depends, ultimately, on our evolution. Had our brains evolved differently, we might now have a math so different that with our present brains we cannot even imagine it. Yet that math would have appeared as certain to us under those circumstances as our present math does to us with the brains we now possess.[10] In this way, the biological aspect of reality is seen to explain our knowledge of all the aspects.

The perspectives cited above are not the only ones to have been adopted in the history of mathematics. Besides the view of Plato and Leibniz, the logicism of Russell, the empiricism of Mill, and Dewey's instrumentalism, there are still other competing "schools of thought." There are, for example, the formalists such as David

Hilbert and the intuitionists such as Henri Poincaré, Hermann Weyl, and Luitzen Brouwer.

6. What Difference Do Such Theories Make?

These differences among theories *about* the science of mathematics have created very important differences *within* it, resulting in wide disagreements over the practices and procedures of doing math. Take, for example, the resistance to the use of irrational numbers by the Pythagoreans. The Pythagoreans, like Plato and Leibniz after them, believed numerals represent a realm of invisible mathematical entities upon which the visible world depends. Since these mathematical entities are supposed to be the ultimate units or building blocks of the world, they were thought to be indivisible. Because of this conviction, the Pythagoreans had a horror of division, fractions, and irrational numbers. This is why they translated fractions into ratios or line segments and insisted there could not be genuinely irrational numbers. The discovery that there are in fact ratios which cannot be expressed as fractions (numbers which are unending decimals such as π) is supposed to have been made by Hippasus of Metapontum in the fifth century B.C. The story goes that at the time he thought of his discovery he was at sea with a boatload of Pythagoreans who were so incensed by his discovery that they threw him overboard![11]

Similar to the Pythagorean resistance to irrational numbers was the resistance of Leibniz to negative numbers. Though he allowed them into equations on the ground that their form was proper, he did so with the proviso that they were to be regarded as purely imaginary quantities.[12] In other words, he insisted that only positive numbers are real, while the negative numbers are fictions. Since he believed math is a reflection in thought of an unseen, eternal realm, each numeral we use must stand for one of the hypothetical entities, a collection of them, or the relations among them. How, then, could a number be negative? How could it stand for nothing?

These instances of math being done differently because of a philosophical perspective may seem to be no more than historical curiosities, so let us consider an example which is a burning issue in our own time—the differences in doing math caused by the perspective of the present-day intuitionist theory.

Intuitionists, like the advocates of the number-world theory, maintain an inter-aspectual perspective which sees the mathematical aspect as utterly independent of all other aspects. But whereas Plato and Leibniz lumped logic in with math, intuitionists regard math as basic to logic in such a way as to leave math partly independent of logical rules. They insist that the intuited mathematical truths are more basic and more reliable than those of any other aspect—including even logical truths. Thus, for intuitionists, if logical paradoxes arise concerning a mathematical system, that is a problem for *logic*, but need not trouble the mathematician. As Morris Kline describes the position of the great intuitionist, Luitzen Brouwer:

> Logic belongs to language. It offers a system of rules that permit the deduction of further verbal connections which are intended to communicate truths. However . . . logic is not a reliable instrument for uncovering truths and can deduce no truths that are not obtainable just as well in some other way. . . . The most important advances in mathematics are not obtained by perfecting the logical form but by modifying the basic theory itself. Logic rests on mathematics, not mathematics on logic. Logic is far less certain than our intuitive concepts and mathematics does not need the guarantees of logic. . . . Paradoxes are a defect of logic but not of true mathematics. Hence consistency is a hobgoblin. It has no point.[13]

And the intuitionist mathematician, Hermann Weyl, put the point this way:

> classical logic was abstracted from the logic of finite sets and their subsets. . . . Forgetful of this limited origin, one afterwards mistook logic for something above and prior to all mathematics, and finally applied it, without justification, to the mathematics of infinite sets. This is the Fall and original sin of set theory, for which it is justly punished by the antinomies.[14]

One of the practical consequences of this view is the rejection of the so-called "new math" introduced into the public school curriculum in the United States in the 1960s (which is now largely discontinued). The new math was based on a view like that of Russell and proceeded first by teaching logical rules such as commutation, association, and distribution, and then by applying them to sets which were taken to be what math is really about. In the quote above, Weyl warns that set theory runs into logical paradoxes and is therefore unsuitable as the basis for teaching mathematics.

Another important consequence of the intuitionist view is their rejection of any proof which rests upon the logical law of excluded middle. (This is the law which says a statement has to be either true or false and cannot be neither: there is no third—or "middle"—alternative to being true or false.) As a result, they reject any proof in the *reductio ad absurdum* form. They also disallow any proof which rests on the logical rule that if one of two options has to be true, and one of them can be shown false, then the other must be true. Both these consequences lead to sharp differences in what intuitionists will accept as proper proofs as over against what mathematicians holding other positions will accept.

Despite accepting a perspective similar to that of Plato and Leibniz (maintaining the complete independence of the mathematical aspect), intuitionists differ with the entity hypotheses of the number-world theory; they deny any hypothetical realm of mathematical entities. They insist that math is exclusively mental, and for that reason everything which goes on in mathematics must completely correspond to what we can actually conceive. Thus many of them rejected as meaningless both the complex numbers and irrational numbers (that had so upset the Pythagoreans)—though these are accepted by Platonists, formalists, and logicists. For the same reason, intuitionists also deny there is any actual infinity. As the intuitionist Poincaré put it:

> Actual infinity does not exist. What we call infinity is only the endless possibility of creating new objects no matter how many objects exist already.[15]

This denial of the existence of actual infinite sets forces intuitionists to yet another denial. They reject *an entire branch of mathematics:* the theory of transfinite numbers developed by Georg Cantor.

These are only a few examples of how the differences in philosophical theories about the relations among aspects have affected the practical doing of mathematics. It is because of just such disagreements and their severe and important consequences that Kline has written:

> The current predicament of mathematics is that there is not one but many mathematics and that for numerous reasons each fails to satisfy the members of the opposing schools. It is now apparent that the concept of a universally accepted, infallible body of reasoning—the majestic mathematics of 1800 and the pride of man—is a grand illusion. . . . The disagreements about the foundations of the "most certain"

science are both surprising and, to put it mildly, disconcerting. The present state of mathematics is a mockery of the hitherto deep-rooted and widely reputed truth and logical perfection of mathematics.[16]

Of course, it is possible that people who frequently work in math are never bothered by the sorts of issues we have been discussing. While many thinkers in math can honestly report that they do their work without puzzling over which perspective is the right one, we should remember that a perspective need not be conscious to exert its influence. What is important is whether the procedures and techniques of mathematics in fact presuppose philosophical perspectives, not whether everyone is always aware of them.

It should also be pointed out that because they can be unconsciously presupposed, perspectives on the nature of reality do not always function as hypotheses. If a certain perspective is consciously proposed as a provisional explanation, and its merits are debated relative to those of other perspectival hypotheses, then it is being treated as a theory (as the thinkers quoted above all did). But when a perspective is unconsciously assumed, it cannot then be a *theory* proposed to explain something since theories are always conscious. In this case the perspective is dogmatically presupposed rather than proposed as a theory to be debated. This is why one and the same belief may be a hypothesis to one person, and a presupposition to another.

7. The Role of Religion in These Theories

But even if a case has been made for the involvement of philosophical perspectives in mathematics, what has this to do with religion? How can the second step of the argument be made? The truth is that religious belief—as defined in Chapter 2—has been at the heart of every one of these perspectives. In each case the adoption of a perspective was controlled by a belief in something as divine. Theories like Plato's propose a separate realm of mathematical entities and view our grasp of mathematical truth as the result of the connection of our experienced world with the entities of that independently existing mathematical realm. The truths we obtain are supposed to be eternal, and not affected by the experienced universe. But by regarding this hypothetical realm as having independent existence they accord it the status of divinity!

Remember, it is not because the hypothetical realm is regarded as populated by entities which are supposed to be eternal, changeless, or logically necessary that it is divine. These characteristics alone would not be sufficient. Even if eternal, they could still be eternally dependent on something else. Likewise, mathematical truths could express necessary connections among quantities but still depend for their existence on something else. It is only when someone regards the hypothetical entities and laws as existing independently of *all* other reality, so that mathematical truths would be the same whether *anything* else existed or not, that the person has ascribed utterly non-dependent self-existence to the hypothetical realm, and has thereby regarded them as divine.[17] Furthermore, any such ascription of self-existence to the quantitative aspect is not only a religious belief, but one which perfectly fits the pagan dependency arrangement. For although it is true that the hypothetical realm of mathematical entities is supposed to be invisible, nonphysical, eternal, and changeless, it is still viewed as continuous with the rest of the natural world which we observe in two respects. The first is that even though it is taken to be more than just an aspect of the world of our everyday experience, it still remains true that it is one aspect of that world. The second is that both the hypothetical realm and the observable world obey the same laws. Indeed, the self-existent laws of the mathematical world make the experienced world possible.

To see its pagan character more clearly, consider a contrast between this theory's idea of the relation between the observable world and the hypothetical realm on the one hand, and the biblical idea of the relation between God and the universe on the other hand. On the Platonic view, the laws governing the hypothetical realm *are* the order of the observable world as well. In fact, the unseen (divine) realm is the very core of the being of the world which appears to us. This, clearly, is a pagan position. According to the biblical idea, God brings into existence (out of nothing) *all* that is true of the universe. Thus, he has created all the kinds of orderliness which govern the universe. For that very reason he is not himself subject to the laws which govern creation. The laws he has created do not automatically apply to him, and only apply at all insofar as he freely abides by them in order to make himself known to humans.

Having pointed out the pagan character of the number-world theory, I must at least mention here that there is a long-standing tradition of Jewish and Christian thinkers who believe this theory can be adapted to be compatible with belief in God. They recognize that simply regarding mathematical entities as self-existent is unacceptable, so they attempt to neutralize its pagan character while retaining its basic idea. This is done by regarding the mathematical realm as either part of God himself or as ideas in God's mind. In this way they thought they could account for the necessity and eternality of the hypothetical realm without admitting anything is self-existent distinct from God. I believe there are insurmountable difficulties with this view, but to treat this topic here would require far too long a digression. Instead we will return to it in chapter 10 when we examine the scholastic tradition in greater detail.

The role religious belief plays in the number-world theory can be seen to recur in Russell's theory. The chief difference is that for Russell the divine principles which govern all reality are those of logic, rather than math. The logical laws, he says, are those to which all reality—actual or possible—must conform; they are the heart and immutable essence of all things. Once again, this position amounts to abstracting an aspect of the universe and regarding it as having divine status. Thus Russell's theory, as it stands, is also a piece of pagan faith. Here, too, a tradition of Jewish and Christian thinkers has attempted to reconcile this theory with belief in God in the same way as the number-world theory is reconciled. They propose that logical laws, sets, etc., be regarded as part of the being of God or as ideas in God's mind in order to preserve their eternality and necessity while still finding a sense in which they may be said to depend on God. In chapter 10 I will argue that this view no more succeeds for logical laws and entities than it does for mathematical laws and entities.

The theory of Mill is, perhaps, even more obviously pagan. On Mill's view, mathematical truths and laws are all generalizations about our sensations and we have sensations because all reality is made up of purely sensory realities, each of which is a "permanent possibility of sensation." When Mill was asked why there are such permanent possibilities and what their causes are, he replied that they are "just there." This shows that, once again, we are confronted with a theory that proceeds to abstract some aspect of our experience of creation and elevate it to divine status. Mill's theory thus presupposes a pagan religious belief.

The same is true of the theory of Dewey, though he is much vaguer on the status of the physical-biological aspect(s) which he takes as the basic nature of reality. Dewey does not specifically *say* that those aspects have independent existence, so far as I know. But throughout all his theorizing, he regards all other aspects as dependent on the physical-biological and never regards them, in turn, as dependent on anything. To further complicate this point, Dewey at times denies that *anything* has utterly independent (he called it "absolute") existence. But he is also adamant in denying that there is anything outside the universe on which it depends. Thus we are entitled to say he is simply inconsistent on this point: it cannot be that there is nothing but the universe and that the universe is not divine. For if there is nothing but the universe, then there is nothing for it to depend upon, and it has "absolute" self-existence. Thus it seems fair to say that Dewey's theory is another case of pagan religious belief controlling a perspective from which a theory of the nature of mathematics is developed.

The same state of affairs—in which religious belief controls a perspectival view of the nature of reality and that view of reality controls the entity theories of math—can be found in logic as well. Any number of thinkers in philosophy (and those who agree with Russell's view of math) have tended to regard modern logic as a problem-solving method based on truths possessing indisputable neutrality. But the issue of inter-aspectual perspective cannot be shut out of logic any more than it can be shut out of math. Logical laws have also variously been understood as: existing in another absolute and immutable realm, a product of the structure of language, rules by which we cannot help but think because of the way our brains evolved, and so on. Even some of the most highly formalized symbolic systems of logic are quite incompatible with one another because of these and similar differences.[18] And as in math, these views either take logical truth to be self-existent or to be made possible by some other aspect(s).

It may now be clearer how the varieties of pagan religious belief evince the restless and wandering character which I mentioned earlier. From the standpoint of biblical religion, paganism appears to ransack the dependent, relative universe for that which is self-existent and absolute. Each aspect of the creation, when divinized, seems to evoke a counter-divinity, each just as plausible (and therefore just as implausible) as the others.

But, how should we spell out the difference for theories of mathematics were they to presuppose belief in God rather than the pagan belief in the divinity of some aspect of creation? To answer this adequately would require that we first elaborate and defend a theory of reality which presupposes belief in God, and then show the consequences of that overview of (created) reality for the concepts of the entities proposed in math and other scientific theories. This will be undertaken in chapters 11, 12, and 13, but I will try to give a very rough approximation of some of the differences belief in God should make to scientific entity theories here.

Belief in a transcendent creator should lead us to the view that no aspect of creation is self-existent or makes any other aspect possible. They are all dependent on God alone. The aspects we experience are equally real, and all created things exist under the laws of, and have properties of, every aspectual kind. This requires that the natures of the entities proposed in the sciences should never be understood as identified with any one or two aspects. Nothing has a nature that is either basically or exclusively one or another of its aspects in the ways pagan-based theories have always assumed.

Among the things such a view of reality would mean for math are the following. Numerals represent the quantitative properties of things. We abstract this aspect of our experience of the world around us and symbolize discrete quantity as 1. We can then symbolize additional quantity by a series of numerals in which each succeeding symbol—2, 3, 4, etc.—stands for an increase over its predecessor by the amount of the first. We may, by further abstraction, discover relations and laws which hold among quantities. But the abstractions we arrive at, such as numbers, sets, etc., will never be seen as independently existing realities. They are never more—or less—than the properties, relations, functions, etc., of the quantitative aspect of things. Thus they are neither members of Pythagoras' or Leibniz's self-existent number-world, nor are they total fictions of our invention as the nominalists would have it. At the same time, they are not to be interpreted as made possible by some other aspect in the way that Mill or Russell or Dewey maintained.

The reasons for even this much will have to wait until chapter 10 and the succeeding chapters which outline a theory of reality.[19]

8

THEORIES IN PHYSICS

Next to mathematics, the science most commonly thought to be independent of religious belief is physics. But here, too, theories exhibit conflicts which presuppose different perspectives about how the various aspects of our experience relate to one another. And these perspectives, again, presuppose different beliefs about what it is that is divine.

1. Some Misunderstandings to Avoid

Before proceeding to show this, however, I want to point out some possible misunderstandings which are important to head off. One concerns the adjective, 'physical'. In ordinary speech we often speak of something as *physical* meaning that it is real rather than imaginary. But in keeping with our earlier definition of an aspect, I will be using the term 'physical' to refer to the physical properties and laws which we find true of the objects of our everyday experience or which are postulated as true of the entities whose existence is proposed by theories in physics.

Another possible way the term 'physical' can be misleading is when it occurs in expressions like "physical object." This could be taken to mean that an object is *only* physical. While there are theories that propose such entities, we never experience anything as exclusively physical. For example, a tree is a physical object, but it also appears to have many more kinds of properties and to be subject to many more kinds of laws than just physical. It also displays qualities and orderliness of such aspects as the quantitative, spatial, biological, sensory, logical, aesthetical, and so on. Of course, working in the physical sciences requires that the physical aspect of things be abstracted and focused upon, allowing the remaining (nonphysical) aspects of things to fall from the center of attention. But this fact does not show there are things that have only that aspect. From the standpoint of our immediate experience, it is simply false that there is a particular class of things that are solely physical and which are therefore the subject matter of physics. Rather, physics, like all the other sciences, starts with the multiaspectual objects of our ordinary experience and abstracts the aspect which becomes the special field of its investigation.

This point is important because, as was noted above, many prominent thinkers take the view that physics deals with *exclusively* physical objects. As we review their opinions, therefore, it must be kept in mind that regarding the domain of physics this way is itself the result of a perspectival hypothesis (or presupposition) which needs to be defended if they are to be entitled to it.

With these points out of the way, let us look at physics to see whether disagreements arise because physicists presuppose different views of the essential nature of reality. To see this we need only examine the most widely accepted theory in all of physics, the atomic theory.

Roughly, atomic theory holds that the objects of the universe are made up of parts (atoms) so small that they cannot be directly observed. My claim about the religious control of theories does not mean that thinking of this proposal at all depends on one's religious belief. Instead it is connected with my earlier comment that it is not enough simply to say, "There are atoms." We have to know what sorts of things these atoms are and how they relate to each other so as to explain the objects and events we experience. To do this explaining the concepts must be specific about the essential nature(s) of these entities. But the fact is physicists disagree over their essential nature. As a result, they also differ over both *what* atoms and their constituent particles explain and *how* they explain. It is the differences over the natures of the entities proposed which presuppose differing overviews of reality which, in turn, presuppose differing ideas of what is divine. To illustrate these differences, let us briefly consider three modern interpretations of atomic theory.

2. The Theory of Mach

The first interpretation of atomic theory we will discuss is that of Ernst Mach. Most people have heard of Mach's name without realizing it, because to honor his work his colleagues named the speed of sound "Mach 1," and double the speed of sound "Mach 2," and so on. Another fact most people do not realize about Mach is that he *did not believe that atoms exist!* Nor was Mach alone in holding such a view. During his lifetime a large number of very distinguished scientists and philosophers came to agree with him, so that he became the founder of a distinct movement in science which was enormously influential through the first two-thirds of this century. But despite Mach's rejection of the reality of atoms and their particles, he still insisted that atomic theory is not to be discarded; it is too successful for that. Instead it is to be accepted the way Dewey accepted talk about numbers and the procedures of mathematics—a useful way of explaining what we experience, even though the entities it employs are not real!

Mach and his disciples adopted a perspectival hypothesis about the nature of reality which sees all the aspects of our experience as collapsed to the sensory aspect. It was on that basis that Mill had taken the position that the formulae of mathematics are nothing more than generalizations about sensations. Mach applied this view of reality to the science of physics in detail. The result was, of course, that he rejected the existence of anything other than sensory perceptions.

In order to understand his reasons for this view, and its far-reaching consequences for physics, it may be helpful to fill in the background of this philosophical perspective a bit more. The theory of reality which maintains that all things have an exclusively sensory nature began in the early seventeenth century, when the belief arose that the human mind works much like an eye or a camera. According to this view, we must distinguish the reality which is outside the mind from the reality which is inside the mind, just as the world of things outside an eye or camera is distinct from the images which appear on the retina or film. Thus the mind came to be thought of as the retina or film on which the sensations of sight, touch, smell, sound, and taste recorded representations of the things which are external to the mind.

In the eighteenth century, such thinkers as George Berkeley and David Hume showed convincingly that if this picture of the mind is correct then all we can know are the purely sensory images *inside* our minds, so that it is impossible to be sure about what is outside them. In other words, if your mind is the camera and everything you know is what is on your "film," you could never tell whether the world outside your mind is like what is on your film, or—for that matter—be sure there is anything outside your camera at all. For all you know, what is inside your camera could be internally generated!

This bizarre conclusion is very close to what Berkeley, Hume, Mill, and Mach ended up accepting. They concluded that so far as we could ever know from experience, reality is *made of* sensations. According to them, when we observe a tree in a field, we ought not to suppose that what we are seeing is physical either in the sense that it possesses distinctly physical properties or that it exists independently of being perceived. What we are seeing is actually a bundle of sensory perceptions registering in our own minds. Consequently, they believed that all we can ever know of what the tree *is* is that it is a collection of all the possible sensations we could ever get from it. The tree (or any other object) is an arrangement of color patches, touch-feels, sound-impressions, tastes, and smells. And though it may be natural to want to argue that there is a "physical" tree outside our minds causing our tree-sensations, they pointed out that there is no way we could ever know that. It was on the basis of this assignment of priority to the sensory aspect that Mach and many other physicists came to believe that it is a *theory* (a proposal!) that there are physical objects at all.

Earlier I made the point that from the standpoint of our immediate experience there are no good reasons to suppose that any objects are exclusively physical, since in our experience everything appears to be multi-aspectual. So you may be wondering why I made that point, and then proceeded to talk about the theories of Berkeley, Hume, Mill, and Mach, which claim not that everything is exclusively physical, but that everything we directly experience is exclusively sensory. The reason is that the point applies equally to each theory, and each provokes the other as a response.[1] Thinkers who took the position that objects outside our minds were exclusively physical (like Galileo and Descartes) admitted that the sensations inside our minds are purely sensory, not physical. They then had to show that the sensations in our minds are faithful copies of the objects outside them. That is what Berkeley and Hume showed could not be done. So they, and Mill and Mach after them, regarded the existence of external (purely) physical objects as a theory which it is difficult to confirm. It was on this ground that

Mach dismissed the existence of external physical objects as an unscientific theory, and proceeded to show how physics could be conducted without it.

However, Mach did not throw out the *theories* which speak of external physical objects. Atomic theory, for example, was accepted by Mach as a "useful fiction" which helps us to make predictions about future perceptions. As Mach himself put it:

> If ordinary 'matter' must be regarded merely as a highly natural, unconsciously constructed mental symbol for a ... complex of [sensations], much more must this be the case with the artificial hypothetical atoms and molecules of physics and chemistry.[2]

And again:

> What we represent to ourselves behind the appearances exists *only* in our understanding ...[3]

> To us investigators, the concept "soul" is irrelevant and a matter for laughter, but matter is an abstraction of exactly the same kind ... we know as much about the soul as we do of matter.[4]

In this way, Mach accepted both our ordinary talk about matter and the atomic theory as playing a role in physics very like the role Dewey gave to numerals in mathematics.[5] That is, although the terms and symbols of atomic theory do not stand for realities, they are still useful in dealing with the perceived world. But remember, it is not just atoms and subatomic particles which Mach's perspective rules out of reality, but any physical objects whatever. This is clearly shown by the fact that his perspective also rules out of reality all physical *laws* as well as all physical objects. In his book *Knowledge and Error,* Mach specifically extended this view to the laws of physics, regarding them as merely our own inventions. He said they are nothing more than "the product of our mental need to find our way about in nature," and "subjective prescriptions for an observer's expectations."[6] At the same time, however, he wanted to keep them in the theories of physics because "within certain limits" they lead us to right expectations (about perceptions) and so should not be abandoned.

3. The Theory of Einstein

Not all physicists agreed with Mach. Some, like Planck and Einstein, maintained that our sensations really are caused by unperceivable, exclusively physical objects that are external to our minds. But even they felt compelled to admit that this belief was only a theory. For example, Einstein, in affirming this belief against Mach, wrote that

> Our psychological experience contains... sense experiences, memory pictures of them, images, and feelings. In contrast to psychology, physics treats directly only of sense experiences and of the "understanding" of their connection. But even the concept of the "real external world" of everyday thinking rests exclusively on sense impressions... what we mean when we attribute to the bodily object "a real existence"... [is] that, by means of such concepts... we are able to orient ourselves in the labyrinth of sense impressions.[7]

In this quote we can see that Einstein also accepts the perspective on reality and knowledge which says that all we directly experience is of a purely sensory nature. So he, too, accepts the requirement that the test for whether something can be *directly* known to be real is whether it is perceivable. All else must be hypothesis. Thus he admitted that he could not be sure there are real "bodily" objects. He nevertheless disagreed with Mach by insisting that the theory that there are physical things lends so much rational understanding to our sense perceptions that we are entitled to believe it is true. The difference between Einstein and Mach, then, was that Einstein believed that there are (purely) physical objects outside our minds which cause our sensations, while Mach denied it.

Einstein held that much of what goes on in our minds is also logical/mathematical reasoning. He believed that the *logical/ mathematical properties and laws are as real as the sensory properties and laws, and that rational thought is independent of perception.* This is shown by the fact that it is possible to conceive of things we can never perceive. As he put it:

> the concepts which arise in our thought... are all... the free creations of thought which cannot be gained from sense experiences....[8]

Because he attributed such independent reality to the logical/ mathematical properties and laws, Einstein maintained that rational thinking is also to be taken as a rule for what counts as real. Notice that at the end of the first section quoted from him, he said that believing "bodily objects" have "real existence" is justified by the way that belief helps us understand the "labyrinth of sense impressions." In other words, because the theory that there are physical objects makes rational sense, physical objects as well as sensory perceptions should be accepted as real. Thus physical objects, like all other entity hypotheses, may be viewed as indicative of reality provided they comprise "a conceptual system . . . firmly enough connected with sensory experiences" which shows "as much unity and [economy] as possible" in its task of "ordering and surveying sense experience. . . ."[9]

This perspective, which takes the logical/mathematical in addition to the sensory as the rule for what counts as real, stands in a long tradition which comes down from the work of the seventeenth-century mathematician and philosopher, Rene Descartes, who proposed that the rule for both philosophy and physics be that

all things which, generally speaking, are comprehended in the object of pure mathematics, are truly to be recognized as external objects.[10]

At the heart of this proposal is the assumption that the laws of mathematics and logic govern external reality as well as our thinking, and do so in such a way as to guarantee a correspondence between the two. This assumption may be expressed as the belief that whatever is rational (mathematically calculable) is real. Einstein admits, however, that his confidence that nature is rational cannot be demonstrated. It is, he says, "a matter of faith that nature—as she is perceptible to the five senses—takes the character of such a well-formulated puzzle." But, he adds, the successes of science "give a certain encouragement for this faith."[11]

This faith that the essential nature of reality is, in part, rational is precisely what Mach denied because he thought reality to be exclusively sensory in nature. And that denial led to some very sharp disagreements with other physicists such as Einstein. For one thing, his denial requires adopting an attitude toward theories which assumes that they are not discovering reality but merely serving as devices to predict what we can expect if we do such and such. This means that in an important sense, theories do not discover anything about the world we live in. They are kept and used because they succeed in predicting future experience, but all the while it is the greatest mystery *why* some succeed and some do not. In this way, Mach's perspective lends a different *meaning* to the entire enterprise of physics, because it takes a different interpretation of what physics *is*.

4. The Theory of Heisenberg

Werner Heisenberg disagreed with both Mach and Einstein. For Heisenberg, the elementary atomic particles are not to be thought of as realities in the way observable objects are real, and yet they are not outright fictions as Mach thought. Instead, he holds the view that they are essentially *mathematical possibilities.* In explaining this, Heisenberg says that elementary particles not only lack any sensory qualities, but that it is not even accurate to say they have being. He says:

> If one wants to give an accurate description of the elementary particle—and here the emphasis is on the word "accurate"—the only thing which can be written down as a description is a probability function... not even... being... belongs to what is described. It is a possibility for being or a tendency for being.[12]

This does not mean that the essential nature of reality is *only* mathematical, however. Heisenberg goes on to make it clear that reality has a dual nature: there is energy, which is "the primary substance of the world." And there are the mathematical laws which make possible the specific forms which energy can take. So he confidently predicts that

> In modern quantum theory there can be no doubt that the elementary particles will finally also be mathematical forms... the mathematical forms that represent the elementary particles will be solutions of some eternal law of motion for matter.[13]

In fact, Heisenberg conceives of elementary atomic particles as so thoroughly mathematical that there can be nothing about them that is not mathematically explicable. So he says that

> when modern science states that the proton is a certain solution of a fundamental equation of matter it means that we can deduce mathematically *all possible properties of the proton* and can check the correctness of the solution by experiments *in every detail.*[14] (emphasis added)

This view of reality as essentially mathematically explicable is behind Heisenberg's famous interpretation of what are called "uncertainty relations," the relations which exist between finding the momentum of a subatomic particle and finding its position. The uncertainty arises because the way to find out the location of a particle is to have it hit something massive enough to stop it. In that case we know where it is, but we can no longer find out how fast it was going. On the other hand, the way to find out a particle's momentum is to have it collide with something which is not massive enough to stop it. Then, provided we already know the mass of whatever the particle strikes, we can calculate the particle's velocity by how far it moves the object it hit. Once the particle has collided with the other object, however, its location is not knowable because it bounces off at such high speed. For this reason, finding out the position and momentum of a particle *simultaneously* is impossible; whichever of the two we discover prevents us from discovering the other.

This in itself is not such a strange thing. There are many uncertainty relations in our everyday experience, for example, trying to ascertain the temperature of water in a glass by inserting a thermometer changes the temperature. The very operation of trying to find that information makes it uncertain.

But the view Heisenberg held of the nature of atoms and their particles required him to take a very special position on the uncertainty between the momentum and location of particles, a position that has come to be known as the "Copenhagen interpretation." Since he was committed to the view that reality is mathematically formed energy, he said that particles do not have both speed and location, but only whichever one we choose to measure! That is, if we find a particle's velocity, then it had no location; if we find its location, then it had no velocity. Heisenberg admits this seems a strange thing to say:

> this is a very strange result since it seems to indicate that [our] observation plays a decisive role in the event and that the reality varies, depending on whether we observe it or not.[15]

He goes on to comment, however, that we should be prepared to give up our ordinary ("classical") concepts when we deal with the world of subatomic entities.[16]

But we could just as well regard the uncertainty between a particle's velocity and location as a limit to our ability to calculate and discover subatomic events—in the way putting a thermometer in water limits our ability to discover its temperature. This was the way Einstein understood the uncertainty. The difference between these physicists is the different status they give to the mathematical aspect in relation to all the others. Einstein takes the mathematical aspect of our thought to be equally as real as its sensory aspect, so that the explanatory successes of math warrant us in believing in the existence of the entities physics proposes. But he does not take his esteem of math as far as Heisenberg who regards as unreal anything not mathematically calculable.

5. What Difference Do Such Theories Make?

We have now seen that there are at least two very different conceptions *of* physics which correspond to two very different ways of theorizing *in* physics. And we have seen that these differences are directed and controlled by differing philosophical perspectives about the nature of reality. As in the case of math, these theory differences result in physics being done differently. For example, from Mach's view it would make no sense to attempt to confirm the existence of entities such as atoms and subatomic particles.

On the other hand, physicists who reject Mach's perspective have engaged in extensive efforts to discover whether the entities proposed by their theories really exist. For example, take the hypothesis of the neutrino proposed by Wolfgang Pauli. Of course, Pauli did not initially *discover* neutrinos, but *invented* the proposal that there are such particles (the word 'neutrino' is Italian for "little neutral one"). His invention was intended to make sense of a number of observations and also to preserve the law of conservation of energy. It did those jobs very well, and later on solved other explanatory gaps in atomic theory as well. But it still bothered physicists that the neutrino was supposed to be undetectable; they were concerned that it might *only* be an invention.

According to the theory, neutrinos are so small that they rarely bump into anything. One scientist estimated that to collide with the nucleus of an atom, a single neutrino would have to "pass through the equivalent of 50 light years of solid lead," and that a "shielding wall capable of thinning out a beam of neutrinos would have to be as thick as 100,000,000 stars."[17] This is why so many scientists initially thought the neutrino would always remain impossible to detect.[18]

This seemingly impossible task was accomplished, however, in 1965. Getting the evidence took a tremendous amount of ingenuity, equipment, time and money. This expense and effort highlights the *motive* which drove the physicists involved. Clearly, their motive was the belief that theories are attempts to know reality; that is, to discover what exists and to know its nature. This belief presupposes a philosophical perspective which accepts the logical/mathematical and physical aspects of experience as (at least part of) the nature of reality, not as merely useful fiction.

The upshot is that even though all these thinkers would say that they accept the atomic theory, they mean something very different by it. For Mach, accepting it means inventing a system of micro-entities that is useful though populated with fictions. For Einstein, it means inventing hypotheses which correspond with the purely physical objects which we never experience. For Heisenberg it means discovering the micro-entities that comprise reality which, while they have physical properties, are essentially mathematical in nature. The placid-appearing surface agreement of these thinkers conceals a deeper level at which they have sharp disagreements over the nature of atoms and their particles—disagreements which mirror their disagreements over how to make the correct priority assignment among the aspects of experience.

6. The Role of Religion in These Theories

Even if such sharp differences in the interpretation and practice of physics have now been traced to differences of perspective on the nature of reality, can it also be shown that these perspectives presuppose some religious belief? As in the case of the differing perspectives in math, I find the perspectives involved in physics are, indeed, grounded on religious belief. For example, in a comment similar to that of Mill, Mach said of sensation that

> One must not attempt to explain sense-perception. It is something so simple and fundamental, that the attempt to trace it back to something simpler, at least at the present time, can never succeed.[19]

What he says about sensation in this quote accords it the status we found to be the defining characteristic of divinity. So, as in the case of Mill, I find Mach's declaration to be a confession of a religious faith.

On the other hand, Einstein opposed Mach by insisting that the logical and/or mathematical aspects are also part of the nature of our knowledge and of reality. In fact, he ended by regarding our sensations as caused by physical objects outside our minds, so that what is sensory is denied independent existence. But since Einstein does admit that the objects of our direct experience are purely sensory, he then has to attribute to rational thought a status which fits the definition of divinity. In order for the rationality of a hypothesis to justify belief in the reality of the entities it proposes, it must be accepted that whatever is rational is real. Thus human rationality (rather than perception) is the rule for explaining what exists. But the only reason for believing that whatever is rational is real is to believe that the laws of logic and mathematics not only govern human thought but all reality, and are the principles which make all else possible, so that they are self-existent and thus divine.

Finally, from all that Heisenberg says about the special status of mathematical concepts, he is clearly accepting this rationalistic position, and explicitly states it in terms very similar to the quote given earlier from Descartes.[20] He says that while all our other concepts are doubtful and "we do not know how far they will help us to find our way in the world,"[21] the concepts of math are immune from doubt of any kind and reflect the nature of reality in such a way that not only what they can calculate is real, but whatever they cannot calculate is not real. The presupposition to this rule for what counts as real is the belief that mathematical laws are the principles which make all else possible. In speaking of his hope that all yet unsolved problems of physics will turn out to be mathematically calculable, and of the fact that this hope is based on an unproven religious belief, Heisenberg says:

> we may hope that the fundamental law of motion will turn out as a mathematically simple law. . . . It is difficult to give any good argument for this hope for simplicity—except the fact that it has hitherto always been possible to write the fundamental equations in physics as simple mathematical forms. *This fact fits with the Pythagorean religion* and many physicists share their belief in this respect, but no convincing argument has yet been given to show that it must be so.[22] (emphasis added)

Thus it appears that Heisenberg's theory about the uncertainty relations is based on a deification of the mathematical aspect of our experience. This is why, from a biblical point of view, this "Copenhagen" interpretation accords to mathematics the status that belongs only to God.

I conclude, therefore, that the theories considered in this chapter are one and all based upon overviews of reality which presuppose some aspect(s) of the universe to be divine. Their advocates all insist on finding the basic nature of reality by identifying one of its aspects as that which is self-existent and makes all else possible. It further appears that the differences in physics that are generated by conflicting religious presuppositions extend to the very understanding of what physics is and how it should be carried on. Moreover, because the perspectives we have considered all presuppose the pagan type of religious belief, they are one and all theories which should be unacceptable to any Jew or Christian.[23]

9

THEORIES IN PSYCHOLOGY

1. Introduction

As in mathematics and physics, disagreements among theories in psychology run deep. Here, too, differences concerning the very nature of this science result from different perspectival overviews of reality. This is because here too differences over the nature of reality determine how the aspect of experience which is its field of investigation (in this case, the *sensory* aspect) is seen in relation to all the others. And as we look at several of the controlling overviews of psychological theories, we shall find—once again—that they are, in turn, rooted in differing presuppositions as to what is divine.

Before examining the sample theories that will illustrate this claim for psychology, let me warn that the theories of reality assumed in psychology are not as readily indicated by their advocates as they were in math and physics. In those sciences, conflicting perspectives were reflected in the titles of the theories—formalist, logicist, intuitionist, phenomenalist, etc. In psychology, the names of the major theories do not correspond to the perspectives which regulate them, and even the most widely accepted definitions of this science are too ambiguous to indicate precisely how its aspect is understood to relate to all the others. The two definitions which have been most widely held in this century are: (1) psychology is the study of the human mind, and (2) psychology is the study of human behavior. To be sure, these definitions represent a serious disagreement over the subject matter of psychology. The first (and older) definition takes human consciousness as the focus of investigation; the second concentrates on bodily behavior. But while the newer definition rejected the first for its supposed imprecision and vagueness, the irony is that both are afflicted with the same sort of conceptual fuzziness.

141

To see why neither of these two definitions can properly delimit the field of psychology or clearly indicate the perspective of those advocating it, we need to recall what a science is. In our discussion of scientific theories, we noticed that they arose to investigate distinguishable aspects of experience or to theorize across two or more aspects and attempt to relate them. The problem with the two popular definitions of psychology is that they leave its aspectual delimitation entirely in the dark.

The older definition provides no help by saying that this science concerns the human mind, since it does not say which *aspect* of mental life is being examined and explained. Human mental life includes acts of thought, feeling, desire, and volition which may be about mathematics, art, ethics, politics, or economics. Not only can such mental acts be *about* any of the aspects of experience but—from the standpoint of our pretheoretical experience—they also *have* these aspects themselves (they may be counted, beautiful, loving, treasonable, or worth money). And, of course, the properties and laws of the spatial, biotic, sensory, and logical aspects are true of them as well. But until we know which aspect of the acts or objects of consciousness is to be explained, we have an insufficient circumscription of the science doing the job.

This same vagueness is true, however, of the newer designation "the science of human behavior": we need to know which aspect of human behavior is to be studied and explained. Human behavior exhibits all the aspects which have become fields of study for the entire range of the sciences. An act of dancing, for example, can be aesthetically beautiful, economically rewarding, physically demanding, biologically healthy, and sensorily tiring. It may at the same time celebrate a religious festival, require a lot of space, and exhibit characteristics typical of a particular culture or period in history. Obviously, no one science can claim to explain *all* these aspects of it. Psychology must have its own "home ground": an aspect which serves as the point of entry for its own particular study of human behavior.

Interestingly, some recent psychologists have noticed these difficulties with the accepted definitions, but dismissed them as unimportant. Isaacson, Hutt, and Blum, for example, admit that:

> Many branches of science other than psychology attempt to explain
> behavior by formulating hypotheses and testing them; and many of the

interests evidenced by psychologists in their theories are *exactly like those of scientists in other areas.*[1] (emphasis added)

Their conclusion is that *if* psychology can be distinguished from other sciences at all, it is by

the relative emphasis on understanding the individual as a total functioning unit.[2]

But, of course, the problem is exactly that no one science can possibly deal with a total human. As soon as it offers biological explanations it will be biology, and when it offers physical explanations it will be physics, and if it offers historical explanations it will be history. This is why we must look beyond the two prevailing definitions of psychology to find how any particular theorist delimits its field and relates that field to the other aspects of reality. Only in that way can we penetrate to the roots of a theory's differences from competing theories, and thus to the religious belief that drives it.

Our provisional list of aspects included a sensitive, or "psychosensory" aspect, the kind of properties and laws which include the perceptual (red, soft, loud, tart) and emotional (angry, sad, joyous). This aspect was preceded in our list by the physical and biotic aspects and followed by logical, historical, linguistic, and social aspects. It is no surprise that conflicts among perspectives on psychology largely concern how the sensory aspect relates to these neighboring aspects. Curiously, it has been philosophers such as Berkeley, Hume, and Mill, along with the physicist Mach, who have tried to collapse the other aspects to the sensory, while most of the thinkers in psychology have tried to explain the sensory in terms of some other aspect!

These trends in theories of psychology have been noticed by Jean Piaget, who comments at length on the theories of psychologists that regard the sensory as explained by some other aspect. He divides them into those which explain it by biology or physics (downward on our list), and those which explain it sociologically (upward on our list).[3] Referring to these trends as "reductionist," Piaget opposes both in favor of what he calls a "constructionist" view:

In its search for a specific standpoint between the organic and the social, psychology turned towards the study of behavior in particular. . . . Behavior, however, can be analyzed from various standpoints. . . .

It is interesting to show that once the reductionist approach has been discarded in order to determine in behavior as such the specificity of the psychological phenomenon, a constructivist approach is being taken. . . .[4]

While we agree with Piaget about the abandonment of "reductionist" theories, our reasons for doing so include the pagan religious presuppositions which inspire and sustain them. To illustrate the religious control of theories of psychology, let us begin by surveying some of the theories which exemplify the "downward" reduction of psychology to the physical and/or biological aspects—the theories which are called "behaviorist."

2. The Theories of Watson, Thorndike, and Skinner

The term 'behaviorism' was coined by J. B. Watson to indicate a view of psychology which is restricted to what can be observed. By this he meant to break with theories, such as those of William James, which accept the definition that psychology is chiefly centered on consciousness. As Watson himself put it:

To show how unscientific is the concept [of consciousness], look for a moment at William James' definition of psychology. "Psychology is the description and explanation of states of consciousness as such." Starting with a definition which assumes what he starts out to prove, he escapes his difficulty by an argumentum ad hominem. . . . All other introspectionists are equally illogical. In other words, they do not tell us what consciousness is, but merely begin to put things into it by assumption; and then when they come to analyze consciousness, naturally they find in it just what they put into it.[5]

Watson went on to say that as he and his colleagues looked at how progress was being made in such sciences as medicine and chemistry, it appeared that the advances were always the sort that could be confirmed by repeatable laboratory experiments. With these sciences as models, Watson set out to remake psychology. He advocated that the behaviorist drop from his vocabulary "all subjective terms such as sensation, perception, image, desire, purpose, and even thinking and emotion as they were subjectively defined." To take their place

The behaviorist asks: Why don't we make what we can *observe* the real field of psychology? Let us limit ourselves to the observed and formulate laws concerning only those things. Now what can we observe?

Well, we can observe *behavior*—what the organism does or says. And let me make this fundamental point at once: that *saying* is doing—that is, *behaving*. Speaking overtly to ourselves (thinking) is just as objective a type of behavior as baseball.

The rule, or measuring rod, which the behaviorist puts in front of him always is: Can I describe this bit of behavior I see in terms of "stimulus and response"?[6]

Needless to say the simple reflex arc of stimulus-response has never been sufficient to explain all animal, let alone all human, behavior. This is why E. M. Thorndike tried to expand the behaviorist theory beyond the limited explanatory power of the reflex action. Thorndike called this supplement the "law of effect." It meant that the consequences of past behavior play a role in determining future behavior. His way of putting this point was to say that if a stimulus-response is followed by a "satisfier" or reinforcer, the connection is strengthened; if it is followed by an "annoyer" or aversive stimulus, the connection is weakened. Although the terms 'satisfier' and 'annoyer' seem to refer to unobservable inner states of pleasure and pain, Thorndike did not slip into allowing these into his theory. In keeping with Watson's program, he defined even these terms behaviorally:

> By a satisfying state of affairs is meant one which the animal does nothing to avoid, often doing things which maintain or renew it. By an annoying state of affairs is meant one which the animal does nothing to preserve, often doing things which put an end to it.[7]

In this way Thorndike also avoided all mention of *purpose*, since that is also subjective and unobservable.

Skinner built on the work of Thorndike. His task was to explain non-reflex responses and for this, he developed the concept of "operant" responses. These differ from reflex behavior, because a simple reflex can be explained by laws that relate an unconditioned stimulus to an unconditioned response, or a conditioned stimulus to a conditioned response. (Doing this for the latter pair, of course, requires knowing the history of the organism's past conditioning.) The operant laws go beyond these, however, by relating behavior to Thorndike's idea of reinforcing stimuli. As Skinner puts it: "the operant is defined by the property upon which reinforcement is made contingent."[8] The laws Skinner wants to formulate are therefore not merely those which relate a stimulus to a response, but those which relate a response to its reinforcers. Operant laws allow the prediction or control of a particular response by relating the reinforcing stimuli to the class of responses of which the particular response is a member. In operant behavior, then, we

> deal with variables which unlike the eliciting stimulus, do not 'cause' a given bit of behavior to occur but simply make the occurrence more probable. We may then proceed to deal for example, with the combined effect of more than one such variable.[9]

All this can be fairly described as an attempt to elaborate on Thorndike's "law of effect" which, for Skinner, becomes the focal point of the entire science of psychology. On this view, the work of the psychologist is to predict or control a particular behavior by establishing the probability of its reoccurrence in relation to its reinforcers. He calls such relations the "contingencies of reinforcement":

> An adequate formulation of the interaction between organism and environment must always specify three things: 1) the occasion upon which the response occurs, 2) the response itself, and 3) the reinforcing consequences. The interrelationships among them are the contingencies of reinforcement.[10]

Common to all these theories is the total rejection of allowing into psychology anything about human mental life and experiences such as thoughts, feelings, purposes, and even perceptions.

Even this brief summary should be sufficient to establish that something very odd is going on. Since all of us constantly experience our own thoughts, feelings, perceptions, intentions, etc., why are these to be ignored by psychology? Notice how Watson spoke of James's definition as *assuming* just what needed to be *proven* when it referred to consciousness. Are not the stimuli and responses that are supposed to take the place of thought and perception themselves known by perception and interpreted by thought? Why, then, do these theorists regard thoughts and perceptions as *assumptions?* Why do they say thoughts and perceptions need to be *proven?*

Such a view can only be understood as the product of these thinkers' perspectival overview on the nature of reality. To get an accurate idea of that perspective, let us approach it by considering their view of human nature. Most other psychological theories had seen humans as comprised of two things: a mind and a body. For them, such sciences as biology and medicine study and treat the body, while the science of psychology studies and treats the mind.

By contrast, the behaviorists reject the mind-body duality. Instead, they see a human as only one thing: a body. Therefore, it is the body alone that is to be studied and explained, no matter which science does the explaining. But why do behaviorists reject the belief that there is a distinct entity called a mind? The reason is their *materialist* perspective on reality.

That a materialist theory of reality is behind behaviorism can be seen in several ways, but the most obvious is that it alone can supply the reason why all inner experience is to be excluded from any explanation of behavior. For it is not necessary to dismiss all inner experience just because one rejects the mind-body view of human nature. A theory could very well deny that a human is two things—deny, that is, that the mind is a distinct *thing*—but still accept that humans have inner experiences which are crucial to understanding their behavior. But if one accepts a materialist perspective, then not only would belief in a nonphysical mind be precluded, but also belief in the existence of inner, nonphysical experiences as well.

Consider the same point from a slightly different angle. If—theories aside—we simply describe what we all directly experience, we would have to say that humans exhibit all the aspects that everything else does. People take up space, move, eat, feel, reason, and speak, for example. Such deeds have, respectively, spatial, physical, biological, sensory, logical, and linguistic properties. People also have values. Acts of valuing may be aimed at truth, economy, beauty, justice, or love. *But—once again—we never experience anything which is an exclusively physical body or an exclusively nonphysical mind.* Those are entity hypotheses invented to explain human nature. And they are invented under the control of some perspectival overview of reality which is either proposed as a theory or simply presupposed. The perspective which regulates the mind-body duality is one that sees two particular aspects as those upon which all the others depend: the physical and the logical. From this overview, it is easy to accept that there are wholly physical things (bodies) and wholly thinking things (minds). The remaining aspects can then be seen as generated by the interaction of minds and bodies.

But the perspective guiding the behaviorist theories is one that sees all reality as restricted to, or dependent on, the physical aspect. It holds either that: (1) there exist only physical bodies and their actions, or (2) any nonphysical entities involved are entirely caused by physical bodies and their actions. This is why the crux of the difference between the behaviorists and other theories cannot be understood simply as an argument over whether there are nonphysical minds. The behaviorist perspective not only disallows minds as explaining anything, but everything else which is supposed to be nonphysical. It views the sensory aspect, along with all the others, as either collapsed to the physical aspect of experience, or as entirely dependent on it. In either case, the real scientific explanation is always physical.

The two versions of materialism distinguished above are reflected in the difference between the way Watson reduces the sensory aspect to the physical and the way Skinner does it. Watson takes the first version. For him, consciousness itself, along with its states and contents, are outright fictions: there are just no such entities. He says that "consciousness" is as fictional as "soul," and ranks all concepts of mental life in the same class as the superstitions of medicine men.[11]

Skinner, on the other hand, does not deny outright that there are inner experiences. Moreover, so far as he is concerned, the inner experiences may even have distinctively sensory and perhaps other nonphysical properties. Nevertheless, he still maintains that such inner experiences are not to figure in the science of psychology. His reason is that these experiences never cause behavior, but are instead always caused by behavior.[12]

On either version, however, the physical aspect is given the status of self-existence. It explains and causes everything because everything depends on it, while it does not depend on anything in turn. In this way, the materialist perspective presupposes a faith in the divinity of matter, a faith which is of the pagan variety since it regards some aspect of creation as divine. It should be clear, therefore, why behaviorism cannot be acceptable to anyone who believes in God.

As with the other Casebook chapters, the purpose here is not so much to critique the theories being reviewed as to show how they are regulated by religious belief. All the same, it is worth noticing the powerful grip the materialist faith and perspective exerts on these thinkers so that they maintain their position despite the incoherencies that afflict their theories. One such incoherency can be seen in the way Skinner speaks of how conditioning controls behavior:

> The same thing is true when a man writes books, invents things, manages a business. He didn't initiate anything. It's all the effect of past history on him. That's the truth, and we have to get used to it.[13]

But if the writing of books is just like all other human activities in being controlled by our past conditioning, what does this say about Skinner's own books? What does it say about the theory of behaviorism? To be consistent, the behaviorist would have to admit that his own theory is the product of his own conditioning. Once that is admitted, however, there is no reason for the behaviorist or anyone else to regard that theory (or any other belief) as true. In fact, it would mean that even if behaviorism happened to be true, no one could ever know that it is true because the theory requires that every belief is held only because the believer's conditioning makes him/her helpless to do anything else. Skinner's claim is therefore self-referentially incoherent. Yet he says, "That's the truth, and we have to get used to it"!

Another incoherency concerns the behaviorists' avowed dismissal of inner states of consciousness from psychology. We have already noticed the implausibility of this claim compared with a description of what we directly experience, but I am now referring to another difficulty. This is that the behaviorist must assume that in establishing the laws which correlate stimuli or reinforcers to responses, he has shown something that will continue to be true of the organism being studied. The laws would yield no scientific prediction or control if what was discovered were true only for the moment it was discovered. But for the laws to continue to apply, what is found out about an organism would have to describe an enduring disposition or tendency of the individual tested. Skinner flirted with this problem when he said that if being thirsty meant only having a tendency to thirst, that was acceptable. It was only objectionable if it was supposed to refer to an inner state of thirst which is a contributory cause of a person's drinking.

The problem, of course, is that dispositions and tendencies are inner states and are just as unobservable and nonphysical as are any of the other entities he and Watson wanted to ban from psychology. Yet Skinner has to admit that he cannot do without dispositions. What is worse, it seems obvious that even if someone could come up with a way to avoid explicitly mentioning them in the theory, the entire explanatory and predictive power of behaviorism would still require them. The claim that inner states are banned from psychology is at odds with the assumption that people have tendencies, so this part of the theory is self-assumptively incoherent.

Finally there is a large explanatory gap left by the laws which are supposed to show how the reinforcers are related to stimulus-response patterns. These, Skinner said, are to be arrived at by establishing statistical correlations between reinforcers and responses. But even granting that the many variables involved in such a task can be sorted out and accorded their relative causal weights (and it is by no means obvious that this can be done), what would the resulting probabilities explain? Suppose we can show, for instance, that more people will vacation in the mountains than at the seashore relative to how severe the winter is. What have we explained? As Piaget has pointed out:

> This is merely expressing, in terms of calculation, de facto states and observed laws, and the reason for the probabilities still has to be explained.[14]

The point of mentioning these difficulties is to highlight the way the materialist faith and perspective exercises its control over those who are captured by it. It illustrates that what makes the theory of behaviorism attractive to its advocates is not its explanatory power, since it is patently incoherent. Rather, its attractiveness stems from a particular vision of what science *should* be, which is based in turn on a specific view of the nature of reality. It is the materialist view of reality which sets the limits as to which hypotheses look plausible and which do not. It is thus much more than a "working hypothesis" or "methodological assumption" that is easily surrendered if it proves unfruitful. On the contrary, it remains a hope and a prophecy commanding loyalty in the face of the most insurmountable incoherencies. The real explanation of such loyalty is that it is rooted in a religious belief: a faith in the divinity of matter/energy. This is the driving motive of the perspective, and the real source of its power over those who do science under its direction.

To be sure, this perspective is excused by its defenders on grounds of wanting to maximize in psychology such laudable features as precision, measurability, and economy of thought. But desirable as such features are, their importance can never override the one concern which must outweigh all others: does the theory account for the relevant data? Here it seems they have forgotten Aristotle's sage advice:

> Our discussion will be adequate if it has as much clarity as the subject matter allows, for precision is not to be sought for alike in all discussions . . . it is the mark of an educated man to look for precision . . . just so far as the nature of the subject admits . . . (*Nicomachean Ethics* 1094b12-25)

So even if states of consciousness are not observable, it is still hard to imagine what could be more relevant to understanding human behavior than what people think, feel, desire, and—especially—*believe*. Is not behaviorism itself a belief of those who advocate it? Is that belief not the reason that they "behave" as they do in pursuing psychology? The moral of the story seems clear: rather than producing genuine explanations of human perceptual and emotional experience, behaviorism has committed theoretical suicide on the doorstep to psychology.

3. The Theories of Adler and Fromm

The second of the reductionist tendencies mentioned by Piaget is one that tries to explain the perceptual and emotional aspect of life as a product of social, rather than physical and/or biological, causes. This does not mean that the advocates of such socially oriented theories ignore altogether the physical or biological aspects of humans. Rather, it means that while the physical and biotic components of humans set the basis and limits for their psychical life, they do so without *determining* how people think, feel, or act. By theorizing in this way, thinkers such as Alfred Adler broke with the earlier theories of the behaviorists and Freud. Whereas Freud had developed theories from a perspective which reduced psychology to one of the "natural" sciences, Adler insisted that psychology is a *social* science.[15] He held that the goal of psychology "is not to comprehend causal factors, as in physiology, but the direction-giving . . . [social] forces and goals that guide all other psychological movements."[16]

Thus while admitting that our genetic make-up determines the sort of bodies we have and the biotic necessities of life, Adler says that even biological innate drives are handled in different ways according to people's *social* orientation.[17] This, he maintained, is true not only of such things as sex drives,[18] but even of the way people perceive the world. Perception, said Adler, is never merely sensory copying but the product of the way people collect and arrange sensations due to the factors of their social life. As a result, people literally do not see the same thing. Because of this, it is possible for psychology to infer far-reaching conclusions concerning an individual's inner life from the way he or she perceives.[19]

What, exactly, are the social factors which lead human feeling, perception and behavior? According to Adler,

> one's own prejudices, one's "unconscious" presuppositions, like all human expressions, exist within a social context, and somehow express the striving for power, significance, and security.[20]

In a word, everyone strives for "superiority." It is this which is "the general goal of man" and "the principal conditioning factor of human life."[21] Because the drive for social superiority is the "life goal" of every person, "no person can tolerate the feelings of real or apparent inferiority."[22] (It was in this connection that Adler coined the term 'inferiority complex'.)

The social drive of each individual for power and superiority is, however, in direct conflict with that same drive in others. Left unrestrained, it would produce a chaos of constant strife which would make human society impossible. For this reason, Adler contended that the goal of superiority is "ridiculous from the standpoint of reality" (by "reality" here, he meant social reality). The individual, he insisted, makes little impression on society. What is more, each individual depends upon society for existence, so that the restraint which blocks the drive for superiority is really insurmountable: the sexes need each other, children need parents, and the family depends in turn on the larger social group. Thus the drive which is the principal determining psychological factor in human life is also in hopeless opposition to the social conditions necessary for each person's survival. These social conditions can be preserved only through adjustments—chiefly the division of labor—by which people cooperate in order to survive rather than compete for superiority:

> If the conditions of our life are determined in the first place by cosmic influences, they are also further conditioned by the social and communal life of human beings, and by the laws and regulations which arise spontaneously from communal life.[23]

Adler called the dependency of the individual on the social group the "logic of communal life" (here "logic" refers to whatever is "universally useful" and necessary to the individual's survival).

He then used these terms to express his point that everything which characterizes humans as distinctly human developed because of the "logic of communal life." Adler claimed that not only speech, but

> thought and concepts, like reason, understanding, logic, ethics and a esthetics, have their origin in the social life of man.[24]

On Adler's theory, then, every human is involved in a great collision. On the one hand, a solitary individual can neither survive nor reproduce, and every distinctly human capability has evolved to meet social needs. On the other hand, it is precisely society which is the source of the individual's feelings of inferiority, and is therefore the obstacle against which the individual struggles. The contest, however, is totally one-sided: no individual can win against society. So the conflict can only be resolved in one way:

> Our sole recourse in this quandary is to assume the logic of our group life . . . as though it were an ultimate absolute truth.[25]

Thus, the needs of society are to be regarded as paramount, and the individual must adjust to them. These needs then become the ultimate standard by which all values, practices, relationships, etc., are to be judged. That is, they are the standards for what is normal and abnormal in psychology.

> What we call justice and righteousness, and consider most valuable in the human character, is essentially nothing more than the fulfillment of the conditions which arise in the social needs of mankind . . . we can judge a character as bad or good only from the standpoint of society.[26]

The way individuals cope in adjusting their drive for superiority with the social conditions of survival, Adler called their "lifestyle," which could be either psychologically normal or abnormal. In abnormal people their "maladjustment is always incongruity between lifestyle and social demands rather than inner conflict,"[27] so that "the cure is always to strengthen social feeling rather than attempt to restrain 'bad' impulses."[28] Generally speaking, an abnormal lifestyle may be characterized this way:

> Division of labor is an absolute necessity for the preservation of human society. Consequently, every person must fill a specific place at some point. If a person does not participate in this obligation, he denies the preservation of social life, of the human race altogether.[29]

This general point is applied to the more specific example of sex and marriage in the following way. In a normal lifestyle,

> sexual attraction . . . [is] always molded along the lines of a desire for
> human welfare. . . . A good marriage is the best means we know for
> bringing up the future generation of humanity, and marriage should
> always have this in view.[30]

So when a man courts a woman, he does this in a psychologically
normal way if we can see by what he does that he is saying "yes"
to the future of mankind.[31] In this, as in every other case, it is "the
immanent rules of the game of a group . . . [which are the] absolute
truth" for the individual.[32]

Adler's emphasis on adjusting the individual to the needs of the
social group led him to take a great interest in the social theories
of Marx and Engles. In fact, he admired their work so much that he
once said "Karl Marx . . . showed the way toward the final realization of social interest."[33] Nevertheless, Adler rejected the historical determinism of Marx's theory. He realized that if everything is
predetermined by the flow of history, there could be no norms: no
right or wrong, no normal or abnormal. "If man were completely
determined by circumstances," he said, "we could not speak of
errors."[34] So he reversed the Marxist idea of economically controlled history, and held instead that

> In each immediate present the economic conditions are reflected and
> answered by each individual and each group according to their pre-
> viously acquired lifestyle.[35]

He thus acknowledged the need for a theory to allow that humans
have genuine freedom to recognize the truth. He saw that if all
thought, belief, feeling, and choice are determined (i.e., forced on
humans by outside conditions) then so is the determinists' acceptance of the theory of determinism forced on them by those same
conditions. In that case they could never claim to know their theory is true since the theory making that claim would be self-
referentially incoherent. In other words, the theory requires that
no belief is ever a judgment made on the basis of experience or
reason, but is always a compulsion over which the believer has
no control.

Adler was aware that if he were simply to supplement the physical determinism of the behaviorists with social determinants, he
would not end up avoiding the dilemma of determinism but would
only have a more complex version of it. He would be allowing for
two determining forces (physical and social) rather than only one
(physical), but would not have avoided the incoherency of assum-

ing he is free to ascertain the truth of his theory. Nevertheless, despite his apparent recognition of this point, Adler never provides a theory of human nature that allows for genuine freedom with respect to the acquisition of knowledge. Instead he falls into precisely the two-sided determinism he seemed to realize should be avoided by regarding thoughts and feelings as rigidly determined by a person's social orientation which is set in early childhood:

> Perhaps there will be some readers who have the impression . . . that we are denying free will and judgment. So far as free will is concerned this accusation is true. . . . In our examination we must ferret out the history of [a patient's] earliest childhood days, because the impressions of early infancy indicate the direction . . . in which he will respond in the future . . . the particular pressure he has felt in the days of earliest infancy will color his attitude toward life and determine . . . his world-view. . . .
>
> It should not surprise us to learn that people do not change their attitude toward life after their infancy. . . .[36]

Another problem Adler left unsolved arises from his acceptance of the needs of society as the standard for psychological normalcy. In his view, it is always the social needs of the group to which the individual must conform. This rules out raising the question as to whether a society itself may be abnormal. Moreover, another result of making normalcy the same as subordinating the drive for superiority to the needs of society (*any* society), is that he is forced to regard every leader, political or religious, who actually did achieve social superiority as abnormal.

Eric Fromm undertook to correct these two faults in Adler's work. In his earlier works, Fromm called himself a *social* psychologist and, like Adler, rejected theories which regard humans as determined by the physical/biotic aspects of their nature. He said that whereas Freud had viewed psychology as a "natural science of man,"[37] a human's true nature is that of "free, conscious activity."[38] These free conscious activities are not determined by the "natural" drives of sex or hunger, but include the ways people need and deal with such things as beauty and love.[39] Moreover, like Adler, Fromm had a great admiration for Marx. He saw the class and economic factors emphasized by Marx as determining the social side of human life. These factors are transmitted to individuals through the family, which is "the psychological agency of society."[40] Since the family itself is a product of the economic and class conditions of society, Marx gave us the way to critique and judge the sort of society and family we *ought* to have. A fully *social* psychology is not, then, left merely to deal with the individual's adjustment to society, but can also say whether society itself is what it should be.[41]

But Fromm's pushing social psychology in a more thoroughly Marxist direction allows him to avoid only one of the two problems Adler had bequeathed to him. It avoids the problem of having to admit that there is no standard by which to judge a society, by allowing him to say that any type of society other than a socialist one is deficient. But it does not avoid the problem that Marx's own theory of history and society was as deterministic as the theories Fromm was rejecting. For Marx, people's perceptions of justice or love, as well as their conceptions of normal and abnormal, are totally determined by their socio-economic conditioning. How, then, can we be free to ascertain the norms by which to judge society if our very ideas of norms are socially determined?

At first, Fromm tried to find a way around Marx's determinism by saying that Marxist theory should not be understood to mean that each individual is psychologically determined by economy and class. Rather, it is only the institutions of society which are structured by economics. Thus Marx should not be interpreted as teaching that the "acquisitive drive" is the overriding motive of every act of each individual, but only of the social structures in which the individual lives.[42] But having made that point, Fromm hedges, for he also says that

> In the interplay of interacting psychic drives and economic conditions, the latter have primacy.[43]

He repeats that this does not mean that the economic factors are always the strongest, but only that they are "less modifiable" by the individual. Yet, at the same time, he again insists the role of "primary formative factors" goes to economic conditions, so that the "task of social psychology is to explain... psychic attitudes and ideologies—and their unconscious roots in particular—in terms of the influence of economic conditions on libido strivings."[44] At this point, Fromm wants humans to be "essentially conditioned by history" for purposes of psychological explanation, while at the same time he wants human life to have an "inner dynamism of its own" so as to be free to discover truth.[45]

This inconsistent wavering between two poles of thought comes to a head in Fromm's *Man for Himself* (1947), but is most clearly addressed in *The Art of Loving* (1956) and *The Heart of Man* (1964). In the latter two works Fromm is explicit about the dilemma. Already in *The Sane Society* (1955), he had acknowledged that Marx had not solved it. While Marx had seen much that is true of the way society determines individuals, his view was not only "economically simplistic"[46] but unrealistic. For Marx thought not only that socialism is *necessary* to heal society but that it is *sufficient* to do so.[47] In *The Heart of Man*, Fromm repeats this criticism in more detail. He chides Marx for everywhere presupposing that man has an essential nature, while also saying that man creates himself in the process of history and is nothing more than the "ensemble of his social relations."

At this point Fromm asserts that man does, indeed, have an essential nature, but that nature is to be "a contradiction inherent in human existence"![48] The contradiction is, of course, precisely the one which he criticized Marx for not solving: on the one hand man is an animal, natural, and determined by nature and society; on the other hand man is conscious ("life aware of itself"), rational, and is "free in thought."[49] It is through this free rationality that humans are able to know that the norm for both individuals and society is the rule of love: love thy neighbor as thyself. Thus, for Fromm as for Kant before him, human freedom lies in the (practical) reason which knows ethical truth. And like Rousseau, he sees man as essentially good in his innermost self. It is the outer determinants of the social order which make him evil.

This, however, is nothing more than saying that both sides of the inconsistency are somehow true. A human is free and is not free in the same sense. This, of course, logically entails that there is and is not a science of psychology as Fromm conceived of it. For if human thoughts and choices are genuinely free, and if they cause human actions, then neither the choices nor the behavior resulting from them can be wholly explained in terms of any aspectual laws—let alone be predicted or controlled through knowledge of such laws.

Needless to say, attempting to accept mutually contradictory beliefs rather than develop a theory that avoids them raises even worse problems than those Fromm thinks it solves. Logical axioms

mandate that for any concept whatever, it either includes a particular characteristic or it does not, and that a concept cannot both
include and not include, exclude and not exclude, the same elements at the same time. Any (putative) concept that failed to
abide by these axioms would not merely be fuzzy or uncertain, but
would literally have no meaning whatever and would fail to be a
concept. Yet Fromm advocates that we reject the axioms of logic
and accept his claim that such mutual contradictions are illusory.

In *The Art of Loving,* [50] Fromm attempts to develop this point in
more detail. Western thought, he says, has been dominated by acceptance of logical axioms ever since they were clearly formulated
by Aristotle, who added that the axiom of noncontradiction in particular is "the most certain of all principles". Simply put, this law
says that nothing can both be true and not be true in the same
sense at the same time. An object cannot, for example, be both
blue and not blue at once, and a statement cannot be both true
and false. Over against this, Fromm claims that there is the option
of "paradoxical logic," which accepts that things can both have
and not have the same quality at the same time, so that a statement
can be both true and false at once. He cites the fact that this was
accepted long ago by some Chinese and Hindu thinkers, and in
more recent times by Hegel, Marx, and other dialectical philosophers. So he concludes that the way to resolve the apparently in-
solvable dilemma of determinism and freedom is to accept both as
true. We cannot see *how* both are true, of course, but that is because "the human mind perceives reality in contradictions." [51]

However, the program of rejecting logic in order to accept contradictory beliefs is not just a harmless, whimsical hope that somehow logically incompatible beliefs can both be true. It results in
nothing less than *the destruction of any and every concept we
could possess.* Even the concept of rejecting the law of noncontradiction depends on assuming and using that law, since without
it the (logical) concept of rejecting it could neither be thought
nor stated. And Fromm himself sees the concept of rejecting the
law as *excluding* the concept of accepting it, which thereby assumes the truth of the law. Thus Fromm's proposal is self-
assumptively incoherent.

Nor is this dire consequence avoided by Hegel, Marx, or any of
the other dialectical thinkers Fromm cites in the hope of convincing us that he is in good company. They one and all use the law of

noncontradiction to form their concepts, to state their case, and to criticize opposing views. They then deny the very law which makes it possible for them to do those things. The only way they bring off the sleight of hand which makes such a trick appear plausible is that they employ their denial of logic *selectively*; they embrace just the contradictions they wish to excuse, while otherwise reasoning in a consistent fashion and criticizing competing theories when they are inconsistent. If they were to employ their denial of noncontradiction at every point throughout their theory, the result would be a nonsense jumble that would fail to express, assert, or deny any belief whatever.

Fromm's position is an example of this same dogmatic selectivity. He presents his view as though there are reasons for rejecting the law of noncontradiction, and then argues that his view of the divine (he calls it "ultimate reality") *logically follows* from that rejection. He ignores the fact that to make any logical inference—to see that something "logically follows from" something else—*means* that something is required *on pain of contradicting oneself*. Having denied this basis for inference, Fromm nevertheless proceeds to infer that reality itself must be an all-encompassing mystical unity which harmonizes all the contradictions which logical thought thinks to be real. He then further infers that since human thought cannot help but be contradictory, ultimate reality cannot be known by thought. He gives a summary of the Hindu, Buddhist, and Taoist expressions of this same view, and infers that accepting their view of the divine requires him to reject the biblical idea of God as a knowable, individual, personal creator. He then offers still another logical inference when he insists that

> Opposition is a category of man's mind, not itself an element of reality . . . . Inasmuch as God represents the ultimate reality, and inasmuch as the human mind perceives reality in contradictions, no positive statement can be made about God.[52]

In this way Fromm ends by adding self-referential incoherency to the self-assumptive incoherency already asserted by his theory. For he makes the positive statement about God that no positive statements about God are possible.

We cannot help but ask ourselves what drove Fromm to such an extreme position. He started with the desire to develop a social psychology, but ended in the abandonment of logic and therefore of all science. *The real motive for Fromm's radical shift of thought was nothing less than a religious conversion:* he went from a pagan faith which saw some aspects of creation as divine to a pantheist type of faith in which the creation we experience is but an illusion contained within an all-encompassing, totally inconceivable, divinity. This is why, along with the pantheist religions, he is prepared to dismiss every difference and "opposition" found in human experience as mere appearance or illusion—logical laws included.

Fromm began with a rejection of the biblical idea of the divine. He regarded belief in Yahweh, the transcendent creator, as merely the projection of a desire for a heavenly Father to care for us. Fromm called this "a childish illusion." So he theorized on the presupposition of the pagan type of religious belief.[53] He looked *within* the universe available to human experience and thought for the self-existent reality on which all else depends. But pursuing psychology from this pagan presupposition, Fromm ran into one incoherency after another. At the same time, he noticed ever more clearly that the best of the thinkers before him had also run into them, and never solved them. Consequently, he came to believe that it was not simply coincidence that so many theories built upon of pagan presuppositions had run into contradictions, but that contradictions would arise in any theory governed by such a faith. Confronted with this realization, Fromm's religious faith was shaken and took a new direction. He saw, as Marx had not, that giving up the logical laws and regarding all contradictions as illusory would also mean giving up materialism along with the entire pagan standpoint for theorizing. Like the Hindu, Buddhist, and Taoist thinkers, he came to regard logical thinking as intrinsically contradictory and misleading, yielding only illusion and not reality. For anything whatever, he said, the truth is that "it both is and it is not."[54] He joined with the pantheistic traditions in advocating a nonrational, mystical experience as the way to know the truth of this doctrine about the one, inconceivable, divine reality. In later works and lectures he adopted a specifically Buddhist version (*Zen Buddhism and Psychoanalysis,* 1960).

4. Human Nature

We have now seen how theories of psychology vary in their explanation of the psycho-sensory aspect depending on their overview as to how all the aspects relate. In this respect they are no different from theories having other aspects as their subject matter. But in the case of psychology the aspect characterizing the perspective for this relation is also the one (or two) the theory assumes to be the essential nature of human nature. As Soloman Asch has observed

Each discipline possesses its special spirit, which consists in a particular way of viewing its data. The study of man . . . also requires its own perspective, which must start from some conception, however tentative, of what it is to be a human.[55]

J. A. Brown has applied the same point specifically to psychology:

All schools of psychology . . . inevitably begin with a belief about man's essential nature which forms the implicit frame of reference into which their facts and the results of their observations are fitted, rather than the reverse as they would have us believe.[56]

Since the issue of human nature is one we have identified as among the revealed truths which can guide theorizing (chapter 6, note 5), we should now look briefly at what Scripture says on the topic. Of course, we cannot expect a detailed *theory* of human nature from Scripture, but what it does tell us can help form a distinctly biblical perspective for our theory making.

The central scriptural teaching about human nature that is relevant here, is that it is centered in what is called the "heart," "spirit," or "soul." Each human is thus seen as an essential unity, no matter how many diverse functions an individual may display in the various aspects of creation. The term 'heart' is not, for example, used to mean simply emotion. We may speak of being guided by our head (intellect) or following our heart (feelings), but Scripture speaks of the heart as the central identity or selfhood of a person from which flow all the issues of life (Prov. 4:23). It is the center of thought, belief, knowledge, will, and feeling; it is thus the root source of the good or evil a person thinks or does (Ex. 28:3; Ps. 90:12; Matt. 12:34,35 and 15:18; 2 Cor. 3:14,15). In this connection it is significant that Scripture asserts that only God can know the human heart (1 Sam. 16:7; 2 Chron. 6:30; 1 Kings 8:39; Jer. 17:9,10), since that is what we would expect if the heart were the ultimate subjective pole of all human activity. In that case it could not become an object to itself, and would be incapable of analysis since it is itself the agent of analysis. Moreover this comports well with the biblical idea that humans can understand themselves only as "in the image of" God, and that failing to have the true God they understand themselves in the image of whatever false divinity they substitute for him.[57]

The view that the "heart" or selfhood is the agent of all the functions of human life is, for our purposes, the main guiding point to be gained from Scripture about human nature. So before going on to show its significance for theories, I should acknowledge that this view is at odds with the popular notion that a human is not an essential unity but a duality—a soul and a body. In fact, many Jews and Christians believe this to be taught by Scripture itself and to be the basis for the doctrine of life after death. The popular view is that only the body dies while the soul never does, so that the body is not essential to being human.

This view has been challenged often in recent years by Bible scholars who have shown that the popular view is derived from Greek philosophy rather than the Bible itself. Scripture does not view the body as merely an external, unnecessary shell for the soul. Neither is its promise of everlasting life based on the teaching that the soul is naturally immortal. Rather, the scriptural idea of everlasting life is that it is assured only because God promises it, and what God promises is the resurrection of the whole person— the resurrection of the *body*—at the day of judgment.[58] This topic cannot be dealt with at length here, so I will merely stipulate that in what follows I will be assuming this wholistic, rather than the popular dualistic, view of human nature.

The wholistic view thus refuses to identify the human body exclusively with certain aspects of creation (for example, the spatial, physical, and biotic) while assigning other aspects exclusively to the soul (the sensory, logical, and volitional, for example). It rejects the position of Plato and Aristotle that the soul can exist separate from the body because it knows eternal, rational truths and may therefore be immortal like those truths.[59] The importance of this is that it refuses to identify human nature with any of the aspects of creation in which it functions, thus overestimating their role in life as compared to the others. Instead it regards the human heart as more than the sum of all its aspects; while it functions in all the aspects alike, it cannot be identified with any one or combination of them. There is that about the heart which exceeds the aspects and stands in direct relation to the creator. *This view thus avoids every reductionist view of human nature.*

As Gordon Allport has observed, the reductionist views of human nature result in a series of one-sided theories. Allport says, "it is only *aspects* of our total life that are like computers, like bio-chemical compounds, rats in a maze, or like the social behavior of insects." The way to avoid reductionist theories, he suggests, would be to have a "systematic pluralism," but he despairs of it ever being accomplished owing to the many competing definitions of human nature.[60] What Allport does not see is that the compet-ing definitions are themselves a result of various pagan religious presuppositions. It is because thinkers have already identified the nature of all reality with one or more aspects that they then iden-tify human nature with those same aspects.

It is exactly for that reason that the Christian philosopher Her-man Dooyeweerd started his biblical reform of philosophy by re-jecting reductionism as pagan-based. And that reform started with his recognition of the significance of the biblical doctrine of the heart for human nature. It was that insight he called

> the great turning point in my thought whereby a new light was shed on the failure of all attempts, including my own, to bring about an in-ner synthesis between the Christian faith and a philosophy rooted in faith in the self-sufficiency of human reason.[61]

As a consequence, he expressed the significance of the biblical view of the heart this way:

> There are many special sciences which are concerned with the study of man. But each of them considers him from a particular viewpoint or aspect. Physics, chemistry, biology, psychology, history, sociology, eth-ics and so forth, they all can furnish interesting information about man. But when one asks of them: "What is man himself, in the central unity of his selfhood," then these sciences have no answer. . . . The ego is not to be determined by any aspect of our temporal experience since it is the central reference point of *all* of them.[62]

Then, by taking this point about human nature as microcosm, Dooyeweerd was able to expand and apply the same insight to the rest of created reality as macrocosm. It led him to see that while various types of nonhuman things each have a definite character, these things are like humans in that *they do not have an intrinsic nature that makes them what they are because it is God who makes them what they are*. Their most essential feature is to de-pend on God.

Simple as these points sound, they have far-reaching conse-quences for theory making. The next chapter will examine in greater detail why these biblical insights require the construction of a distinctive theory of reality.

PART IV
Radically Biblical Theories

10

THE NEED FOR A NEW BEGINNING

1. Introduction

The Casebook chapters illustrated how scientific theories constructed within specific aspects of experience are directed and controlled by some philosophical idea of the essential nature of reality. The control arises because ideas of the nature of reality are always ideas of the *kind* of general connectedness that holds among all aspects. We saw that different ideas of that connectedness alter the understanding of each specific aspect in ways that influence the theorizing going on within it. These ideas thus provide what I called perspectives or overviews of reality. The result is that different overviews make us more likely to notice certain features of things, alter what we see as important, and determine both the questions we ask and which hypotheses will look acceptable as answers to them. Finally, we found that the perspectival overviews themselves vary according to whatever is believed to be self-existent or divine.

This appears to be such a pervasive and unavoidable pattern in theory making that it will now be accepted as (part of) our understanding of the biblical claim that religious belief underlies and directs all knowledge. The remainder of this chapter, and those which follow, will try to spell out what it would mean to theorize so that our theory making is thoroughly controlled by belief in God in this way. According to the understanding we have now reached, this will require first that we devise a theory of reality which is governed as intensely as possible by the presupposition that God has created everything other than himself, and second that we employ that theory of reality as our guide for all other theorizing.[1]

At this point, however, many thinkers who believe in God may object. After all, a host of distinguished Jewish and Christian theologians and philosophers have theorized about the nature of reality without seeing the need for any such radically new beginning. This, of course, is true. But in most cases it is because these thinkers were guided by the scholastic assumption that human reason—and thus theorizing—is at least partially autonomous with respect to religious belief. As a result, they felt free to adapt theories of reality which have pagan presuppositions in the belief that theories about nature need only be *logically* compatible with revealed doctrines concerning supernature. For this reason, many Jewish and Christian thinkers have deemed theories of philosophy and science to be religiously unobjectionable even if they are not internally guided by belief in God. On this view, religious beliefs are understood to influence theories only by acting as external checkpoints.

The main burden of this chapter will be to show why the program of adapting pagan-based theories so as to make them compatible with belief in God cannot succeed. The chapter will continue to lay out the case that religious control of theories is always present and cannot be expunged. It will carry forward our argument that this control is never simply a matter of a theory's external compatibility with a belief about what is divine. And it will show why even the accomplishment of external compatibility merely cloaks a deeper religious incompatibility since it ignores the internal driving religious presuppositions from which a theory can never be free. Religious belief is (to borrow Jesus' metaphor) "the yeast which permeates the whole lump of dough."

But to make the reasons for this position as clear as possible, we must first review what any theory of reality tries to do and the traditional strategies by which they have tried to do it.

2. Retrospect

In chapter 5, we saw that theories of reality are concerned with the basic nature of reality; they attempt to answer the question "What *kinds* of things are there?" We then noticed that the traditional theories have answered this question by identifying the essential nature of reality with some one or two of the aspects displayed by the things and events we experience. We found that although there is no single list of aspects that all scientists and philosophers agree upon, they all accept some list or other from which they begin to theorize. We then proceeded to work with a (provisional) list which is both intuitively plausible and which includes every aspect that has even been made a distinct field of study or been proposed as the nature of reality. We discovered that the list greatly facilitated our examination of all sorts of theories.

So far as theories of reality are concerned, the list of aspects which any thinker assumes at the outset is very important. As we have seen repeatedly, the traditional approach to constructing a theory of reality has been to select candidates for the essential nature of reality from that list. Such theories are then defended by arguing that the aspects selected as the nature of things are not merely aspects *of* reality, but are to be enthroned as the essential nature of what all things *are*. As we saw earlier, there are two basic strategies which these theories have used in arguing for their selections. The first strategy is for a theory to argue that its selected aspect is the only real one; all other alleged aspects are either to be dismissed as mistakes or subsumed under the one it selected. The second strategy is for a theory to admit that there really are many aspects, but to argue that the one or two it has selected are basic to the rest. The sense of "basic" is that the aspect(s) supposed to be basic make the rest possible; the basic aspect(s) can exist without the others, but the others cannot exist without the basic one(s).

A good illustration of the difference between these two strategies is found in the difference between Watson's and Skinner's versions of materialism. Watson took the first strategy. He argued that the physical is the only real aspect of things; nothing whatever has any qualities other than physical qualities or is governed by any laws other than physical laws. Skinner, on the other hand, took the second strategy. He allowed that there are nonphysical properties to things but saw them all as dependent on the physical in a one-way causal relation. In chapter 9, I followed Piaget in using the term 'reductionist' to characterize these strategies. To distinguish them, let us now call the first reductionist in a strong sense: it reduces the list of aspects by eliminating all but the one the theory selects. On this strategy a theory does not try to solve problems about how various aspects relate, but to *dis*-solve them. The second strategy is still reductionist; we will call it weak reduction. Instead of trying to eliminate the existence of all other alleged aspects, it is content to reduce their status. They are argued to be second-class citizens of reality because their existence is made possible by the first-class aspect(s). To paraphrase George Orwell, the weak reductionist strategy allows that all aspects are real but some are more real than others.[2]

Most philosophers use the term 'reductionist' only for what I have here called the strong sense of reduction, but I think my use of it to describe both versions is justified when we notice what they have in common. Both attempt to identify *what* all things are (their basic nature) by finding *why* they are (what makes their existence possible). For this reason, both the stronger and the weaker senses of reduction are driven by the same presupposition, namely, that both the nature of, and the reason for, the existence of created things is to be found *within* those things. It is only that presupposition, and its resulting selections, which mandate the (strong or weak) reduction of the remaining aspects as the way to justify a theory of reality. *Thus the presupposition to both reductionist strategies is a religious belief of the pagan type.* Both strategies elevate certain aspect(s) of creation to the status of divinity. From the standpoint of their religious presuppositions, therefore, they are equally reductionist.

The strategies can, of course, be used in favor of whatever aspects a theorist may pick—not just for the physical aspect favored by versions of materialism. For example, in Aristotle's theory of reality, the physical is only one part of the basic nature of all things rather than the whole story. According to his theory, there is also a rational component which is actually the more important since it gives matter its orderliness. This orderliness he characterizes as essentially *logical* in nature. He expresses this by insisting that the fundamental laws which make ordered things possible are the logical laws, and he also proposes that there are logical entities called *Forms.* These are not merely shapes, as might be suggested by the way we use the word 'form'. For Aristotle, a logical form is a real, nonphysical entity which, when combined with matter, imposes an order on the matter which produces things of a certain type. So he calls the form of a thing the "what-it-is-to-be" that type of thing, as well as "the cause of the being of a thing."

A thing's form is therefore called its substance. The literal meaning of "substance" is that which stands under (supports) a thing in the sense of making it possible. So although Aristotle sees the entire array of forms as existing in a scale of increasing complexity, he still regards them all as equally eternal and uncreated. It is substances which make possible the things of everyday experience. And these things, which are observable composites of form and matter, come into existence and pass away. But the forms, and the matter they combine with, are just there; all else depends on their combination while their existence does not depend on anything, not even each other. They are self-existent.

As should be clear even from this brief description, Aristotle used the weak reductionist strategy to defend his theory. He did not deny that there are any other kinds of properties and laws than the physical or the logical, even though these are the basic kinds. Instead, he held that when form combines with matter to produce individual things of a certain type, it also produces all the other kinds of properties and orderliness true of those things. In fact, he thinks of that orderliness as an internal program determining each thing to behave in just the ways we find common to things of that type. It is these programmed regularities of behavior which we observe and call laws of nature.

I have taken the time with the theories described above because they illustrate the traditional strategies so well. And it is important to make them as clear as possible because I want to argue for a new beginning in theory of reality by undermining the other theories all at once by attacking their strategies, rather than by tackling the theories that use them one by one. I will start by offering a *religious* critique of them. I will contend that their pagan presuppositions cannot be effectively neutralized so as to allow them to be adapted by those who believe in God. That will be followed by a *theoretical* critique of the explanatory power of the reduction strategies. I will argue that they both fail the criteria of coherency offered in chapter 4.

3. The Religious Critique of Reduction

The central religious objection to the reduction strategies has already been indicated: it is abundantly clear that no matter which aspect the strategies are used on behalf of, *their success consists of showing that something within creation is what everything else depends on for existence.* They are therefore strategies for showing which aspects of creation are divine. This is not to say that a materialist would *call* matter "divine," but that regarding matter/energy as self-existent is to accord it divine status and is therefore a (core) religious belief whether that is acknowledged or not. Of course, a theory *may* recognize that regarding something as the most basic reality is a religious belief. Aristotle insisted not only that both forms and matter are eternal and make everything else possible, but that especially forms, as the causes of being of things, are thus divine. He even calls the highest form "God."

My point here is not anything new. The majority of Jewish and Christian thinkers have agreed that theories such as those just mentioned are pagan-based, but they have nevertheless continued to accept and use the strategies themselves. They have been convinced that these strategies can be adapted to make the theories using them compatible with belief in God. Of course, the details of just how any particular theory is rendered compatible with the Faith has varied from thinker to thinker. For now, however, it is only necessary to examine the central idea of the adaptation scheme since it is not merely the details of this plan that are objectionable, but its essentials.

The central idea of the scheme for adapting reduction theories is ingeniously simple. All that needs to be done is to introduce a split between the essential *nature* of things on the one hand, and what everything in creation *depends* upon on the other hand. That is to say, there need be no religious objection to accepting a theory of reality that identifies the basic nature of creation with one or two of its aspects *so long as those aspects are, in turn, held to be dependent on God.*

This attitude seems plausible if we accept the scholastic view of the general relation of religious belief to theory making. Once knowledge is partitioned into natural and supernatural realms, and the biblical claims about the religious basis of all knowledge are restricted to the supernatural realm alone, there appears to be no reason to seek a whole new approach to theorizing about the realm of nature. So, too, there appears to be no reason to be suspicious of the traditional strategies; their pagan connections seem obvious, but easily avoided.[3]

We have already discussed some of the reasons for finding this scholastic approach seriously deficient with respect to the role of religious (core) belief in theorizing. We saw that the biblical claims on that point were much stronger than scholasticism has taken them to be, and we have now seen how a number of pagan core beliefs guide theories internally. So the question is: why should we think that pagan faith can give more guidance to theory making than can belief in God? At the very least we should expect that our faith can also provide a distinct perspective which delimits a range of acceptable hypotheses, just as pagan faiths do.

Besides, doing theory of reality by using the reduction strategies is still to begin by trying to find which aspects of creation are basic to all the rest. It therefore begins by assuming that some one or two aspects have a relation to all the rest which is the same as the relation God has to creation. At its best, then, the adaption scheme leaves the aspects selected as basic to the rest in a semi-divine status; they are not fully divine, but they are more like the divine than the rest of creation. In this respect they correspond to the pagan idea of a god, if not divinity itself. For this reason, regarding any aspect of creation as having such a status runs counter to the biblical doctrine of creation. It accords to certain aspects of creation the status of crypto-divinities which mediate between God and the rest of creation, whereas Scripture always speaks of God *directly* sustaining everything other than himself.[4]

Consider the same point from a slightly different angle: apart from pagan religious belief, what would be the reason for trying to construct a theory of reality by reducing all the rest of its aspects to some one or two? If theory of reality had begun on biblical presuppositions without inheriting a pagan tradition, the doctrine of creation would have led thinkers in the reverse direction. Had they theorized under the grip of the biblical doctrine that God has brought into being everything other than himself, they would have taken for granted that it is God alone on whom all else depends for existence; thus, one of their guiding principles would have been the denial of that status to anything else. Instead of seeing how close their theories of reality could come to a pagan view without being outright pagan, they would have been guided by a religious horror of reductionism. Instead of elevating certain aspects as more real than the rest by claiming that God funnels his sustaining power through them, the theories would have started with the assumption that all creation depends on God equally.

At this point many thinkers will surely object that I have gone too far, and will contend that the biblical doctrine of creation is not nearly so explicit as to rule out reduction theories. After all,

Scripture is not a technical treatise. It is written in ordinary language and cannot be expected to deal with theoretical issues. In particular, it does not deal with the abstract entities which populate the theories of science and philosophy. So the fact that God brought the observable universe into existence out of nothing does not require us to hold that he also brought into existence such abstractions as laws, properties, kinds, universals, propositions, sets, etc. Such abstract entities may very well have a status intermediate between God and the things he called into existence.

Further, these critics will point out that this doctrine of creation does not fit with the prevailing doctrine of God found in classical theology. According to that doctrine, at least the qualities attributed by Scripture to God himself cannot have been created by him. God's own goodness or justice or power must be as uncreated as he is. Furthermore, it seems clear that God and creatures share some of these properties in common; at the very least he shares characteristics with *humans,* since they are "created in his image." This is why humans, too, can be wise or good or powerful or just. Of course, there is a difference between these qualities as they exist in God and as they exist in humans, but that is because God possesses those properties in an infinite mode while humans possess them in a finite mode. In God these qualities are perfections; he possesses the highest possible degree of goodness, power, justice, etc., while we possess them in a very limited and imperfect way.

The important point here is that humans possess finite modes of the *same* qualities as God. And this means that these qualities are uncreated in humans as well as in God—even though humans possess them imperfectly. These qualities have not, therefore, been created by God in the sense of having been called into being out of nothing. Rather, God has seen to it that finite degrees of some of his perfections have been *imparted* to creatures whom he has—in other respects—called into being. As Thomas Aquinas puts it: " 'God is good' . . . means that what we call goodness in creatures exists in God in a higher way. Thus God is not good (merely) because he causes goodness, but rather goodness flows from him because he is good" (*ST* Ia q.13, a.2). And again: ". . . God is known from the perfections that flow from him and are to be found in creatures yet which exist in him in a transcendent way" (*ST* Ia q.13, a.3).

Our critics will also point out that according to the prevailing theology it is God's imparting finite degrees of some of his (uncreated) qualities to creatures that makes it possible for human language to apply to God. For it is the finite modes of these same properties which we know by experience and represent in language. When religious language speaks of God, therefore, it must do so by *analogy* so that the meaning of our terms is partly the same but also partly different from when they are used of creatures. The possibility of our terms applying to God so as to tell the truth is guaranteed by his possessing the same qualities as are signified by our terms 'good', 'wise', 'just', 'powerful', etc. What our language cannot convey is the infinite mode in which he possesses those properties. Our critics could even end this objection by pointing out that not only has the analogy theory of religious language been widely accepted for centuries, but it seems to have no plausible alternative. Even Karl Barth, the most prominent theologian of this century to reject it, had to admit he had nothing to put in its place.[5]

Here, then, is an impressive array of reasons for retaining the traditional strategies for theories of reality. It appears that Jewish and Christian thinkers retained these strategies because they fit so well with assumptions needed to make sense of the biblical doctrine of God. Traditional theology's account of both God's nature and the possibility of religious language require that there are qualities possessed by creatures which are uncreated. So on either account, there is nothing wrong with regarding certain aspects of creation as having a mediate status between God and the other aspects. Indeed, some must be more real than the others unless classical theology is wrong about both the nature of God and how religious language is possible. Since God is *one*, for example, it would mean that numerical unity is uncreated. Why not then regard other numbers as uncreated if they can be generated by certain operations with the number one? Or again, since God knows everything, why not regard the laws of logic as eternal and uncreated—as laws of God's knowing as well as ours? If these are correct inferences then there are at least two aspects of creation (the numerical and the logical) which include uncreated properties and are governed by uncreated laws. So these aspects not only *can* but *must be* regarded as aspects which are more real than the others, and hence those on which the others may significantly depend. Here, then, is not only a clear reason for retaining the traditional strategies for theories of reality, but a reason which seems to derive from the doctrine of God itself. The attributes that comprise the nature of God can serve as guidelines for which aspects are to be regarded as basic in theory of reality.

This objection reflects a theology that has had a long hegemony in the Judeo-Christian tradition. Indeed, it has become so widespread and entrenched since the time of Augustine that the majority of theorists in that tradition find its denial virtually unthinkable. But since what is at stake here is nothing less than the interpretation of the very dependency arrangement which distinguishes biblical religion from all others, it is worth taking the time to reexamine just what Scripture says about how creation depends on God.

A. Pancreationism

There is no doubt that the biblical writers assert God's creatorship of the world of everyday experience. The sun, moon, stars, along with earth and the life forms that inhabit it, are all explicitly said to be brought into existence by God. Moreover, these writers teach that this creating was not, at first, simply forming something that was already there; it was a bringing into existence out of nothing, not mere cosmic interior decoration. Repeatedly Scripture declares that God created "all things." Is it the case that this is a rough expression, too imprecise to be of value to theories? Is it used by Bible writers only to refer to objects of ordinary perception? If so, the prevailing theological tradition could be quite right to say that certain features of creation may be uncreated. And in that case the doctrine will indeed be too vague to require the surrender of the traditional strategies for theories of reality. On the other hand, if the doctrine of creation is stated in stronger terms— if it claims, for example, that God brought into existence everything other than himself *and that there is nothing uncreated about what he brought into existence*—then the traditional doctrine of God's attributes is in need of a serious overhaul, one that would also mandate the abandonment of the traditional strategies for theories of reality.

Of course, the Scriptures are written in ordinary language and do not reflect the technical concepts of science or philosophy. We cannot expect them specifically to raise the issue of the existence of abstract entities, any more than we can expect them to offer a technical account of how human language applies to God. But there is no reason to suppose that only abstract technical language could express the claim that everything about creation has been called into existence by God and that there are no exceptions. (Indeed, my last clause just did exactly that.) So it is at least possible that the Scriptures teach this even if they are devoid of technical language. Whether it does so or not cannot be settled in advance simply by saying it's written in ordinary language. What is needed is an examination of just how Scripture uses the expression "all things," and what its assertions about "all things" can be seen to presuppose when compared with one another.

Another misguided attempt to settle the issue in advance is the simplistic inference that since God is said to have created all *things*, then the meaning of expression alone shows it refers only to ordinary objects of perception. This will not work because the word 'thing' cannot carry such interpretive weight. It cannot imply that God's creating does not extend to abstract entities for the simple reason that the word 'things' does not occur in the Hebrew or Greek expressions that are translated as "all things." In each language the expression is one word meaning "all." The terms themselves are therefore indefinite with respect to the issue before us so that their extension can only be settled by examining their use; their lexical meanings alone will not suffice.

To start, we can notice that in several places the Hebrew Scriptures speak of God as sovereign over the laws which govern the world (cf. Ps. 119:89–91 with Ps. 148:6). They are said to be his servants, and are mentioned as parts of creation with which God stands in covenant relation and the means by which he rules creation (Jer. 31:35, 36; 33:25; Job 38:33). Moreover, their abiding reliability is said to depend on God (Gen. 8:22); God is not trustworthy because some laws can be seen to show him so, but just the reverse. The laws can be relied on just because God promises to keep them in force. So it is clear that they depend on God. Since the orderliness of things is included among God's creations in this way, it is already clear that the expression "all things" does not refer only to observable objects (2 Sam. 23:5). Other statements, such as Isaiah 45:7, also support this last point. In them God is said to create the course of history, including whether there is peace or disaster. So once again, the "things" which depend on God are more than just ordinary objects.

The New Testament extends the reference of "all things" even further. God is said to be the creator of every sort of principle and power (Eph. 1:10–22; 3:9–10), of space (Rom. 8:38–39) and, yes, even of time (Titus 1:2; 2 Tim 1:9; Rev. 10:5–7).[6] But there are even stronger statements than these. In Colossians 1:15, 16 God is said to have created all things "in heaven and on earth, *visible and invisible.*" Now since everything whatever—even abstract entities—are either visible or not, the literal meaning of this passage logically entails that nothing about creation is uncreated. Nor is this remark alone in requiring "all things" to extend to everything other than God. In Romans 1:18–25, Paul speaks of false religion as the changing of the truth about God into a lie so that people "worship and serve something created instead of the creator." Here, too, the creator-creature distinction is viewed as exhaustive: everything is either God or something he called into being and depends on him.[7]

This review of the biblical use of "all things" is far from exhaustive. Nevertheless, it is sufficient, I think, to show that the pattern and tenor of its use runs counter to the scholastic adaptation scheme.

No doubt the scholastic objector will find this account unconvincing. None of these passages specifically mentions abstract qualities, and it still seems that at least those qualities attributed to God would have to be uncreated. Besides, unless God shares certain qualities with creatures, there would be no way for our language to apply to him. So once again we are forced to a looser interpretation of the doctrine of creation. But the remarkable thing is that there is at least one place where Scripture comes very close to speaking of a property in abstraction. Moreover, it is speaking of a property possessed by God! It is found in Proverbs 8:22–31 where, in a personification, wisdom is represented as saying of herself:

> Yahweh possessed me from the beginning of his way, the first of his works of old. I was set up from everlasting, from the beginning, before the earth was. When there were no depths, I was brought forth. . . . While as yet he had not made the earth . . . nor the beginning of the dust of the world. When he prepared the heavens, I was there . . . I was by him as a master workman; and I was daily his delight . . . and I was with the sons of men.[8]

Now it is never good procedure to rest too much on any single passage of Scripture, so I am not about to claim that these remarks alone are sufficient to establish a theological doctrine. At the same time, however, the passage is too important to ignore. However brief it may be, and however poetic its style, it is one of the rare Scriptural hints about how God possesses his qualities. Taken in conjunction with what we have seen about the way Scripture writers speak of God's creating "all things," the Proverbs passage beautifully comports with the strict interpretation of the doctrine of creation—the view I will call "pancreation." Even allowing for poetic license, it seems clear that no one could have written these lines who held the scholastic view of the doctrine of creation or the traditional theology of God's attributes. For it says that the quality of wisdom is created by God even if it is everlasting in time,[9] even though it is possessed by God himself, and even though it is also present with, and perhaps shared by, humans. Thus while it does not deny that God shares properties with humans, *it denies that God's qualities must be uncreated because he is.*

The cumulative force of this evidence convinces me that the Bible is not silent on whether anything is uncreated other than God or on whether certain features of creation are uncreated. It simply does not allow for exceptions. The passages cited not only give the clear impression of trying to teach pancreation, but it is hard to see how they could have made it plainer.

For this reason I am prepared to accept the result that there is, indeed, something seriously askew in the classical theological tradition. That something is the pagan religious belief, derived from ancient Greek philosophy, that there are entities other than God and/or features about creation which are uncreated and thus divine. Since that belief has penetrated and corrupted the very understanding of God himself, it is not surprising that thinkers accepting the classical theological tradition have failed to exorcize the pagan-based strategies from their theories of reality. In the next section I will offer a sketch of the lines along which the doctrine of God needs to be reconstructed and will integrate that with an indication of what that reconstruction would entail for an account of religious language. The account will necessarily be brief, and virtually every issue raised will be left in need of further discussion. But it will be sufficient, I think, to show that we can safely reject the traditional view without being in danger of have no coherent alternatives. The account of religious language to be offered will reject the view that it need be analogical in the sense that traditional theology has proposed, and will hold instead that it is ordinary language with its own distinctive qualification in the universe of discourse of faith. In this way it will directly meet the claim made by some contemporary thinkers that either some form of the analogy theory works or the question of how human language can apply to God has no conceivable answer at all.[10]

B. The Nature of God and Religious Language

We have found that the reduction strategies for theories of reality have pagan religious roots, and that the scheme employed by Jewish and Christian thinkers for retaining those strategies works only if the biblical doctrine of creation is not interpreted strictly. More precisely, the adaptation scheme works only if there can be qualities and laws true of creatures which God did not create. A closer look at the biblical sources of the doctrine of creation showed they do not support this scheme, however. If anything, those sources teach pancreation: not only has God brought into existence everything other than himself, but nothing *about* creation is uncreated. So the adaptation scheme does not succeed in rendering the strategies compatible with biblical teaching.

A strong objection to this interpretation comes from the traditional theology of God's nature and the prevailing explanation of how our language can apply to him. It is claimed that both require the weaker interpretation of creation, the interpretation which also makes room for the retention of the reduction strategies. This is because the traditional view of the nature of God and religious language insist that the properties possessed by God himself (and perhaps certain others as well) are uncreated both in him and in creatures.

Despite its widespread acceptance, however, the traditional theology of God's nature has deep-seated and formidable difficulties even aside from its incompatibility with pancreation. Consider first that on this view, God's nature consists of perfections, that is, of infinite degrees of certain qualities that exist in lesser degrees in creatures. God's nature, on this view, is as uncreated as he is and is something he cannot help having. The problem here is that if God's being is thought to be distinct from the properties constituting his nature, then he would be dependent on them.[11] Put another way, since these properties are essential to God, if they constitute what he *must* be, then if there were no such properties as perfect goodness, knowledge, or power, God could not have existed. Therefore this view of his nature does more than merely allow there to be entities other than God which are equally as uncreated as he is; it denies that God is self-existent altogether. This attempt to combine the pagan idea of self-existent perfections with the biblical doctrine of God leaves the perfections divine and demotes God.

To avoid this consequence, Thomas Aquinas proposed that God's nature be taken as identical with his being; God just *is* his nature, so it is not something distinct from him. Thus while God's nature does consist of perfect qualities (some of which creatures share imperfectly), the only sense in which he could be said to depend on them is harmless: it is nothing other than his own self-dependency. Thomas develops this position in the doctrine he calls God's "simplicity," and he proposes it precisely to safeguard God's self-existence.[12] There are two problems with this solution, however, which I find insurmountable.

The first is that if God is identical with each of his properties, then it logically follows that each of the properties is identical with each of the others. This means, as Aquinas admitted, that God's justice, power, knowledge, and goodness are all the same. But this would vitiate any possibility of our language applying to God. If God's goodness is identical with his power, then what we mean by the words "goodness" and "power" are just not what God has at all for we have no conception or idea of goodness that is not different from power, knowledge, and an indefinitely large host of other perfections. This difficulty can be illustrated if we think of God's perfections as represented by colors. In that case we would say that God has perfect redness, blueness, greenness, etc, but according to the simplicity proposal we would have to add that in God all these colors are the same! In that case what we experience and what we mean by our color words could not be what God has at all. He might, to follow the analogy, have some other color we cannot experience or imagine which causes us to see red, blue, etc., but whatever he had would not be the same as what our color terms mean. Thus the simplicity doctrine ends up requiring that God does not have infinite degrees of the qualities we know, share, or name. And in that case the analogy theory of religious language (which Thomas himself advocated) is destroyed.

The second difficulty is that if God is identical with his properties, which are all identical with one another, then God *is* a single
abstract property. This is an even worse consequence than the first
difficulty for it makes no sense to say that an abstract quality created the world or offers humans a covenant of forgiveness, love,
and redemption. In short, the simplicity doctrine—against its own
intentions—implies that God is not a person at all and thus un-
dermines *every* (secondary) religious belief Jews and Christians
derive from the Scriptures about how to stand in proper relation to
him.[13] This difficulty is not, therefore, a minor theological flaw
which can be safely tolerated pending some subtle variation that
will smooth out the theory. It is totally unacceptable.

For these reasons we are led back to the position that God's revealed nature must be distinct from him, but with the constraint
that it must also be dependent on him. This, I propose, can be
done provided we follow the line of thought indicated by the passage quoted earlier from the Proverbs.[14] There God's wisdom is
said to be dependent on him precisely because he created it. Proverbs denies, to be sure, that there ever was a time when God did
not have wisdom; it says wisdom was with him "from the beginning." But that fits well with the other Scriptures which indicate
God created time also. If God created time, then there is nothing
incoherent in supposing that God brought his wisdom into being
along with time itself, so that even though wisdom is created by
him there never was a time he did not have it.

My proposal, then, is that we take the Proverbs passage as a
model for understanding all the other properties God has in common with creatures. *On this account, it is not the case that creatures share some of God's uncreated properties, but that God
reveals himself by giving to creatures some of the properties he
has created and assumed to himself.* These constitute God's revealed nature which is the only nature that is humanly knowable.
On this view, then, the fact that we can know truth about God
does not require that creation is partly divine, but that God has
taken on created relations and properties.[15] So while we affirm
that God really has both the relations to creatures and the qualities
that Scripture ascribes to him, we insist that he does not have them
essentially; that is, he does not have to have them to exist. Rather
he freely abides by created laws and norms, stands in created relations, and possesses created properties, so as to accommodate

himself to our creaturely limitations. In fact, Scripture ascribes to God properties of virtually every aspect of creation. He is quantitatively one; spatially he is omnipresent; physically he is powerful; biologically he is the living God and our Father: sensorily he sees us, and feels love, anger, or pity toward us; logically he is both consistent and all-knowing; socially he is a friend, etc. Following the line of thought laid down in Genesis, we will hold that he has taken on these characteristics in order to make himself known through the covenant he offers to all humanity. In short, God's revelation of himself is the revelation of the characteristics he has taken on for the sake of covenantal fellowship with humans.

This would mean, of course, that God's uncreated, unrevealed being is unknowable by us. It is not governed by any of the (created) laws which govern creatures, and so cannot be conceptualized by us. Nevertheless, his revelation of himself conveys to us all we need to know in order to stand in proper relation to him. He has sworn by his covenantal oath that he will everlastingly remain the same towards those who put their trust in his promises, to those who have subscribed to his covenant by placing their faith in him and loving him with all their "heart, soul, and strength." On this latter point, I find our accommodationist view of God's nature to fit much better with the overall covenantal form of Scripture than that of the prevailing theology. The idea of a covenant is that of an oath of agreement in which God has made certain demands and promises. It would be strange for God to *promise* to have certain characteristics if he just cannot help having them. If that were the case, we would expect Scripture to say that God is merciful or faithful or just because he simply could not be anything else rather than representing him as freely promising to be so. On the traditional view, God's promising these things makes no more sense than it would for you or I to promise to be human, or not to be uncreated.

Furthermore, the accommodation view is in accord with the biblical idea of God's perfection, which is misrepresented by the traditional theological idea of perfection. The traditional theology works with a pagan-based philosophical notion of perfection (derived from Plato), a notion in which a perfection is the highest possible degree of a quality. But the biblical writers use the term 'perfect' to indicate fullness and constancy; to be perfectly just, for example, is to be *unfailingly* just rather than just in an unimaginable degree. An outstanding instance of this distinctively Hebrew sense of "perfect" is found in Jesus' admonition to his disciples: "Be perfect as your Father in heaven is perfect." This would make no sense whatever from the point of view of the traditional theology, for it would amount to telling them that they should be God! But on the Hebrew view of perfection it instead means that they should be as constantly faithful to their end of the covenant as God is to his end.

This proposal about how to understand God's attributes can perhaps be made clearer if we now introduce a refinement into the schema used in chapter 3 to represent the biblical dependency arrangement. Figure 5 reflects both the biblical idea of pancreation and the idea of accommodation suggested by the Proverbs.

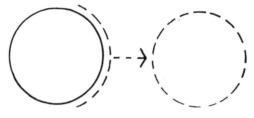

Fig. 5

On the accommodation theory it will still be true that there are differences in the ways God possesses his properties and relations from the ways creatures do. We have already touched on one of these, namely, that while he is unfailingly good, just, wise, etc., we are not. But there are other differences as well. One of these is that God possesses the characteristics he reveals himself to have in combinations which elude creatures altogether. For example, God stands in relations to humans which Scripture describes as fatherly, kingly, and in one place at least, motherly, yet God has no body and so is neither male nor female. So although it is ordinarily a natural—almost irresistible—inference that if one is fatherly one is a male, or if one is motherly one is a female, these inferences cannot be drawn in the case of God.

For this reason, the accommodation view counsels extreme caution in dealing with the nature of God. First, it cuts off all speculation about God's own being. We cannot spin out an extended account of God's nature beyond what he has revealed on the assumption that he conforms to the laws of logic (or any other created laws) in such a way that we can reconstruct his nature by doing rationalistic metaphysical theology. Our trust in God, for example, is based on our experience of the truth of his word, and not on some logical proof that it is impossible that he lie.[16] Running a logical credit check on God is to subject the creator to the laws he has set over creatures, and thereby reduces him to creaturely status. Second, it requires that we confine ourselves as much as possible to precisely what God has revealed of himself. Some inferences from what is revealed may be necessary and unavoidable, but for the most part our knowledge of how he accommodates himself to us depends on his telling us about it. (Here I am reminded of Calvin's sage advice "never to think or speak of God beyond what we have Scripture for our guide.") We should especially be reluctant to extend our idea of his attributes beyond what he declares their consequences to be, since he has taken them on in specific respects. For example, we must learn from his word the respects in which he offers to be good to those who love him, rather than spin out *our* conception of what an infinitely good being would have to do and could not do. Just as with fatherliness, God may take on part of what we ordinarily mean by goodness but not the whole of it. For this reason the human enterprise of theology should never be allowed to become a project of rational theorizing by which we suppose ourselves to have extended our knowledge of his nature or promises beyond what he has revealed. Still less should it ever be allowed to replace Scripture itself as the guide to life. There is no substitute for the immersion of our hearts and minds in the Word of God.

Another difference in the ways God and creatures possesses the same properties is found simply in the fact that it is God, the transcendent creator, who possesses them. It is this which generates the distinct faith-meaning which accrues to the terms designating the properties in each case.[17] It is not, however, the sort of meaning difference that is generated by the difference between the infinite and finite degrees of qualities as the traditional analogy theory teaches. Rather it is an analogy which preserves sameness of meaning along with a distinctive difference which results from the fact that more is at stake when it is God who offers us forgiveness, or God who loves us, or God who is angry with us. But the difference in meaning is no greater for the universe of discourse of faith than are the differences which occur in nonreligious language among the various (aspectually distinguished) universes of discourse. The term "good," for instance, exhibits a difference in meaning when applied to an art work from when it is applied to a law. And we recognize that difference without any trouble because of their respective aesthetic and justitial universes of discourse. So, too, there is a fiduciary universe of discourse in which terms acquire additional meaning whenever they are ascribed to something taken to be unconditionally trustworthy (divine). But this is no greater a difference than is to be found among other universes of discourse restricted to creatures.

Because the accommodation theory takes the revealed attributes of God to be created, there is no threat to God's difference from creatures generated by his sharing properties with them. He differs from creatures radically by being the self-existent creator. There is no need to propose analogical or other elaborate theories about changes in the meanings of the terms designating his shared properties. What Scripture attributes to God is just what we ordinarily mean by those terms with the additional meaning that accrues them from knowing that it is the creator who possesses them. (Think of the heightened "pitch" to which the meaning of our terms is raised in the liturgy!) On that basis we know what to expect of God everlastingly, given the nature he has revealed himself to have.

Because this view of the matter is so different from that of traditional theology, it is worth pointing out that something very close to it was held by the Protestant reformers, Luther and Calvin, though it has not been followed by any significant number of Protestant theologians. For example, Luther once remarked:

> Now God in his own Nature and Majesty is to be left alone; in this regard we have nothing to do with him, nor does he wish us to deal with him. We have to do with him as clothed and displayed by his Word, by which he presents himself to us. That is his glory and beauty in which the Psalmist proclaims him to be clothed.[18]

Calvin picks up the same line of thought, but applies it more directly to religious language:

> [I]n the enumeration of his perfections, [God] is described [in Scripture] not as he is in himself, but in relation to us, in order that our acknowledgement of him may be a more vivid actual impression than empty visionary speculation.... [E]very perfection... set down [in Scripture] may be found in creation; and, hence, such as we feel him to

be when experience is our guide, such he declares himself to be by his word. (*Institutes* I, x, 2)

This is not an isolated comment by Calvin. He repeats the point often and never offers any other view of religious language:[19]

> [H]ow can [human reason]... penetrate to a knowledge of the substance of God while unable to understand its own? Wherefore let us willingly leave to God the knowledge of himself... we must conceive of him as he has made himself known, and in our inquiries make application to no other quarter than his word. (*Institutes* I, xiii, 21)

And again:

> But as for those who proudly soar above the world to seek God in his unveiled essence, it is impossible but that at length they should entangle themselves in a multitude of absurd figments. For God—by other means invisible—clothes himself, so to speak, with the image of the world, in which he would present himself to our contemplation.[20]

C. Replies to Objections

Although a number of objections have been lodged against the accommodation view of God's nature, there is not the room to deal with them all here.[21] But since it is such an unusual position, and since it has such important consequences, I want to deal with at least a few of them to indicate the lines along which they can be handled.

The first says that even if God possesses his revealed attributes as a result of taking them on, that cannot be true of his self-existence. Yet the accommodationist account of religious language proposes that the meaning of the terms we apply to God are derived from our experience of creation. If nothing in creation is self-existent, how can we explain the fact that we have the concept of self-existence?

The notion of existence is a notoriously difficult one, and I will not pretend to resolve the debates that surround it here. I will simply start by saying that it is, to be sure, derived from our experience of creatures. The term 'existence' literally means "to stand out from," or to be distinct from. It reflects the fact that we come to recognize the existence of something by distinguishing it from other things. But the existence of something cannot be *defined* as its ability to be picked out; that is at best a circumscription of it. The fact that we can distinguish a thing is made possible by the fact that it exists, and so is not identical with it. As a result, even the literal meaning of the word 'exist' does not name what we are really after when we use it but points beyond its own meaning to the fact of existence which lies behind it and makes it possible. To complicate things further, it seems that the existence of each thing we confront in experience is uniquely individual to that thing. It is not a quality a thing possesses alongside its other qualities, because a thing would have to exist in order to possess qualities. And it certainly is not a universal quality shared by more than one thing; two or more things do not have the same existence. (The distinguishability of things which forms the literal meaning of the term 'exist' may be shared, but not the bare fact of their existence which makes them distinguishable.) For these reasons, I think that even the existence of creatures is not something we ever really conceptualize. It is an unanalyzable, basic fact of creation which we confront in our experience but which we are unable to grasp in a concept. Therefore I will call the meaning it has for us a "limiting idea" rather than a concept.

When we speak of God's self-existence, then, we are applying to God our limiting idea of existence which is thereby put under even further constraints: it is existence which does not depend on anything in any way, is outside time, and is not governed by any law that holds for creatures. It is thus a limiting idea that is largely negative. Even the circumscription 'distinguishable' is true of God only in his relation to creation, since aside from what he has created there would be nothing for him to be distinguishable from. What is left of the idea is only this: God's own being is what all creatures and his own revealed nature (including his distinguishability) depend on. It is beyond us to grasp what that is at all, which is why so many theologians have said that "we do not know what God is, but only what he is not, and how he relates to creatures."[22] And we come to know this fact about him only because in the course of revealing his accommodated nature, God has also revealed that every feature of creation has been brought into existence by him out of nothing. Thus his uncreated being is something which we cannot conceptually characterize at all.

Another criticism of the accommodation theory is that it is self-assumptively incoherent. By proposing that God chose to take on the attributes which comprise revealed personality, the theory is assuming God's uncreated essence to include a *will*. Likewise, if the theory admits that God knew which attributes he wanted to take on, then the theory has assumed his uncreated essence to include a mind. So, the accusation runs, it turns out that the accommodation theory is assuming it knows about God's uncreated essence after all.

But the theory need not do this; it does not need to admit that Scriptural talk about God's mind or will goes behind his accommodation. The will of God, or the plan of God, is also part of God's accommodation to creatures. It is by his accommodation that he performs acts in space and time which we can understand as acts of choosing or knowing, and not those acts by which he accomplishes his accommodation. The accusation therefore amounts only to reading part of the classical theology into the accommodation theory, for the latter did not say anything about how God accomplished the accommodation; that is quite beyond our ken. We cannot get "in back of" his revealed nature, and so are not entitled to do a "theopology" on God's nature analogous to an anthropology of our own. Just because we are constituted with a will and a mind does not mean that (aside from his accommodations) God is, too. At the same time, however, we must not suppose that God is not really personal. It must always be kept in mind that "accommodation" means it is *God* who has taken on the characteristics he reveals himself to have. They are no less true of him simply because they reveal the nature he has assumed in relation to creation. Consider, for example, that aside from having creation depend on him, God would not be a creator. Being the creator is not essential to him because he does not need to create in order to be. But that does not mean that he somehow does not really stand in that relation to all else. And the same is true of his other accommodated attributes.

By far, however, the most often raised criticisms concern the doctrine of pancreation which underlies the accommodation proposal. It is pancreation which is especially objectionable to those thinkers who regard logical (and perhaps mathematical) laws as uncreated and necessary for God as well as creatures. Their criticisms amount to saying that if this is denied all sorts of self-contradictions and absurdities would result for we would then be committed to saying that contradictions are not impossible for God.[23] In that case we would be required to admit it is possible that God not be logically identical with himself or that God could bring it about that triangles lack three interior angles. In short, denying that logical laws are uncreated and govern God will allow that nothing is impossible since there would be nothing so absurd that God could not do it.

This criticism reflects a serious misunderstanding of our position. So far as the first is concerned, saying that God has created the laws of math, logic, and other necessary truths, does not mean that God *violates* them. A law can be violated only by something to which it applies in the first place. You and I may disobey a health rule, for instance, by eating things that are bad for us. Or we may disobey the traffic law that says not to make a left-hand turn at a particular intersection. But a rock cannot disobey these rules because they just do not apply to it. The rock can neither be healthy nor unhealthy, nor can it do acts that are legal or illegal. And this is what we are saying about the uncreated essence of God. As creator of all the laws of creation, God is not automatically subject to them as creatures are—though in his accommodation he may abide by them in certain specific respects so as to be understandable to us. Aside from his accommodation, God transcends rather than violates the laws of logic.[24]

So far as the second point is concerned, God's not being governed by the laws of creation does not release us or any other creatures from them. What is possible and impossible for creatures is a result of the laws God has set over creation, and this includes what it is possible and impossible for us to conceive. As a consequence, neither creatures nor God's revealed nature are ever rightly conceived by us if we violate the necessary truths God has built into creation (not even the miracles caused by God should be construed as violations of created laws). There is thus no reason to suppose that the floodgates of absurdity are thrown wide open unless what is necessary for creatures is also necessary for God.

This religious critique of the reduction strategies has tried to show why they were not abandoned by theistic thinkers despite their pagan roots. Our claim is that the classical understanding of God's nature in both Jewish and Christian theology has been so seriously infiltrated and compromised by pagan belief that the residual paganism of the reduction strategies can pass almost unnoticed. We shall now turn to a closer look at those strategies themselves to compare them with the criteria for theories laid down in chapter 4.

4. Theoretical Critique of Reduction

We will begin by recalling some things noted earlier about perspectival theories. First, we noticed that adopting a particular perspective tends to entrench it as a mindset; the more one looks at things from that perspective, the more that perspective appears to be the right one. Part of the reason for this is that aspects are kinds of properties and laws true of everything, so all things can be viewed—and in some sense, explained—from the standpoint of virtually any of them. The longer any particular aspects are regarded as the basic nature of reality, the more they will yield fresh explanatory insights that will seem to confirm the perspectives which correspond to them. In this way, a perspective carries its own persuasive power with it and tends to blind its adherents to the fact that the same sort of confirmation is possible from other perspectives. This is why, so far as accounting for the nature of (created) reality goes, the crucial issue is the original adoption of a perspective. If any perspective is ever to be justified theoretically, its justifiability must be initially plausible at the least. Unless this can be shown, spelling out the explanatory advantages of a particular perspective will never thereby show that an equal job could not be done from another perspective. Given sufficient time and talent, any perspective might turn out to be capable of transposing the same tune to its own key.

It is here that the significance of our criterion of self-performative coherence comes into play. For no matter how well developed its defense, no matter how cleverly elaborated its explanations, every reductionist theory of reality must start by selecting some aspect of the world of our experience as the nature of what is. *But to abstract any aspect of experience and proclaim it self-existent is to make a self-performatively incoherent claim.* The claim simply ignores the act of abstraction by which any candidate for the basic nature of reality comes to be isolated and conceptualized in the first place. In this way, the claim depends upon a mistake which (to recast a Marxist expression) ignores the "means of its production." Such claims turn a blind eye to the extent to which the artificial isolation of an aspect may have altered—even partly falsified—the conception of the aspects chosen, and of their relations to the remaining aspects. They ignore the extent to which the apparent independence of the chosen aspect(s), which made them seem attractive candidates, may itself be a by-product of their abstraction, and thus fail to correspond to any real state of affairs. In this way, the entire reduction strategy is analogous to putting a thermometer into a glass of water and claiming that its reading shows what the water's temperature was prior to the thermometer's insertion. It might, but how could we ever know?[25]

This criterion is based upon such a simple, straightforward point, that I fear it may easily be underestimated. It might be objected, for example, that all it has done is raise the possibility that an aspect's status is distorted by abstraction. But since abstraction is necessary to theorizing that is a risk we have to take since there is no alternative. The answer to this is that there is good reason to suppose that any attempt to abstractively isolate an aspect completely destroys our idea of it. To see that this is so, we must consider the self-performative incoherency from another angle. Doing this consists of the thought experiment of trying to conceive of a reduction theory being true; that is, try to conceive of any aspect of experience existing in total isolation from the rest.

Take, as a first example, Plato's search for the basis of our experience of justice. He makes it clear he is asking for the essential core of justice, not merely for instances of it. As he puts it, he wants to isolate the quality of "justice in itself" and understand that quality apart from any thing or act that may have it or any other qualities with which it may co-exist. So let's begin by subtracting from our idea of justice every connection of its meaning to other aspects. Drop from it everything having to do with quantity, space, and matter. Then delete from it every reference and connection to biological life, sensory perception and feeling, and logical conceptualization. Next peel away every connection of the idea of justice to language, culture, and society; divest it of everything economic, ethical, aesthetic, and fiduciary. What is left? By eliminating the connection of the idea of justice to the other aspects, the entire content of the idea itself is also eliminated.[26]

Perhaps it will be objected that this experiment only succeeds for something as ethereal as the ideas of justice. What about other aspects that have really been touted as the self-existent nature of all things—the physical, the sensory, the logical? Our reply is that the experiment produces the same results no matter which aspects it is tried on. What is left of the meaning of "physical" once it is stripped of every connection to the properties and laws of quantity, space, perception, or logic? Or what is left of the meaning of "sensory" if it is deprived of its relations to the aspects of quantity, space, matter, life, and logic? What meaning would be left to logic if there were no nonlogical properties of things to be governed by logical law? Even the fundamental logical axiom of non-contradiction refers to (aspectual) *respects* in which a thing cannot both be and not be, and says that nothing can be true and false at the same *time.*

I believe this experiment shows not only that we never *experience* anything to be purely physical or sensory or logical or whatnot, but that we cannot even *conceive* of that being so. We may succeed at isolating aspects from the things which exhibit them to our pretheoretical experience, but we never succeed in isolating them from one another. It shows, therefore, that the criterion of self-performative coherency has hit on a condition for theorizing which cannot be ignored. No matter how hard we try to isolate them, all aspects continue to display unbreakable tendrils of meaning connecting them to all the others. That is, concepts formed in any one aspect cannot fail to contain elements from and display connections to all the others. This is nothing less than a mortal blow to the justification of any reduction theory. For how can the claim that any aspect or combination of them is capable of existing independently of the others be justified when we literally cannot even conceive of that being so? This may not show every reduction theory to be false, but it is surely good reason to think they are all theoretically unjustifiable *in principle.*

It could be replied, of course, that even if the initial selection of aspects as the essential nature of reality cannot be justified at the outset, there is nothing to prevent our comparing their explanatory power afterward. We could simply judge one perspective better than another by the interpretive advantages it offers. The answer to this is that there is no neutral ground from which to do the judging. A thinker holding to perspective X will not think perspective Y's explanations better because they will simply look false. If Y-theories are much more detailed, they will merely appear false in greater detail. This is because the selection of an aspect as self-existent is a religious belief driven by the fact that it is experienced as divine. It is not a neutral decision of "pure reason."[27] In support of this point, I now ask those familiar with the history of theories of philosophy to reflect: isn't this exactly what we find to be true of theories of reality? When did the advocates of one "ism" ever succeed in convincing the advocates of another purely by argument? Do Kantians convert Thomists in this way? Do Thomist sway materialists? Do materialists or mind-body dualists or Hegelians or existentialists persuade each other?

The notable failure of persuasion concerning beliefs about what is divine is evidence that they are pretheoretical convictions brought to theorizing. In fact, they are the convictions which ultimately determine how a thinker understands the very idea of what it means to be rational. The theories deriving from them cannot be the grounds of their choice, since the very weighing of these must already presuppose some perspective. Thus it appears that while theorizing can elaborate the consequences of the religious belief it presupposes, it cannot do so in a way that will (neutrally) justify that belief over any other. This is what I meant when I said in chapter 4 that theories can only be justified relative to the faith with which they begin.

Thus our criticism shows why reductionist theories of reality will never be able to rid themselves of the incoherencies resulting from their initial isolation of the aspect(s) chosen as the essential nature of everything. For every aspect will continue to display its unbreakable connectedness with all the others the whole time a theory proffers arguments to support the belief in its real independence. For this reason, reduction theories cannot supply any genuine justificatory advantage for their pagan-based views of reality in comparison to a theory of reality that presupposes belief in God.

5. Conclusion

The conclusion to be drawn from this critique is that the acceptance of any reductive perspective on the nature of reality is a matter of pretheoretical faith rather than theoretical justification. I do not call such beliefs "faith" only because they are unjustifiable, however, for they bear *all* the characteristics of religious belief. First, they are beliefs in something as self-existent and unconditionally trustworthy. Second, they are basic beliefs not derived from other beliefs, but rooted in the experience of their objects as divine. Finally, the solitary self-existence of any aspect can never be conceived, and so can only be a limiting idea. Thus the pagan belief that any aspect can exist independently is just as much of a (theoretically unjustifiable) limiting idea as the belief that it is God alone who is divine.

There is, however, this difference: on the pagan standpoint, some aspects of experience are believed to be self-existent in the face of the fact that they are all literally meaningless when abstractively isolated from one another. We can form no idea of any aspect in total isolation, so the limiting idea is that whichever aspects are selected as the nature of reality may have that status anyway, even though that is false insofar as we can know them. Thus the idea of any divinized aspect is an idea whose object is known as dependent but is taken to be nondependent by the theories developed from its perspective.

On the other hand, we who believe in God do not arrive at that belief by abstracting any aspect of experience but by encountering God's revelation in his word. And though the properties and relations God is revealed to have would also be inconceivable in isolation, they are not believed to be self-existent but to have been created by God and assumed by him. It is only his uncreated being which is self-existent. So unlike the forms of pagan belief, our limiting idea of God's being, known by revelation, is not believed in the face of the fact that so far as we can understand it at all, it is false.

Therefore: since the Scriptures teach pancreation and pancreation does not entail absurdities; and since neither a biblical doctrine of God's nature nor an account of how our language can apply to him require any aspect of creation be uncreated; and since there is no justificatory advantage to any reduction theory that regards some aspect(s) of creation as self-existent; let us proceed to see what sort of theory of reality can be constructed from the perspective that God, and God alone, is self-existent.

11

A THEORY OF REALITY

1. The Project of Biblical Theories

In chapter 6 I distinguished the radically biblical position from that of fundamentalism. I held that in one sense the fundamentalist's claim is too strong because it assumes that Scripture is like an encyclopedia containing revealed truths about every sort of subject matter. For them, God's word is not the light to our path, but the path itself. This assumption has led them to imagine that the way theories should be religiously regulated is by having them begin with the truths appropriate to their disciplines which can be extrapolated from Scripture or inferred from Scripture by theology. In opposition to this I maintained that Scripture is not an encyclopedia and has nothing to say which can serve as initial data for most scientific theories. I held instead that the most important influence of religious belief is both less direct and more pervasive than that, namely, that some religious core belief always functions as a presupposition guiding the formation of theories in both philosophy and the sciences. The guidance takes the form of providing a perspectival overview of reality which sets the parameters within which other hypotheses appear acceptable. Thus the religious belief regulates theory making even if it does not itself supply specific hypotheses.

At the same time, however, I maintained that the fundamentalist position is in another sense too weak. This is because it regards the influence of religious belief on theories as something the believing theorist should strive for, but which anyone may in fact do without. In opposition, I claimed that some religous belief regulates any abstract theory whatever.

In the intervening chapters, we have seen a number of illustrations of how religious presuppositions extend their control through

196

theories of reality to a variety of scientific theories. In each case, however, the sample theories were all controlled by some version of nonbiblical (pagan) religious belief; as yet I have provided no samples of how theories can differ by presupposing the radically biblical idea of God. The examples considered have nevertheless shown how religious presuppositions exert their influence, and thus prepared the way for seeing what we can expect if biblical presuppositions replace nonbiblical ones.

Since we found that religious presuppositions exert their influence on other theories through a theory of reality, it should be obvious why we are starting with that topic in this chapter. But I should say right here that the following chapters will not then go on to develop biblically based theories of mathematics, physics, and psychology. That is, they will not parallel the Casebook chapters. There are two reasons for this. One is that I do not have the required expertise to do that job. The other is that the theory of reality we are about to examine cannot be adequately explained in one chapter, but must be developed by being applied to a number of diverse issues if its hypotheses and their consequences are to become clear. I believe the issues that best allow the theory to become clear are those of social theory rather than math or physics or psychology. Therefore, this chapter will present a blueprint for a theory of reality that presupposes God alone is divine, and the two following chapters will apply that blueprint first to develop a theory of society, and then to a theory of the state.

For this reason, it is crucial that these chapters be read in the order in which they appear. I emphasize this because dealing with a new theory of reality may be an unfamiliar and difficult project for many readers. The very prospect may therefore tempt them to pass over this chapter to the chapters on society or politics whose titles sound more familiar and perhaps more interesting. But without a biblical theory of reality to guide our further theorizing, we lack the intellectual scaffolding within which distinctively biblical theories may be constructed. And the lack of just such a scaffolding is the main reason why the efforts of so many Jewish and Christian thinkers have fallen short of producing radically biblical theories. So our procedure here will be to completely recast theory of reality—both as to the questions it poses as well as the answers it gives. For these reasons, by-passing the theory of reality about to be sketched will result in a failure to understand both the main proposals of the later theories, and the reasons which recommend them. In fact, it will render totally unclear why they are supposed to be distinctively *biblical* proposals.

Before going ahead, we should take notice of some special difficulties this program encounters which do not plague pagan-based theorizing. The first of these is that a thinker whose theory making is directed by pagan belief is often not only unaware of the religious character of his or her controlling presupposition, but is sometimes unaware of that presupposition altogether. That is to say, pagan religious presuppositions may not only be assumed unconsciously, but they may guide theory making while remaining unconscious. This was not true of the sample theories considered in the Casebook chapters. The thinkers represented there were all fairly clear about the basic presuppositions which directed their theories, and some even acknowledged the religious character of those presuppositions. Many other thinkers, however, are not at all clear about the presuppositions of the theories they endorse. But while theories can be produced under the guidance of a pagan faith even when it is held unconsciously, theories controlled and directed by biblical faith will not spring from the minds of Jews and Christians by means of unconscious guidance. Not only will the production of such theories require conscious effort, but even the sincerest efforts of the ablest of thinkers may meet with only mixed success. There are at least three reasons for this.

The first is the unique way in which biblical faith comes to those who believe in God. According to Bible writers, it comes about by the conjunction of two factors: contact with God's revelation of himself and the operation of God's grace which enables a person to see the truth of that revelation. Scripture everywhere represents this special grace as necessary because it must overcome our sinful human inclination to regard something other than Yahweh as divine. Thus, while people may unconsciously regard part (or all) of the creation as divine, no one ever comes to faith in the transcendent creator unconsciously.

The second reason is the way the residual effects of that sinful inclination makes resisting the influences of unbiblical beliefs and attitudes a struggle within even the most committed believer. The greatest heroes of the Judeo-Christian tradition had such struggles, and we who are their junior admirers can expect no less. So just as our religious weakness requires a conscious struggle for our personal attitudes and behavior to become permeated and controlled by our faith, so, too, it is a struggle to extend the influence of that faith to the task of making, evaluating, and reforming theories.

Finally, the effort required to invent or reform theories on the basis of our belief in God is made even greater by the influence of scholasticism. Indeed, this view has been so dominant among believing theorists for so long that it is very difficult to shake the habits of thought it produces even for those who come to see it as inadequate.

Because of both the innate and traditional obstacles to constructing radically biblical theories, those who attempt this task cannot help but be painfully aware that their efforts may be seriously deficient despite their best intentions. This chapter and the next two chapters should not, therefore, be misunderstood as claiming to reflect the biblical perspective in some final way. Nor does it claim to capture that perspective with perfect purity, or to have hit on the only hypotheses that could be developed from that perspective. Rather, they are an attempt to highlight the perspective itself, and to show how theorizing can be guided by it.

This last point has some important consequences. The most obvious is that with respect to any particular question there may be several hypotheses possible which presuppose belief in God. Thus a hypothesis may be ever so properly directed by our faith and still simply be mistaken. In other words, when we embark on the task of making explanatory guesses we may be within the range and direction of biblically motivated thinking, but still make a wrong entity hypothesis or shorter range perspectival hypotheses. The counterpart to this point is that nonbelievers may theorize from a nonbiblical, false perspective and still make specific proposals which are largely correct. We must always be open to learning from these discoveries, even though we must also strive to recast the interpretation of them from a biblical perspective. It would be a huge mistake, therefore, for believers to reject any theory *in its entirety* just because it presupposes a nonbiblical faith. We need not, for instance, reject the whole of atomic theory and look for a replacement for it.

The second consequence follows from the first. Especially in the sciences, our position is not concerned simply with the truth or falsity of specific hypotheses *considered in isolation*. It is not, for example, simply a matter of: are there atoms or not? It focuses instead on the broader context—the perspectival overview of reality—within which a hypothesis is proposed. Although an entity theory can be guided by a perspective based on a nonbiblical presupposition and still be correct in important ways, the false perspective involved will always guarantee that the nature of the proposed entity will be misinterpreted in ways which distort and at least partly falsify it. Therefore our position is that while a biblically regulated entity hypotheses may turn out to be wholly false, no nonbiblically directed hypothesis can ever be wholly true.

This claim should not be misunderstood as the trivial truism that since everything must be regarded as either dependent on God or not, those who believe in God and those who do not must disagree about everything on just that point. Simply disagreeing over whether what is postulated by a theory depends on God would not by itself make an immediate difference to the use of that hypothesis in the science in which it is proposed. This ultimate religious disagreement does not alone *constitute* the difference for theories. Rather, this ultimate religious disagreement spreads throughout a theory by generating other differences of interpretation. This spread extends through the perspectival overview to what I will call the "working concept" of any hypothesis; that is, to its concept as it relates to other concepts—especially concepts in other aspects—as they are employed in explanation. That is, the proposed aspectual nature of the entity determines how its relations to properties and laws of the aspects not characterizing its nature are interpreted.

The spread of the religious disagreement into concepts of the natures of things is both important and inevitable because regarding any one or two aspects of creation as self-existent (divine) means that the existence of all the other aspects are made possible by them. Such an overview not only puts some aspect into the status of God, it thereby reduces the status of the remaining aspects. The reduced status of the others consists either in their being seen as dependent on the one(s) regarded as divine, or in their being eliminated altogether in favor of the one regarded as divine. Either way, the religious issue (that some aspect of creation is accorded the status of God) results in the overestimation of the power and importance of the divinized aspect(s), and the corresponding underestimation of the power and importance of the rest of them. This, in turn, cannot help but be reflected in the working concepts of the proposed entities. So even though thinkers with widely differing perspectives may agree that there exist a certain type of theoretical entities (such as atoms), their concepts of the nature of those entities, and thus of how those concepts are to be used in explanation, will differ relative to which aspects are regarded as reducible to which others. (This was illustrated by the differences between Mach's, Einstein's, and Heisenberg's concepts of an atom discussed in chapter 8.) Thus while a radically biblical approach to theories does not mandate all new hypotheses in every science, it does require that we rethink and reform the concepts of all hypotheses in a way which reflects the biblical perspective.

Now rethinking a theory of reality in this distinctively biblical direction of thought will lead us to some very new hypotheses.[1] Some of them may sound strangely foreign compared to the past attempts by Jews and Christians to think about theory of reality, despite the fact that we share the same biblical presuppositions. Where this happens, I can only plead with my fellow believers to try to distance themselves from the influences of the scholastic position. No matter how difficult it may be, purifying our theories from pagan elements is obligatory for every Jew and Christian alike. The only alternative is to abandon theorizing about God's creation to those who presuppose it is not God's creation. Our task, then, is to develop theories which are guided by our faith in God. It is not to theorize in order to supply credentials for our faith, still less is it merely to theorize so as to "leave room for faith." It is not our faith which needs to be made intellectually respectable by means of theories, but our theories which need to be made religiously acceptable by being internally motivated and directed by our faith.

2. Some Guiding Principles

The deep involvement of religious belief in both the strong and the weak reductionist strategies has already been demonstrated. We have seen how each strategy tries to identify the basic nature of all things by reducing all the other aspects to the one or two chosen as that nature. The central idea of the strategies is that the essential nature of things can be found by identifying the aspect(s) upon which all the others depend. This is why using the vehicle of reduction to transport us to the goal of the nature of things exacts the price of smuggling in pagan contraband: it ascribes divinity to some aspect(s) of the creation, which is flatly contrary to the biblical doctrine of God as the sole, transcendent creator and sustainer of every thing other than himself. Any method or theory which accords that status to anything other than God is false and blasphemous. In fact, it is this very point which I contend must be made the first guiding principle for a genuinely biblical perspective. It is the **principle of pancreationism** defended in the last chapter: *Everything other than God is his creation and nothing in creation, about creation, or true of creation is self-existent.*

But this principle alone is not sufficient to distinguish the biblical perspective because the principle has so often been combined with theories which regarded some aspect(s) of creation as making the existence of all other aspects possible. To protect the principle of universal creationism from this distortion, a second guiding principle is required, the **principle of irreducibility**: *no aspect of creation is to be regarded as either the only genuine aspect or as making the existence of any other possible.* The principle reflects the biblical view that all creation depends directly and equally on God, so all genuine aspects—whatever the correct listing of them may be—are equally real. This latter principle, together with universal creationism, serves to bring into focus a more thoroughly biblical perspective. It does this by showing that our belief in God permeates and controls our theories *by requiring the complete abandonment of the reductionist strategies* rather than merely the eclectic rejection of objectionable elements in the contents of theories using those strategies.

But the abandonment of reductionist strategies will not simply lead us to a different *answer* to the question of the basic nature of reality. It also results in a new way of framing the *question* itself. We will still want a theory to account for our commonsense experience that various types of things have distinctive natures, but we will not be seeking the basic nature of everything in the senses of "basic" used by the traditional theories. We will deny that any one aspect is more real than any other, or that any makes another possible. Thus, the pagan idea of "basic" will be ruled out of the quest for *what* things are, just as it is ruled out of the quest for *why* things are. Instead, we must now invent or reinterpret theories in a way that is completely nonreductionist.

We have already noted that any list of aspects is initially obtained by abstracting them from our experience; they appear in commonsense experience to be aspects *of* things. Now unless one starts with a pagan religious presupposition, what reason is there to elevate any of them to being more than that? Why can't a theory refuse to enthrone any aspect as *the* essential nature of *all* things? In short, why suppose that some sort of reduction is unavoidable if the natures of things are to be accounted for?

It is true, of course, that things of a particular type appear to share a specific nature which is more "centrally characterized" by certain of their aspects rather than others. But simply focusing on a particular aspect as telling us more about the nature of a particular type of things does not require a reductionist theory. For example, a plant has physical properties as does a rock, but the plant is alive and the rock is not. In this way the "nature" of a plant is more centrally characterized by its biological aspect rather than any other aspect. This does not mean that its other aspects are reduced to its biological aspect, however. It need only be the case that the laws of the biological aspect take the lead in governing the overall internal organization and development of a plant. Hence we characterize its "nature" as that of a *living* thing. In this way, we may single out the biological aspect as telling us something "central" about the nature of a plant without requiring either that the biological makes all the other aspects possible, or that the biological is the essential nature of *all* things.

The further development of such a nonreductionist approach in the next section will open up some exciting directions for a theory of reality which were excluded by pagan presuppositions. If we no longer look for the nature of things by searching for which aspect makes all the others possible, and if there need be no one basic aspectual nature of *everything,* there may be as many different "natures" to creation as are needed to explain the types of things we experience. If this is so, we will be freed from the sorts of bizarre, implausible lengths to which modern reduction theories have been driven in trying to show that the most diverse types of things actually have the same basic nature. We may be delivered from such dead ends precisely by being released from the compulsion to find what it is *in* things which accounts for *both* their natures *and* the possiblity of their existence. So while it is true that knowing it is God who makes things to be what they are does not hand us a theory of reality, it does free us from ransacking the creation for something about it which is self-existent. It thereby delivers us from trying to account for the possibility of all things in terms of one or another of their aspects.

3. The Framework of Laws Theory

We have already noticed that the various aspects displayed by the objects of experience and investigated by the sciences are not only kinds of properties, but kinds of laws. Each aspect exhibits an orderliness among its properties; that is, they are related in ways that determine what is either necessary or impossible among them. For example, it is a law of the physical aspect that all sodium salts burn yellow, while it is a law of the spatial aspect that nothing can be both round and square. Without such an orderliness, creation as we know it could not exist; without statements expressing this order, no explanatory theories about creation are possible. The law statements we formulate are therefore approximations of specific links in the cosmic order. They express relations which, under specific conditions, are *necessary* in that they cannot be violated by any creatures.

The idea of law is prominent in Scripture, too, where it also has the sense of supplying order to things. The most prominent use of the term is, of course, in reference to the religious-moral law which has a central role in the covenant between God and the human race. But Scripture also uses the term for the orderliness of the universe at large. We already noticed that the Psalms (119:89–91, 148:6) and the prophet Jeremiah (31:35ff, 33:25) speak of the order of creation as established and maintained by God. Laws of creation are specifically included among the "all things" which are called his "servants," and part of his covenant is that he will faithfully preserve them. These remarks echo the passage in the eighth chapter of Genesis where God declares that he will maintain the regularities of creation "as long as the earth remains."

Such biblical remarks are not offered in the precise technical language of philosophy or science and do not involve what I have called "high abstraction," but they do emphasize a point which can be developed in a significant way for theory of reality. They encourage the proposal that Jews and Christians begin to rethink theory of reality by elaborating the idea of a framework of laws under which all created things exist and function. Scripture speaks of these laws as created, and therefore not to be regarded as identical with God. Nevertheless, they constitute the orderliness he has built into creation by which it is regulated. This is not to suggest that laws are *things* like planets, trees, or oceans, nor is it intended to mean that they exist separately from the things and events they govern. Rather, "law" is our term for the orderliness God has embedded in his creation, and our theory will start by recognizing a distinct law-*side* to created reality. Moreover, since we have abandoned the reductionist strategies there will be no need to expect that the law framework will be made up of only one or two kinds of laws, or that some one or two kinds generate all the others. Instead, our theory can include all the different kinds of order there seem to be and regard them all as equally real components of the cosmic law framework. Therefore I will preface the further development of this program with a review and clarification of the list of aspectual kinds of properties and laws given earlier.

The members of this list, you may recall, were arrived at simply by taking every large-scale kind of properties and laws which has been distinguished in the history of philosophy and science. The list is not supposed to be final, and the theory to be proposed would not have to be essentially altered should it be convincingly shown that certain members of the list should be deleted, combined, or subdivided, or that entirely new members should be added to the list.[2] Our working list, once again, is as follows:

fiduciary
ethical
justitial
aesthetical
economic
social
linguistic
historical
logical
sensory
biotic
physical
kinematic
spatial
quantitative

I have tried to avoid nouns to designate the members of this list since nouns tend to encourage the misunderstanding that these are classes or groups of *things*. Instead, I have used adjectives to emphasize that what are being listed are kinds of properties and laws exhibited by the objects of our experience. This has resulted in some odd terms and some special meanings for some familiar ones, so I am going to comment briefly on several of them.

The term 'quantitative' is used to designate the "how much" of things, and should not be misunderstood to refer to a realm of numbers or the abstract systems of mathematics devised for calculating quantity. There is evidence that some animals have a sense of quantity even though they cannot count,[3] and it is just such an intuitive awareness of the "how much" of things that I am pointing to here. It is our nonabstractive, intuitive experience of the quantity of things which the science of mathematics abstracts as its field of inquiry. Within that field it then further abstracts the property of discrete quantity, which becomes the basis for the natural number series from which even more abstract and complex mathematical concepts are built. Various branches of mathematics can then be developed corresponding to the different ways quantities can be calculated by formulating laws which hold among them. But all this stems from our intuitive recognition that things have quantity.

'Kinematic' is used to designate the movement of things—their motion in space. Most scientists presently include these properties and laws within the physical aspect, but at least two thinkers have argued persuasively that it is actually a distinct aspect.[4]

The term 'sensory' is used to cover the qualities and laws of both perception (touch, taste, sight, smell, and sound) and of the feelings elicited by perception. They are included in the same aspect because sensation and feeling are both ways in which humans—and animals—are sensitive.

The term 'historical' also deserves some comment even though it is a familiar one. This is because so many people think of it as referring to anything that has happened in the past. That is not what is meant here. Nor is it the way historians use it either, since not everything that has happened is historically important. Judging from what interests historians, it appears that the difference between what is historically important and what is not is the same as what is significant to the formation of human culture and what is not. What history is about is the transmission of culture-forming power. Thus our adjective 'historical' will be virtually equivalent to 'cultural' or 'culturally influential.' It will refer to the human ability to form new things from already existing materials, so that we will speak of all the products of this ability as cultural (historical) artifacts.

The term 'ethical' is not at all unusual as a general term referring to what is right or wrong about human behavior and attitudes. Nevertheless, the term is often used to cover two very distinct senses of "right": what is right according to justice, and what is right according to morality. In the list given above, these aspects are distinguished. The justitial aspect has to do with the obligations which befall our attitudes and actions according to what is *fair.* By contrast, the ethical aspect has to do with obligations which arise according to what is *loving.*

Although different, the two senses are, of course, related. Generally speaking we may be just to someone without also being loving, but we cannot be loving to that person without being just. Love often bids us go beyond what someone strictly deserves, but we would have to be at least as just to someone as circumstances permit before we could succeed in being loving to that person. Our view of the ethical aspect could therefore be called a "love ethic," but in a much stronger sense than that term is usually used. We do not merely mean that it is better to be loving than not, we mean that love is what ethics is *about.*

On this view, love is more than just a feeling. It is a normative principle of action which is circumscribed by the biblical admonition to "love your neighbor as yourself." In other words, we are to balance our self-interest with the interests of others. Ethical obligations are therefore those which arise from this norm for the relationships we have in the various aspects of life such as: love of self, love of husband or wife, love of children or parents, love of friends, or even love of a pet. Since these obligations arise from an aspectual norm, they extend over the spectrum of human experience including obligations to nature, one's work, one's country, art, learning, etc. In short, the ethical aspect is the one whose order includes the norm for human love-life.

Finally, the term 'fiduciary' is used to refer to the varying levels of reliability or trustworthiness a thing or person may have. This aspect is especially important in connection with human social relations of all sorts, which disintegrate rapidly where there is significant lack of trust. Because this aspect includes *all* degrees of trustworthiness and certitude, it also has a special connection to religious faith. This connection appears whenever anyone trusts something to be unconditionally reliable, for only something which has unconditioned existence could be unconditionally reliable. Trusting anything as unconditionally reliable therefore presupposes it to be (at least part of) what is self-existent and all-sustaining in relation to all else, and thus divine.

Even at this early stage, it is possible to see how a nonreductionist idea of such cosmic law framework can free us from the horns of one of the old dilemmas which has plagued traditional theories of reality: the dilemma of objectivism versus subjectivism. This issue can best be understood as a controversy between contrary answers to the question, "What is the source of the laws which give orderliness to creation?" Whereas the objectivist locates the source of order in the objects of human experience, the subjectivist locates the order in the human mind as the knowing subject. Of course, most theories have been partly objectivist and partly subjectivist, but to illustrate the two sides of the controversy I will use theories which are about as exclusively one or the other as any I can think of, namely, the theories of Aristotle and Kant.

For Aristotle, as we already saw, the "cause of the being of a thing" is its substance or form. A thing's form is also responsible for determining the innate nature it shares with other things of the same type, and it is the nature of those things which programs the ways they can behave and relate to other things. Therefore what we call laws are our formulations of the observed behavior of things as caused by their internally programmed natures. This means that there really is no distinct law side to creation. "Law" is but our name for the regularities we observe in experience, and these regularities are guaranteed by the unobservable form for each type of thing. Thus the source of all regularity and order is located in the objects of experience even though that source is not itself directly experienced. On this view, humans come to know the orderliness of things by conforming their concepts to the natures of objects as they exist outside their minds; in other words, by conforming their thinking to "object-ive" reality.

Kant, on the other hand, maintained that the mind of the knower, or "subject," is the source of all the order in experience. He held that what is fed into the mind are chaotic sensory stimuli, which the human mind then orders into an intelligible experience. His theory was that the human mind does this subconsciously and spontaneously in fixed ways it has no control over. So when we observe (or theorize about) regularities in our experience, and when we attempt to formulate them into law statements, these are all conscious dealings with an orderliness we are already unconsciously imposing upon stimuli, thereby creating the reality we experience. So far as our *conscious* knowing is concerned, we are attempting to understand the objects we experience—just as Aristotle believed. But, said Kant, it is possible to do that only because those objects have first been formed by having our mental order imposed on them. In this way the apparently "objective" order of reality is really subjective in origin.

It should be obvious why both objectivism and subjectivism are unacceptable since each presupposes a variety of pagan religion by assigning to some part of the creation the role of lawgiver to creation. From the biblical point of view it is neither the known objects nor the knowing subjects which are the sources of the order of what we experience, for God alone is the law-giver to creation. The biblical way of thinking about the laws of creation avoids the dilemma of objectivism and subjectivism by supplying a third alternative. Since Scripture teaches that God created all the laws which govern creation, we may view the order of things as originating neither in the known objects nor the knowing subjects. Instead, both objects and subjects are governed and connected by being governed by the same divinely ordained law framework.

Returning to the clarification of the aspect list, we need to notice that just as its members are intended to reflect what we find in pre-theoretical experience so, too, is the order in which they occur on the list. Reading from bottom to top, the order of their listing is intended to reflect the order in which they appear in things as we experience them prior to theorizing. That is, experience shows a sequence to the way things exhibit the aspects, so that properties of those lower on the list seem to be preconditions for the appearance of properties of those higher on the list. For example, there are things which have physical properties without being alive but nothing living fails to have physical properties. So having physical properties appears to be a precondition for anything's having biotic properties. Similarly, a biotically living thing may or may not be able to feel or perceive, but nothing capable of sensing is not biotically alive. In the same way, it appears that sensory perception is a precondition for a being's ability to think in logical concepts, which is a precondition for being able to conceive of plans by which the historical-cultural formation of new objects from natural materials is accomplished. This ability, in turn, is the precondition for one of the most outstanding examples of cultural formative power: the invention of language, which is the necessary precondition for the development of typically human social relations and customs. And so it goes on up the list.

Now I have been speaking of this order as one of preconditionality, not of time. This is not to deny there is a lot of evidence that the sequence we can now observe among aspects was mirrored in a real chronological development in the past. The evidence shows, for instance, that there was a period of time on earth when there were physical things but no living things, a period when there were beings which were both physical and living but which did not feel or perceive, after which there were beings that were physical, biotic, and sensory but without logical thought, etc. Nevertheless, this reflection of the aspectual order in time is not the same as the preconditionality I have been pointing to. Even without knowing about the gradual unfolding of these properties through time, the preconditonality sequence would still hold good for the reasons already given.

In fact, confusing preconditionality with the gradual appearance of properties in the past will make it harder to see the order with respect to the first four aspects, since we know of no objects in creation which ever lacked these. So here our argument is to point to the preconditionality sequence alone by saying that a thing would have to be spatial for it to have movement, which is in turn a precondition for anything's having physical properties of matter and energy. By the same token, there can be spatial shapes without their having to be shapes *of* any object which is also physical (geometry deals with spatial shapes abstractly isolated from things which possess them), and these can all be quantified by numbers which do not seem to require even spatiality.[5]

But although the order of the aspect list reflects the sequence in the way we experience properties in things, this sequence cannot be used to support the weak reductionist strategy for theory of reality. According to that strategy, the order we have been noticing is a *causal* one; some aspects—usually ones lower on the list—are said to cause the existence of the others which are higher on the list. But finding that properties of the higher aspects do not appear in things without those that are lower does not at all show that the lower ones *produce* the higher, since being a precondition for something is not the same as causing it. For instance, one of the preconditions for starting a wood fire is that oxygen be present, but the mere presence of oxygen will not start the fire. So we are entitled to notice here that proposing some lower aspect on the list as the reason why the higher ones exist is actually to make a pagan assumption. For to assume that it must be one or another of the aspects which cause the rest is to rule out in advance that there is a transcendent creator who is both necessary and sufficient for the existence of them all—including their order of preconditionality.

Besides this religious objection, however, there are serious theoretical difficulties with any attempt to use the order among aspects as support for a weak reduction theory. We have already seen why the claim that any one aspect can cause the existence of the others fails when applied to their property side: it is self-performatively incoherent to abstract a kind of properties, regard its resulting isolation as real independence, and thus proclaim it to be the essential identity of things rather than just an aspect of them. But there is an additional reason why this claim is implausible when applied to an aspect's law side. For while aspectual properties exhibit an order of appearance, aspectual laws do not. Explaining this point will at the same time allow a major part of the law framework theory to be presented, so it is worth pursuing here. But to make the point clear, I first need to introduce some new expressions that will allow me to speak in ways that will guard the distinction between the law and property sides of any aspect.[6]

The objects of experience (things, events, relations, states of affairs, persons, etc.) will be spoken of as existing or functioning "in an aspect" or "under the laws of an aspect." In this way we will remind ourselves that the existence of creatures is always law-governed, and that we must always distinguish between the entities subjected to the laws and the laws which do the governing. So to say a thing "functions in" an aspect is another way of saying it has properties of that aspectual kind which are governed by that aspect's laws. The law framework theory maintains that both the properties and laws of an aspect exist in mutual correlation. The law order of each aspect sets the limits for what properties are possible within that aspect and guarantees the necessary connections among them, but it does not create those properties. Neither is it the intrinsic natures of certain properties which set the orderliness for an aspect or bring others of its properties into existence. Both the law and the property sides of an aspect depend for their existence on God.

Focusing on this correlation now allows us to notice that there are two ways an object may possess properties of an aspect. I will speak of these two ways by saying that a thing may function in an aspect "actively," or "passively." The two functions are not, however, mutually exclusive. In fact, we contend that all things function passively in all aspects simultaneously, so that it is only the active functions of certain aspects that a thing may lack and which exhibit the sequential order of appearance noticed above. Consider, for example, a rock. According to the distinction being proposed, we would say that a rock functions actively in the quantitative, spatial, kinematic, and physical aspects. It bears these properties and is subjected to their laws so that it impinges actively on other things so far as these kinds of properties are concerned. The rock does not, however, function actively in other aspects such as the biotic, sensory, logical, economic, or justitial. Nevertheless, it does function in these aspects, because there is a sense in which it is subjected to their laws. The ways a thing is subjected to the laws of an aspect without functioning actively in it, I will call its passive properties in that aspect. That the rock does not function actively in the biotic aspect means it is not alive. It does not carry on metabic processes, ingest, or reproduce. But it can have properties which are indispensable to the life of living things and which are biotically important in a passive way. That these properties are passive means they cannot appear except in relation to things having an active function in that aspect. The rock may, for instance, be part of an animal's den; it may be the object on which a seagull drops clams so as to open them; if small enough, it may enter a bird's gizzard and help grind its food. In other words it can have functions which may be biotically appropriated by living things. In similar ways water and other nonliving things may display biotic passive functions without themselves being alive. Such properties remain only potential, of course, until something with a biotic active function actualizes them. But they are nevertheless real properties of those objects made possible by the fact that they are governed by biotic—as well as all other—laws. (Be sure not to confuse "active" with "actual" here. Passive properties can be either actual or potential, while active properties are always actual.)

A rock does not function actively in the sensory aspect either. This means that it does not feel or perceive. But the fact that it can be perceived by animals and humans who have sensory active functions is made possible (in part) because it is subject to sensory laws and has passive sensory properties. Remember in this connection that we do not directly perceive *physical* properties in the strictly sensory meaning of "perceive," though we experience them in the wider sense of "experience." Physical heat, for example, is defined as the rate of molecular vibration but we do not sensorily feel a thing to be vibrating faster or slower when we feel heat. Again, physically speaking, light waves differ in frequency, but what we perceive is red or blue, etc.; and felt weight is the pressure or resistance we feel, while physical weight is gravitational attraction whether felt or not.

Similarly, the rock does not form logical concepts. But were it not (passively) subjected to logical laws it could not be an object of our logical thought so that we could not form a concept of it. Just so, we could not value it economically were it not subjected to the economic law of suppy and demand. Once again, these passive functions can only be actualized in relation to the active functions of other beings. The rock does not have *actual* economic value until someone values it. But were it not passively subject to the order of the economic aspect, it could not become an object of value for us. Its economic potential is a real characteristic of it made possible by its subjection to that aspect's order.

By contrast to a rock, a tree functions actively in the biotic aspect in addition to its active functions in the quantitative, spatial, kinematic, and physical aspects. It carries on metabolic processes, has a life span, and is able to reproduce. Its social function, on the other hand, is passive and is actualized only when, for example, it is used to provide shade for human social affairs. It may also have a passive aesthetic function if it is located or shaped so as to contribute to the beauty of a garden. In contrast to the tree, an animal would also be said to have a sensory active function.[7] Even the most primitive animals are sensitive in ways plants are not, if only at a crude level.

So far as we know, only humans have active functions in all the aspects.[8]

Perhaps the following diagram will help make this part of our theory clearer:

	Rock	Tree	Animal
Fiduciary			
Ethical			
Justitial			
Aesthetical			
Economic			
Social			
Linguistic			
Historical			
Logical			
Sensory			▮
Biotic		▮	▮
Physical	▮	▮	▮
Kinematic	▮	▮	▮
Spatial	▮	▮	▮
Quantitative	▮	▮	▮

▮ Active
Functions

☐ Passive
Functions

This distinction between active and passive properties allows us to appropriate the elements of truth from both objectivism and subjectivism while avoiding the extremes of each. We can agree with the subjectivist that things do not actually possess passive properties apart from our relating to them in specific ways. Nevertheless, we can agree with the objectivist that we do not create these properties wholesale. Instead, we hold that there are real potentialities for the actualizing of such properties, and these potentialities exist independently of us. Unlike the objectivist we do not locate these potentialities *in* the objects, however, but see them as the result of the ways objects conform to the distinct law side of creation.

The distinction between active and passive properties also shows why we maintain the emergence theory to be implausible.

For while there is a sense in which active functions of things "emerge" in the sequential order discussed above, it makes no sense to suggest that aspectual laws also emerged. The orderliness of both active and passive properties in each aspect has been made possible by aspectual laws which would therefore have to exist already. What sense does it make to suggest, for instance, that once things were only physical but that logical laws then "emerged" along with logical properties? That would mean that the supposed emergence was not itself even *logically* possible.

In this way the distinction removes the most plausible objection to our contention that the aspects are all equally real—a point which was earlier defended by the criterion of self-performative coherence and the thought experiment it inspired. That argument showed we cannot conceive of any aspects as really independent of the others. But against this emergence theories urge that the sequential order of their active functions is best understood as showing the lower ones are likely to be causally basic to the higher ones. We have now seen why this is unconvincing, and does not count against our first two guiding principles.[9]

Moreover, this point now puts us in a position to add a third guiding principle. For if all creation is actively or passively governed by the entire law framework, we may now formulate the **principle of aspectual universality.** This principle says that *every aspect is an aspect of all creatures, since all creation exists and functions under all the aspectual laws simultaneously.*

This additional principle forms a complement to the principle of aspectual irreducibility and serves to emphasize two important points already mentioned: (1) aspects are not to be confused with types or classes of things, but are kinds of properties and laws true of all things; (2) nothing we experience is ever experienced as purely a single (aspectual) kind of thing. This is important since so many of the entities that populate the theories of modern philosophy are precisely fictions of that sort. They are supposed to be purely physical objects, purely sensory percepts, purely logical concepts, etc. Compared with our experience, such entities are all clearly hypotheses; we never experience anything that has properties of only one or two of the aspects. And we now have good reason to reject those hypotheses in favor of what experience exhibits.

This is not to say that theories can never correct, enlarge upon, or even contradict certain facets of ordinary experience. Saying that we never experience entities that are purely of one aspectual kind would not, by itself, make those theories false. But, as we have seen, it is not merely the case that the objects of experience display a multiplicity of aspects; it is also the case that the theories attempting to deny the equal reality of that multiplicity are either self-assumptively or self-performatively incoherent. So we insist that the only plausible position is to say that all things and events function in all the aspects, provided passive properties are distinguished from active ones. The lesson, then, is that if a theory of reality is to explain our experience of the natures of things (and what else could a theory of reality explain?), it must take into account how things function in *all* the aspects.[10]

I now want to introduce a more convenient way to speak of a point noted earlier. We briefly observed that although experienced reality is multiaspectual, various types of things display distinctive natures which are "more centrally characterized" by a particular aspect. I mentioned that the way things of a certain type function under the laws of a particular aspect can characterize their nature more strongly than the ways they function in the others, without involving any reduction among aspects. I will now speak of this as the way things of a particular type are "qualified" by that aspect. And I will speak of the way entities are governed by the laws of their qualifying aspect as their "qualifying function." This point can now help to explain the element of truth contained in so many modern theories which regard things as purely physical, or purely sensory, etc.

As examples of this mistake, think again of how much Mach and Einstein believed that the objects of our pretheoretical experience are all *purely* sensory. Even Einstein's disagreement with Mach only took the form of adding that there are also objects outside experience which are *purely* physical. What is happening here, according to our theory, is that the qualifying functions of things are being mistaken for their exclusive nature. For example, we ordinarily think and speak of a rock as a *physical* thing, or of acts of perception as *sensory* perception, but these pretheoretical intuitions of their natures do not show them to be *exclusively* physical or sensory. Our intuition of their natures focuses on the particular aspect which most centrally characterizes them, not which exhaustively characterizes them.

To illustrate the point further, consider the example of acts of human behavior. Human acts are like all other events which occur in the world in that they have many aspects. But they can differ according to their aspectual qualification: acts of buying or selling have an economic qualification, acts of eating have a biological qualification, acts of dancing have an aesthetical qualification, while acts of trying or deciding court cases have a justitial qualification. Even though things of a distinct type have a specific aspectual qualification, they still exist under the laws of all the aspects at once, and can be studied from the standpoint of any of them. In fact, not only *may* they be studied from different angles corresponding to their other aspects, but it is impossible for these other aspects not to enter the explanations of each science. No matter how hard a science may try to exclude all but its delimiting aspect, it cannot avoid dealing with the passive functions its data display in the other aspects.

In addition to supporting the principles of aspectual irreducibility and universality, our critique of reduction strategies and emergence theories also points to yet one more guiding principle for our law-framework theory. The thought experiment in particular suggests what I will call the **principle of aspectual inseparability.** This means that *aspects cannot be isolated from one another; their very intelligibility depends on their connectedness.* Though they may be abstracted from the things which exhibit them, they cannot—even in thought—be isolated from one another. So even though the *meanings* of "quantitative," "physical," "sensory," "justitial," etc., are all importantly distinct and irreducible, they can only be understood in connection with, and by being compared to, one another.[11]

These principles can now guide our further theorizing in at least a negative way. That is, we will take it as a sign that our theorizing has gone astray if any hypothesis it entertains leads us to: (1) deny the distinctness and irreducibility of a multiplicity of aspects, (2) restrict the range of any aspect within creation, or (3) regard any rupture of the continuity and interdependence of the aspects as complete and real rather than as partial and an artificial product of high abstraction.

At this point I am often asked why these principles could not be accepted quite apart from belief in God. If they can, wouldn't that mean that there is no necessary connection between religious presuppositions and theories after all? To this I reply that the new program being sketched here derives from a perspective which, indeed, requires a transcendent divinity. The real reason its nonreductionist program is incompatible with pagan faith is not found in a theoretical argument, but in the religious nature of humans. Of course, anyone may try to view all aspects as equally real and mutually irreducible simply on purely pragmatic grounds without belief in a transcendent divinity. The reason this will not succeed is that unless the lightning bolt of faith is grounded outside creation altogether, it will simply have to come down within creation. In that case it cannot fail to distort all theoretical explanations by divinizing some aspect(s) of created reality, thereby denying or demoting the reality and importance of the others.

4. The Natures of Things

A. Natural Things

Let us now return to the issue of the experienced differences in the natures of things, and see if we can give an account of them which conforms to our guiding principles. We already admitted that the commonsense idea of the nature of a thing recognizes a specific aspect as more "centrally characterizing" its nature. We explained this by the concept of what it means for a thing to be "qualified by" an aspect. This may now be further clarified as follows: the qualifying aspect of a thing is *the aspect whose laws guide and regulate the internal organization or development of the thing considered as a whole.* The reason we intuitively speak of a rock as a "physical" thing or a plant as a "living" thing is that it is the physical and biotic aspects respectively whose laws exercise the overriding governance of the internal organization of those things. It is not that those things are *exclusively* physical or biotic, nor do the properties and laws of those aspects *cause* the properties or laws of the other aspects of these things. Rather, the laws of their qualifying aspects play a more prominent role in their natural internal organization and/or development than do the laws of any other aspect.

Let us now look more closely at what is meant by saying that the laws of a thing's qualifying aspect exercise a "more prominent or overriding governance over it." If we consider the quantitative, spatial or physical aspects of a tree, we see that they do not tell us about the aspectual characterization which is nearest to our intuitive idea of its nature. But when we come to the biological aspect of the tree, we have reached that aspect whose laws guide the in-

ternal organization and development of the tree as a whole. It is
the biological laws which direct or lead the overall arrangement of
its parts, its internal relations, its processes, and the structural arrangement among the properties of them all. This is why it comports with our commonsense idea of its nature to say that it is
qualified as a living thing. And this is what we mean by saying that
its nature is "more centrally" characterized as a living thing than it
is as a spatial thing or physical thing.

This part of our account fits well with the previous distinction
drawn between active and passive functions of things. That distinction recognized a sequential order among aspects so far as the
appearance of active functions is concerned. Now for every example we can think of, the qualifying aspect of a thing is also the last
aspect in that order (the highest on our list) in which the thing
functions actively. That is, a rock is qualified by the physical aspect
which is the highest on the list in which it functions actively. The
fact that it is merely passive in the remaining aspects is partly why
we intuitively see a rock as having a (centrally) physical nature. By
contrast, the qualifying function of a plant is its biotic function
since it is the biological laws which exercise overriding governance of the internal organization and processes of a plant. Here,
again, it is also the biological aspect which is the highest aspect on
the list in which a plant functions actively. Thus there appears a
striking correspondence between our intuitive grasp of a thing's
highest active function and its qualifying function as defined by
the law framework theory.

Now it would take more space than I have here to demonstrate
this correspondence for hundreds more examples. But since this
has already been done elsewhere,[12] and because of the lack of convincing counterexamples, our theory now proposes to accept this
correspondence as part of our concept of the qualifying function
of a thing. Therefore, the fuller definition of a thing's qualifying
function will be: that aspect whose laws govern the overriding internal structure and development of a thing considered as a whole,
and which is the highest aspect in the sequential order in which
the thing functions actively. This deliberately includes both the intuitive recognition of a thing's nature as centered in the last aspect
in which it functions actively, and the theoretical determination of
which laws have the overriding governance of the internal structure of a thing taken as a whole. But the identity of the aspect

intuitively seen as qualifying a thing's nature and the kinds of laws that govern its structure as a whole has not been defined so as to be inevitable. It is instead a prediction of our theory, and is subject to confirmation or disconfirmation by philosophical and scientific analysis of various types of things and events—so long as the analysis follows our nonreductionist principles. Thus the concept of the qualifying function of things provides a way to account for their natures which is at once both thoroughly nonreductionist and subject to empirical confirmation.

But what has been said so far about the concept of a qualifying function and the distinction between active and passive functions is only the start of a nonreductionist account of the natures of things. It is not yet a sufficient account of their natures. First, it is not specific enough. In saying that a tree's qualifying function is biological, our theory has not yet accounted for anything unique to a tree as distinct from other types of plants. Since the natures of things have been only roughly approximated when we identify their qualifying functions, we need to be more specific if we are to account for the difference in the natures of various types of things having the same qualifying function.

The way in which our law framework theory can be enlarged to account more specifically for the distinctive natures of types of things corresponds to the sequence in the appearance of aspectual active functions discussed earlier. That is, the fact that there is order among aspects implies the existence of inter-aspectual laws in addition to those which hold within aspects.

The laws of this inter-aspectual order I will call "type laws." These laws range across aspects regulating just how properties of the various aspectual kinds can combine so as to form things and events of particular types.[13]

The concept of a type law can now be combined with the concept of the qualification of a thing so as to give a more adequate account of the nature of the type to which it belongs. For example, the fact that a tree is biologically qualified can now be coupled with the distinctive structural organization of its parts and functions which make it a tree rather than a mushroom or a daisy. Of course, just what structurings these laws allow cannot be predicted in advance; their discovery depends on our analyzing the realities we find or form. Thus our law framework is a complex, crosshatching network of laws. In addition to the (multiaspectual) causal laws we experience daily, the network includes aspectual laws which determine the necessary relations among properties within particular aspects and type laws which govern the structural combination among properties of different aspects, making possible myriad specific types of things and events. It is the crosshatching governance of both sorts of laws by which our theory accounts for the nature of a type of things. That is, our understanding of a thing's qualifying function, taken together with an analysis of its structural type, comprises the whole account our theory gives for the commonsense idea of the nature of a thing. A more complete account of the significance of the idea of type laws, as well as of the other principles and concepts introduced by our theory, will be given in the next chapter.

With this sketch of the law framework we are now in a position to recognize an important feature of our theory that is implied by what has been said so far, but has not yet been made explicit. It is a feature by which it departs from the majority of theories that have been adapted by Jewish and Christian thinkers. And though I can only briefly allude to it here, it brings greater clarity to what follows by giving a fuller idea of the theory's unique *direction;* that is to say, why its biblical presupposition drives its development along certain lines and not others.

The feature I am referring to is that this theory shows a way to account for the natures of things without needing the idea that things have a "substance." The direction of thought away from this concept took its impetus from the biblical idea that nothing in creation exists "in itself," so that there is nothing *in things* which causes them to be what they are. It is God who causes them to be what they are. The most basic characteristic of all created realities is that they depend on God in every respect. As a consequence, our theory of the nature of created things or events has no need of the concept of substance, but sees them as *individual structural assemblages of properties determined by a type law, and centrally qualified by whichever aspect's laws regulate their internal organization.*[14] It is because no aspect of any created thing is to be viewed as its substance on which all its other aspects depend that we contend it is a mistake to think of a thing or event as anything over and above an individual structuring of all the properties comprising it. This is a consequence of our rejection of the reductionist program of selecting one or two aspectual kinds of properties as what things are, leaving the rest as what they possess. So we deny there is any substance to a thing which *has* the rest of its properties. Instead, we hold that a thing *is* an individual combination of every aspectual kind of properties, given a specific structuring which determines the type of thing it is, within the cosmic law framework.[15]

B. Artifacts

So far the concepts introduced by the law framework theory have been applied only to natural things. We started with them because the natures of artifacts are more complicated than can be accounted for in terms of the qualifying function of their natural material. Nor can that deficiency be remedied simply by adding the type law of the natural material to the account. This is because the structural arrangement of properties which typifies the things serving as natural material will never tell us about what is new in the nature of an artifact—what its natural material has *become.* So whether the artifact is the product of humans or animals, we need to expand our concept of a qualifying function so that it can account for the new nature which appears in an artifact and which was not possessed by its natural materials.

For example, the earth or rock which lines an animal's den or hole would, by itself, have no more than a physical qualification. But once it has undergone transformation in order to meet an animal's biotic or sensory needs, it acquires an additional qualification despite the fact that it has only a passive function in the biotic or sensory aspects. Unless we recognize that such transformation has occurred, we would not recognize the earth or rock as the den *of an animal,* and so we would miss an important part of what it *is.* Thus, our concept of the qualifying function of such a thing needs to be expanded to include the aspect qualifying *the process of transformation* which produced it. For animal artifacts, then, the concept of their aspectual qualification will be subdivided between at least two aspects. We will call the aspect in which the natural materials of such artifacts have their highest active function their "foundational function," and we will call the aspect whose laws governed the process of their formation, their "leading function."

For example, a beaver may construct a lodge out of mud, sticks and other materials, which have physical and biological qualifying

functions in their natural state. But as an artifact, the lodge has acquired an additional *sensory* qualification because the beaver's activity is governed by its sensory instincts and needs (shelter,
warmth, protection of young, etc.). Thus we will say that the lodge
is qualified by a physical or biotic foundational function while the
process of its formation was led by sensory feelings and needs. We
will therefore speak of the sensory aspect as the lodge's "leading
function." This means that artifacts differ from natural things because one part of what qualifies them (their leading function) is an
actualized passive function rather than an active function.

Also in the case of human artifacts, natural materials may be
formed into a new thing whose nature cannot be understood without recognizing some addition to their qualification. Here, too, we
will need to add (at least) the aspect whose laws govern the kind
of process that transformed the materials. Stones, for example,
have no more than a physical qualifying function in nature, but human effort may transform them into a house. Unless the new arrangement of those stones is then recognized as a product of
human formative power, they cannot be recognized as making up
a house. But unlike animal production, human formative control of
natural materials is not simply dictated by sensory instinct. Humans transform natural materials in accordance with a freely conceived *plan.* So there are two additional elements to the nature of
a human artifact, rather than only one. There is not only the aspectual qualification of the process of the natural material's transformation, but also the aspectual qualification of the plan by
which guided the process.

In the case of animal artifacts, we used the expression "foundational function" to designate the highest aspect in which the natural material had an active function. But since human formative
activity adds two new qualifications to the nature of an artifact, we
need to apply our terminology differently. For human artifacts
there are a total of three aspects involved in their qualification: the
kind of natural material, the kind of process, and the kind of plan
that guided the process. Of these, only the aspectual qualification
of its *plan* should be referred to as the artifact's "leading" function. So the other two will both be regarded as foundational functions of the artifact ("foundational" in the same sense that they
provide the means for the accomplishment of the plan). The first
is the qualification of the natural material—the last aspect in

which it functions actively. The second is the qualification of the work or process of formation involved.

What, then, is the aspect that qualifies the second foundational function for a human artifact, the process of human formative control? This question, like so many others about the aspectual qualifications of things, is not answered by being deduced from our theory. Instead, it is answered by examining the objects of our experience. So we may not assume at this point that all artifacts will have the same qualification for their second foundational function. Nevertheless, in keeping with our earlier clarifications of the meanings of our aspectual terms, we may say that the process of human formative power most often involved with an artifact is a "historical" or "cultural" process. Most products of human control of natural material will therefore be regarded as parts of human culture. In the case of our present example of a house, it seems clear that houses are always produced in a style which is derived from and/or contributes to the accomplishments of some historical period and cultural style.

What then is the leading function of a house? One plausible candidate would be to say it is biological. And, no doubt, a house does serve human biological needs. We would form houses very differently were our bodies radically different from what they are. But a house is more than bare biological shelter which is how it differs from a simple lean-to or hut. It provides both a place for social exchange and accommodates the social need for privacy. The size and shape of its rooms, along with their arrangement, usually indicate a varying social status among those who occupy or use them. In fact, unless its formation is seen as led by such social purposes, a building would not be called a house. For these reasons, we say that the second foundational function of a house is historical, and its leading function is social.

The leading functions of historically founded human artifacts vary greatly from artifact to artifact, of course, and need to be analyzed carefully on a case-by-case basis. But the foundational and leading functions are always regarded as correlates in such analysis, since neither can be adequately understood without the other. Together, their analysis helps us to acquire a more complete idea of the nature of any given artifact.

There is not the space here to analyze many more examples to show the adequacy of this threefold distinction to account for the natures of artifacts, though it could easily be done. A book, for instance, would be said to have a historical foundational function and a linguistic leading function. The poetry printed in a book, on the other hand, would have a historical foundational function but an aesthetical leading function. So would a painting, a sculpture, or a piece of music. A warehouse, with its loading platforms and large storage area, shows a specific type of purpose which led its construction, while the teller's stalls and safety vault of a bank show another specific type. But both types are economically qualified purposes, so the leading function of both buildings is their economic aspect. By contrast, a church building or synagogue have the fiduciary leading function of faith. In this way, the more complicated natures of artifacts are accounted for by a combination of an expanded concept of a thing's qualifying function and the concept of a type law. For the natures of human artifacts are described not only in terms of their foundational and leading functions, but also in the ways they are related by type laws so as to determine each type of artifact.

The concepts introduced in this sketch of the law framework theory will be fleshed out and illustrated in the next chapter where they will be used to develop a blueprint for a theory of human social communities. In the last chapter they will be applied in some detail to a more specific theory of the political community or state. I realize that such communities are not usually referred to as "things" in the way we call a tree, a painting, or a building a thing. Nevertheless they deserve to be regarded as things since they, too, are realities which function in all the aspects of experience, have specific natures analyzable as qualifying functions, and exhibit specific structures made possible by type laws. Moreover, they are things formed by human activity, and so should be recognized as being specific types of human artifacts. Our theory will therefore proceed to analyze them as such. This means that the natures of specific types of social communities will be established by analyzing their foundational and leading functions and the relations between them as determined by their type law. The procedure of this analysis will be, first, to see how our theory of mutually inseparable but irreducible aspects provides us with an overview of human society as a whole. This will give us a social principle for determining in a *general* way the proper roles and relations of various kinds of communities to one another in society. Then in chapter 13 we will analyze the specific internal nature of the state according to its type law. This will allow us to see important points about the proper role of the state in society, where the conceptions of its duties and limits are determined not by the demands of other institutions, but rather by very nature of the state itself.

But since the chapters on society and the state will need to make free use of our new terminology, and since that terminology is apt to seem strange to most readers, I thought it best to append here a short glossary. Here, then, is a summary of the concepts so far introduced by the law framework theory:

1. Aspect—a basic kind of properties and laws.
2. Active function—the way a thing is directly governed by the laws of an aspect so that it has properties in that aspect independently of their being activated by other things. In every aspect but the quantitative and spatial, a thing's active functions are exhibited by the effects it produces on other things.
3. Passive function—the way a thing is indirectly governed by laws of an aspect so that it only has potential properties in that aspect until they are activated by another thing having an active function in that aspect.
4. Qualifying function—the aspect of a thing or event whose laws govern its internal organization and/or development taken as a whole.

In a natural thing this is always the highest aspect in which it functions actively. In a human artifact, it includes the aspect qualifying the process of change that produced it as well as the aspect qualifying the plan or purpose governing the process.

5. Foundational function—the aspect whose laws govern the process of change by which humans produced an artifact.
6. Leading function—the aspect whose laws govern the plan or purpose which guided the process by which humans produced an artifact.

It should be added that the concept of purpose used here does not mean any subjective whim about the use of an artifact once it is formed. We all know a teacup can be used as an ashtray, or a chair as a stepladder. We refer instead to the leading function of the plan by which the artifact was formed, which is embodied in its structure and reflects its type law. The purpose meant here is therefore the artifact's "structural purpose" which cannot be altered without altering the artifact itself.

7. Type law—laws which range across aspects determining the combinations of properties which characterize types of individuals.

12

A BIBLICAL THEORY OF SOCIETY

1. Introduction

This section will define some basic terms so they can be used in the succeeding sections to apply the law framework theory to a theory of society.

The first term in need of clarity is 'society.' As I use it, this term will refer to individual persons and/or groups of persons standing in any one of three relations: individual to group, group to group, and individual to individual. The term 'group' as used here is intended to mean a durable one which joins its members into a recognizable unit, rather than a chance collection of people such as those who happen to be waiting for a bus. But since the term 'group' can be taken either way, from now on I will use the term 'community' for a durable social unit. In what follows, the discussion of various communities will include only the first two of the three basic social relations, since these are more important to understanding the theory of the state to be sketched in the next chapter.

Social communities will be regarded as falling into two major divisions which I will call "institutions" and "organizations." Only the strongest sort of social community will be called an institution. This use of 'institution' will mean only a community which has all of the following three characteristics: (1) their members are united to an intensive degree; (2) membership carries the intention of being life-long; (3) membership is (at least partly) independent of the member's will. The communities with these characteristics are marriage, family, state, and religious communities such as a temple, mosque, or church.

Membership in institutions is independent of the member's will in two senses. One is that a person is usually born into a family, a state, and some religious affiliation. The other is that changing membership in such institutions is not done easily and simply by unilaterally deciding to do so. To change one's citizenship or one's membership in a religious institution requires being accepted by the new institution involved, and legally ending a marriage requires that the divorce be recognized by the state. And no matter how the bonds of familial affection may break down, one is a biological member of one's family so long as it exists. By contrast, social "organizations" are ones in which the member's bond is less intense and less permanent. Organizations also decide who may or may not join them, but membership is not intended to be life-long and their members are free to come and go more easily. Examples of organizations are businesses, hospitals, labor unions, political parties, and schools.

In the last chapter we saw why our theory regards most artifacts as having a historical foundational function. As we used it, the term 'historical' was equivalent to 'cultural', and referred to the free exercise of the power humans have to form artifacts from natural things. We noticed that social communities are among the new things humans form, so that most of these also have a cultural foundational function. There are two institutions which are exceptions, however. These are marriage and the family. For even though the social forms given to marriages and families are under human control and can vary culturally, the process of their formation is not a cultural achievement but is rooted in our biological nature and so is governed by biological laws. This point is supported by the fact that these are the only institutions that must cease to exist when all their original members die. These communities will therefore be called "natural institutions" meaning that they have a biological foundational function. However, any view of marriage or family which sees them as *restrictively* biological has a reductionist view of them. While the biological order of creation regulates their formation, their leading function and structural purpose is ruled by the ethical norm of love. This is clearly the view Scripture takes of marriage, which is spoken of as essentially a community of love (Gen. 1:28, 2:18, 24; Eph. 5:25–33). The book of Genesis, for example, views the sexual relation of Adam and Eve as necessary to their love bond and as good for both of them *prior to their fall into sin.* Our ordinary language reflects this as well when we speak of the sexual union of husband and wife not merely as "mating," but as "making love." Thus, anyone who insists, as Aristotle did, that the single purpose of sex is to perpetuate the species has made a serious mistake.

No doubt marriage and family do accomplish the purpose of perpetuating the human race. This fact does not, however, alter what we called the "structural purpose" of these institutions, which is ruled by their leading function. This is because the purpose embedded in the structure of a thing or community does not rule out the presence of other purposes in connection with them. For example, partners to a marriage may have their own private purposes for marrying, such as social climbing or financial gain, but the purpose of the marriage institution, which is guaranteed by its leading function, is exhibited only by its inner spirit: the perpetuation and enhancement of the sort of love which forms the closest of all human ties.

Though all communities have a fixed qualifying function and are structured by a type law, each type exhibits a number of varieties. There are varieties of states, for example. There are varieties of families, often connected with how the family's living is supplied. Consider, for instance, the variation in the relations among the members of a farming family, a laboring family, a royal family, and a family which runs its own business. We also recognize that just as there can be deformed natural things, there can be deformed social communities as well. Two examples are a state which is an absolute dictatorship and a polyandrous family. But neither the varieties nor the deformities in acutal social communities affect the structural principles which make them possible. These principles reside in the law side of creation, which guarantees the qualifying functions and type laws which structure every actual community.

Calling attention to the aspectual and inter-aspectual laws of creation is one of the main interpretive advantages which our theory provides. It allows us to focus on the fixed principles which underlie the differing types of human social communities, so that we are not led astray by every variation or deformation they may have. Our understanding of them in each case begins with the recognition of the irreducible aspectual differences which, in turn, allows us to analyze their aspectual qualification (their foundational and leading functions). Then we look for the most basic ways the members of these communities must relate in all the aspects in order for that type of community to exist. By formulating a general statement of these relations, we approximate the type law which makes them possible. Without this idea of the law framework to guide a theory of social communities, how could one hope to arrive at the aspectual nature of each type? How could one ever tell which social forms are normal and which are aberrations? As Dooyeweerd has put it:

> If we consider a beautiful embroidery from behind, we do not discover any pattern in the confused criss-cross of the interlacements. Similarly, we cannot discover the structural patterns of the different types of societal relationships if we pay attention only to the ... [forms we actually find in existence and the ways] in which they are interlaced with one another. (*New Critique,* vol. III, p. 176)

But does this mean that we cannot do sociology without a philosophical theory? If so, is the science of sociology collapsed to social philosophy? And if not, what is the difference between them?

Pointing to how our theory of reality directs the doing of sociology is merely acknowledging our philosophical presuppositions and spelling them out. Indeed, no theory of society can avoid such presuppositions whether they are admitted or not. The difference between social philosophy and the science of sociology appears to be the same as the difference between philosophy and the other sciences: whereas philosophy—so far as theory of reality is concerned—explicitly theorizes about an idea of how all the aspects relate to one another, the science of sociology presupposes some such idea in its investigation of the actual communities of human society and the ways they interact and influence one another.

One of the main contributions our law framework theory makes to social theory is that it can employ aspectual norms as the standards for what is normal or abnormal about various communities. This is a highly controversial issue. Many social theories claim that no account of society can be scientific unless it deletes all reference to norms. So we now turn to the question as to whether sociology can develop a theory of the natures and interactions of communities simply by describing them as they *are* (the social facts), without any reference to how they *should* be (social norms).

2. Fact versus Norm

The first matter we must be clear about is the meaning of the term 'norm'.

In the last chapter we noticed that there is a sequence among aspects with respect to how things have an active function in them. Active functions in aspects lower on the list are preconditions for things to have active functions in aspects higher on the list. Another difference we may now notice between the aspects which are lower on the list and those which are higher is that the laws of the lower aspects are ones that we cannot disobey even if we try. That is, there is no way we can actually violate the order found in the quantitative, spatial, kinematic, or physical aspects. But from the biological aspect upward on the list, the character of the order changes; the higher we go on the list, the more of each aspect's order can possibly be disobeyed. Rather than being an order determining what is necessary, possible, and impossible, the order of the higher aspects is increasingly made up of norms which are guides for the ways in which plants, animals, and humans ought to act if they are to maximize the purposes which are qualified by those aspects.

For example, the *laws* of the biotic aspect determine the relations among certain biological properties. But there are also biotic *norms* for health which relate other biological properties. A living thing may violate such a norm and still live, but it will be healthier if it conforms to the norm. Or again, think of the laws of logic. There is a sense in which logical laws are inviolable. There is nothing in creation which can exist in violation of the logical axiom of noncontradition: nothing can be true and not-true in the same sense at the same time. But we can disobey it in our thinking by committing logical fallacies of reasoning or by holding incompatible beliefs. Thus, while the logical order of creation has the character of inviolable law for everything other than thought, it is a normative order for our thinking. We *can* disobey it, but we *ought* not to do so if we want any logical assurance we have arrived at truth. For aspects even higher on the list, our ability to disobey their order extends beyond our thought to our behavior. We may disobey economic, justitial, and other norms in action as well as in thought and belief. But the effects of doing so will always undermine the purposes of increasing wealth or achieving justice, etc., unless these are altered by intervening forces. However, our being able to disobey norms does not detract from their reality as parts of the cosmic law framework. Indeed, it is often the consequences of disobeying norms that display most vividly their reality and binding character. Because these parts of the law framework have the distinctive character of being able to be disobeyed by humans, and because they provide the standards for what ought to be, they are called "norms."

Having now indicated what a norm is, I want to warn against several common misunderstandings about them. First, it is important not to confuse what is average or usual with what is normal. "Normal" means that which is in accordance with a norm no matter how often it may be disobeyed. Second, the governance of these norms within their aspect does not depend on our consciously knowing precise statements of them, or upon our deliberately trying to conform to them. Although people often have no conscious formulation of certain norms, their activities are still governed by them in important ways. This is demonstrated by the fact that everyone recognizes certain activities as conforming to norms—as being *norm*al—while other activities are not, even if they cannot say exactly what those norms are. For example, we are not able to state norms of art very precisely, yet we make judgments such as "This is a work of art but that is not," or "This work of art is better than that one." Similarly, in linguistics we recognize that a particular string of words is nonsense rather than a sentence, or that one way of stating something is clearer than another. These judgments presuppose that there are norms in these aspects, even if those who make such judgments cannot state exactly what they are.

Third, a norm is not an absolute perfection as was the pagan Greek idea of a Form. It should not be thought of as a changeless and perfect model for justice, or clarity, or beauty, or whatnot. If it were, then everything would have to copy it exactly to conform to it, and all the things which conformed to it would be exactly alike. Rather, a norm is that part of an aspect's order which serves as a standard to guide the things and activities qualified by that aspect. For this reason many actions, thoughts, and artifacts may all equally conform to the norm of an aspect and yet be quite different. For example, performances of a symphony may differ and still be equally beautiful, different statements may be equally kind, and different judgments or actions be equally just.[1]

There are a number of problems for sociology which center around norms, especially as to whether norms are subjective or objective, and whether they can (or should) be dispensed with in social theory. The subjectivist view is that there are no norms in reality, but merely the subjective feelings and biases which individual theorists bring to their work, or that individuals and societies posit as arbitrary guides to behavior. So subjectivists see the inclusion of norms in any social theory as unscientific. The chief argument for this position is that there is a wide disagreement over exactly what the norms are, and no clear-cut way to settle the disagreements. So the conclusion is that norms cannot be objectively real, and that sociology must stick only to descriptions of the social facts (what "is"), and eschew all normative evaluation (what "ought to be"). Among those who take this approach, however, there is also disagreement about just what the sociological "bare facts" are, once all normative judgments are supposedly stripped away.

In the classical objectivist theory of Aristotle, norms do have a basis in reality. This basis is thought to be the same as the basis for the laws of the "natural" aspects: both laws and norms are statements we formulate to express the nature of a thing as guaranteed by its Form. Although not all objective views of norms are committed to Aristotle's theory of Forms, they are all committed to saying that there is an important sense in which norms can be directy "read" from the book of experience. They then supply arguments to defend their concepts of what the norms are, and to show that it is not really possible to exclude all normative judgments from social theory.

As in theory of reality, our idea of a cosmic law framework gives us a distinctive direction of thought which steers a course different from both subjectivism and objectivism. Since we hold that all things in creation function under all the aspectual laws alike, including their norms, we utterly reject the position that norms of linguistics, economics, art, justice, ethics, etc., are nothing more than subjective biases. Though people do disagree over exact statements of the norms of some aspects, there is no way anyone can avoid the general recognition that human acts and social communities are norm-governed in their very nature. For example, the norm of clarity in language or of supply and demand in economics is unavoidable in speech and business; so is the ethical norm of love (treat others as you would be treated) for doing the loving thing, or the norm of justice (that people get what they deserve) for being fair. These norms are principles which rule the leading functions that make human activities and communities possible *even when people engaged in those activities or communities deny and/or disobey them.*

This fact cannot help but be implicitly recognized, even by a theory that explicitly wishes to deny it. The purpose of a business organization cannot help but be led by economic norms even if the subjective intention of its owner is not economic wealth but fame or besting a personal rival. Similarly, the purpose of the marriage institution is still led by norms of love even if one of the partners has married only for economic gain. It is also why when there is no love between husband and wife there is no real marriage; they have a marriage "in name only." Likewise, the members of a family may in fact hate one another rather than conform to the ethical norms of love. But in that case, everyone recognizes that it is an ab-normal family. Or, again, the purpose embedded in the leading function of a synagogue or church is governed by fiduciary norms of faith even if some of their members participate in those institutions purely for social prestige. This is why we maintained that there is a purpose ruled by the norms of the leading function of acts and artifacts which is unavoidably embedded in their nature. Were these norm-governed, structural purposes eliminated from our view, we would cease to recognize these acts and artifacts as *human* acts or communities and thus omit the greater part of what they *are.* What, for instance, would be left of our understanding of a business if every reference to economic norms were eliminated? What would be left of our understanding of marriage or family if all reference to love were excised? What would be left of our understanding of a synagogue or church if we ignored the norms and purposes of faith? The very *concepts* of these communities would be stripped of their most essential characteristics!

One interesting consequence of our concept of structural purposes embedded in leading functions is that it allows our theory to make sense of criminal activities and communities in a way other theories cannot. A criminal syndicate, for instance, is still structured by economic norms which lead its economic purpose, even though the conduct of its business deliberately disobeys the norm of justice reflected in the legal statutes of the state. In fact, no organization can even be recognized as *criminal* unless the norm of justice has been invoked to make that judgment. Similarly, if we try to explain the rate of crime in terms of poor housing, poverty, and other factors, these conditions can only be recognized for what athey are by the way they violate social and economic norms. To call housing "poor" or an economic condition "poverty" is to make a normative judgment.

The same holds true for other social institutions and organizations as well. A state may act illegally, but it will still have a legal structural purpose led by the norm of justice. This is why the crimes of a government or government officials seem the more reprehensible to us: they violate the very purpose that is qualified by the leading function of that institution. The same is true of a political party whose structural purpose is to generate trust in the policies and people it wishes to have direct the state. For this reason it is qualified by a fiduciary leading function. Nevertheless, a political party may violate the trust people place in it, and may even guide the state into violating its own structural purpose of justice (think of the Nazi party). Nevertheless, the norms cannot be ignored. It is a common saying that even criminal organizations have their own internal ethical and legal rules to which they adhere, so that there is "honor among thieves." Even the most violently anarchistic organization would quickly fall apart if it became devoid of all observance of norms of fairness or trust among its own members.

We are therefore in agreement with the part of the objectivist position which holds that norms are real and cannot be ignored even if we try. In other ways, however, we must disagree with the classical objectivist position. For instance, we cannot agree that norms are only extrapolations from the nature(s) of things, so that those natures make the norms possible. Our theory holds instead that there is a distinct law side to creation, the norms of which exist whether or not there are things of a particular nature. Thus we see the matter in reverse from objectivism: it is not the natures of things that make laws and norms possible, but it is the law framework that determines the distinctive natures of types of things. For if norms were merely our summaries of the self-contained natures of things, *it would be impossible for any thing to disobey those norms without violating its very nature and thus becoming something else.*[2] So objectivism cannot account for the fact that individual activities and communities can retain their identity while disobeying norms.

This is why we say that norms must be regarded as a distinct side of reality, not identical with the things, acts, and communities they govern. So we do not call the purpose of an act or community as it is normed by its leading function, an "objective" purpose. The normative purposes included in the leading functions of human acts and artifacts do not reside in the *objects* of our experience any more than they reside in us as experiencing *subjects.* This is why I called them "structural" purposes, referring to the cosmic law framework whose type laws determine the structural order of every created individual.

Traditional objectivism has regarded human reason as autonomous and neutral in its reading of norms from the natures of things. This is why the severe disagreements about norms count against the objectivist's position. For if norms are really "read" from the natures of things we experience, and theoretical reasoning is neutral, why doesn't everyone see them alike? By contrast, we deny that norms and normative structural purposes are interpreted in a neutral fashion. Instead, we contend that beyond their immmediate intuitive recognition in pretheoretical experience, norms will be understood (and misunderstood) quite differently depending on the religious belief which is presupposed by the view of reality which controls their interpretation. A reductionist view of reality will always overestimate any norms closely associated with the aspect(s) supposed to be the nature of reality, and will correspondingly underestimate or deny the reality of those which are least compatible with its reductive view. Thus, the interpretation—and to some extent even the recognition—of norms is hindered or aided by a philosophical perspective which is in turn controlled by some religious belief. For this reason, the disagreements which are so problematic for the objectivists do not count against the law framework theory at all. On the contrary, our theory expects and accounts for such disagreements.

By the same token, however, we do not see such disagreements as supporting the conclusion of the subjectivist. The fact that people can disagree about norms no more shows that norms do not exist than disagreements over the color of a thing show that there are really no colors. Two people may look at the same object in the same light at the same time and still disagree on whether it is more green than blue. But this does not prove that colors are merely our subjective biases rather than real (passive) sensory qualities of things. At the same time, it should not be overlooked that there is wide agreement on the most general norms of several aspects.

Take, for instance, the impressive similarity in the ways the world religions and greatest moral teachers have stated basic ethical axioms, and the fact that certain specific ethical rules (sexual prohibitions and rules against murder) are found in every human society yet discovered. Similarly, there are norms of justice which have also had a wide cross-cultural recognition for thousands of years.

In sum, the program of eliminating norms in order to deal with the pure facts is, we believe, destructive of social theory and impossible in fact. What "ought" to be is always part of what "is." Norms, like natural laws, have an existence distinct from both subject and object with God as their source; he alone is the law-giver to creation. This is why norms can and do continue to govern creation even when people exercise their freedom to disobey them. Any theory which attempts to pare down human activities and communities to the "bare facts" by eliminating norms is attempting something which is self-defeating. To strip away their norm-governed structural purposes and ignore their leading functions is to destroy their specifically human and social character and render them incomprehensible.

3. Individualism vs. Collectivism

One of the dominating problems of social theory is whether to take an individualist or a collectivist view of society. In fact, every writer on the subject has leaned in one or the other direction for such a long time, that it is now a commonplace assumption that no one can help but be one or the other.

Individualists insist that the basic social unit is the individual person, because individuals can exist without communities, while communities are formed by, and comprised of, individuals. The individualist, Thomas Hobbes, for instance, held that human life was originally completely "solitary," with the formation of social communities coming later. The motive for forming them, he thought, was that a solitary life was also "poor, nasty, brutish and short." He did, however, believe that communities, once formed, were realities whose natures it is important to understand. Some individualists, however, have gone so far as to say that there are no such realities as social communities; all that really exist are individuals and the agreements they make with each other.

Collectivists, on the other hand, assert that some form of community is the basic social reality, since that is what produces and sustains individuals. They view the individual as literally a *part* of a larger social whole, without which the part could not exist at all. For example, Aristotle said:

> Thus the state is by nature clearly prior to the family and the individual, since the whole is of necessity prior to the part.... The proof... is that the individual, when isolated, is not self-sufficient... (*Politics*, bk I, ch 2)

This debate has very serious consequences for both social theory and practice, particularly in connection with our understanding of the more important institutions and organizations of society. Let us deal first with the question of whether social communities are to be considered real.

Even though we do not usually speak of an institution or organization as a "thing," that does not mean they are not real: we do not usually speak of a person as a "thing" either, but that does not mean people are not real.

Surely social communities are recognizable as distinct unities, just as things and people are. Moreover, they must be something over and above the individuals who are their members, since in the case of all social communities except marriage, their identity persists even when their members change. In addition, we have seen that social communities function in all the aspects of experience and have differing qualifying functions determining their natures. In all these respects they are the same as the realities we usually call "things," and so should be regarded as equally real as rocks or trees or the people who are their members.

The heart of the individualist theory is the claim that individuals are more basic than communities. The sense of "basic" intended is the same as that which occurred in reductionist theories of reality. It means that individuals can exist without communities but communities cannot exist without individuals. This, however, is an extremely implausible claim. As Aristotle pointed out, a solitary individual cannot survive. Perhaps the easiest way to see the truth of this point is to think of the extended period of time that human infants are utterly helpless and require constant care and attention. During this time the nursing mother also would need protection and provision of food, so that without some social arrangement they could not both survive. Of course, we can well imagine that an isolated adult could survive in the wild, but that is only because of the knowledge and skills such a person would have already acquired by having been raised in human society. Furthermore, it is pure speculation that there ever was a time when people lived in complete isolation without any social community whatever as Hobbes claimed, or without any ruling authority as was claimed by another famous individualist, John Locke. So far as we know, people have always lived in families, tribes, clans, or villages, with some sort of recognized authority, rules, and traditions.

On the other hand, the collectivist position sees every person as literally a part of an all-inclusive social whole. This position is completely at odds with the nature of social communities. The social community is not self-sufficient in relation to individuals, since it cannot exist without individuals any more than individuals can exist without it. So our first objection to collectivism attacks its fundamental claim. The collectivist theory is wrong because *individuals and social communities exist in a mutual correlation in which neither can exist without the other. Neither is "basic" to the other in the sense required by both individualism and collectivism, because neither was ever the source of the other. Both were created by, and depend on, God.*

Moreover, from the biblical point of view, it is abhorrent to regard individuals merely as parts of any human social community. They are not merely "cogs in the machinery" of the state, or "cells on the organism" of the human family. The most uniquely human thing about people, from the biblical standpoint, is their capacity for fellowship with God. This was the very purpose for their creation, according to Genesis, and it is this which makes it possible for humans to be members of the spiritual kingdom of God which transcends every humanly formed community. This is so pervasively true of humans that even when they reject the true God they cannot help but believe in something else as divine. When this happens, they become members of a corresponding spiritual kingdom of false belief, which also transcends every humanly formed community. For this reason, we must insist that although humans always live and function in social communities, there is no humanly formed community of which they are nothing more than parts.

For these same reasons, we maintain that although humans function actively in all the aspects of creation, human nature is not merely the sum of these functions. As we noticed in chapter 9, human nature is "something more" than all these functions since it resides in the human "heart," or self, which has a unique relation to the creator who transcends creation. Therefore, unlike all other creatures, humans have no single qualifying function. Even their function in the fiduciary aspect, which expresses their faith, is not identical with their heart's relation to God. Rather, it is the heart which directs the exercise of every act of faith. The heart's relation to God thus extends beyond created reality to the uncreated creator, and is that which most centrally characterizes humans: they are essentially *religious* beings. This does not mean that humans, both individually and collectively, do not perform acts and take part in social communities which do have qualifying functions. It is rather to insist that there is another relation to human life than those which are aspectually qualified, a relation which is the ultimate basis of human existence, while the idea of that relation is the ultimate basis of the interpretation of human existence.

Social communities, by contrast, each have a particular qualifying function. They do not have a nature, apart from human beings, by which they can stand in a direct relation to God. They are, to be sure, dominated by norms, ideas, traditions, etc., which serve God or which serve a God substitute. But even those that are qualified by a fiduciary function and conduct worship cannot have the relation to God that a human person has, nor do they have an eternal destiny as persons do. Even the eternal community of believers (the Kingdom of God) that has already begun as God's rule in the hearts of believers, has not yet actually been established as a multi-aspectual reality in creation, and will only be established by God himself. Thus, there is a crucial difference between the nature of any social community and human nature which, again, forbids our construing a person as nothing more than a part of some social whole. Thus, from the biblical standpoint, we must reject the fundamental claims of both the individualist and the collectivist.

For these same reasons, we must also reject the major consequences of each of these traditional theories. For example, individualist theories regard all social communities as artifacts formed by the voluntary association of free individuals who have contracted among themselves to promote some value they hold dear. As a consequence, these theories usually assume that such social contracts will protect the worth and welfare of the individual as being of prime importance and regard the welfare of the larger community as secondary.[3] Collectivist theories, by contrast, argue that individuals are always dependent on social communities, both biologically and culturally. On their view, social communities are not freely invented by people who once did without them, and could do without them if they wished. This usually results in their estimating the worth and welfare of the social community as not only more important than that of any one individual, but also more important than all the sub-communities contained within the larger whole. It is in this way that each theory's answers to the question about whether the individual creates the community or the community creates the individual generate another important difference in social theory, namely, a difference of social priorities. In case of conflict between the good of the social whole and the good of the individual, one theory gives priority to the individual while the other gives priority to the community. Unlike our theory, neither side can strike a genuine balance between the individual and society because each has started by assigning a social priority to one or the other.

This controversy over where the social priority is to be placed does not merely result in vague differences in the attitudes of those on the two sides. It is not simply that in a court case a judge holding the individualist view would tend to lean toward favoring the rights of the individual, while a judge who is a collectivist would tend to lean toward favoring the welfare of society. Such a result, all by itself, would be important enough, and would cause significant differences in the way cases are decided. The significance of the two positions is even greater, however, in that each position *gives a particular slant to the very idea of justice which underlies the judicial procedures and laws which are adopted.*

To appreciate the extent to which this is so, consider that the collectivist views of Plato, Aristotle, and Marx, *defined* justice as the maintenance of harmony among the parts of a society for the preservation of society as a whole. In their view this meant that every social community, other than the state, should be totally regulated by the state for the benefit of the state. They took this position because all other communities were supposed to be parts of the state, which was seen as the all-encompassing social whole. Justice is thereby made to be equivalent to whatever tends to preserve the state *in the opinion of the state.* This view therefore sets no limits on what the state may demand or forbid. Consequently it sees human rights as nothing more than whatever freedoms it is in the state's interest to grant. By contrast, the influential individualist theory of Locke held that the core idea of justice is the protection of the property of individuals. It views individuals as the possessors of "natural" moral and legal rights which the state does not give, and which it should not attempt to take away. The only way any natural rights may be justly lost, Locke thought, is if individuals voluntarily agree to surrender them to the state. But since the very idea of justice is equated with the protection of private property in this theory, there is no room left for state concern with *public* justice where private property is not involved.

I will not pursue the consequences of these two traditional positions any further here since they will be criticized in greater detail in the next chapter. For now it is enough to point out how each of the traditional views distorts the meaning of justice by defining it as more fundamentally the preservation of individuals, or of the collective whole of society. On the other hand, our biblical presupposition and law framework theory will deliver us from having to choose between individualism and collectivism. It points out that since the norm of justice resides neither in individual persons nor in the collective whole of society, neither is to be favored over the other in the administration of justice. Instead of narrowly focusing on one or the other, the law framework theory uses a wide-angle lens to apply the norm of justice equally to both individuals and social communities.

4. Parts and Wholes

In dealing with the collectivist position, we briefly noticed that Aristotle defended it with the argument that a whole is basic to (his term was "prior to") any of its parts. He made this point in reference to the relation of individuals to the state—a point the biblical view of humans vehemently denies. But there still remains the question of whether certain social communities are actually parts of others. This question is important because all social theories accept the idea that since a part is dependent on the whole, any community which is part of another is to be subordinate to that other. Thus any communities which are parts of another are to be ranked lower in *authority,* and the community comprising the whole is given the authority to regulate all the communities which are its parts. This question therefore needs to be answered by any theory of society whether collectivist, individualist, or biblical.

I stress the importance of this question for *any* social theory, because it has generally been associated more with collectivist theories since they almost always regard some single institution as the overarching community which encompasses all individuals and all other communities as its parts. This is how they defend their chosen institution as the supreme authority in human social life. Individualist theories, on the other hand, have a reputation for resisting any all-encompassing social authority. Because they regard individuals as creators of communities rather than vice versa, individualists claim that people have rights which exempt them in certain ways from the authority of any community. But merely exempting individuals from certain sorts of authority will never, by itself, prevent some communities from being subsumed as parts of another. Individualist as well as collectivist theories have invariably ended up seeing certain communities ranked higher than others in authority, which results in a social *hierarchy* of communities with a supreme community at the top to encompass and rule all the others.[4] So our question is unavoidable for every social theory alike: how may we tell if one community is or is not a part of another? How can we know when we are confronted with a genuine part-whole relation and when we are not?

In keeping with our law framework theory, we may now appeal to the idea of each thing's qualifying function, along with the networking of aspectual and type laws, to answer this question. For it appears that the law framework theory can provide new insight into the problem of determining when a genuine part-whole relationship exists by allowing us to make some important distinctions which show that many relations often spoken of as part-whole relations are really not that at all.

We will start by accepting the traditional view, defended by Aristotle, that parts cannot exist separately from the wholes of which they are part. The sort of separation this view denies to parts seems to include two elements, namely, that a part must participate in the internal organization and functioning of a whole, and that it cannot exist apart from the whole. Of course, neither of these two conditions taken by itself is sufficient to identify a genuine part-whole relation. Simply not being able to exist apart from thing Y will not make thing X part of Y, since there are whole-whole relations in which one or both cannot exist without the other. For instance, a tree is an individual whole having its own internal parts, but it cannot exist separated from the earth. It is not, however, *part* of the earth. Likewise, simply functioning in the internal organization of Y does not necessarily make X a part of Y. A small stone can function in a bird's digestive tract to help grind its food, but is still not *part* of the bird. But while neither of these conditions alone is sufficient to identify a genuine part-whole relation, traditional theories have regarded the combination of the two as sufficient to do the job.

We must disagree. We have now seen that humans cannot exist apart from some community, and that they do function in the internal organization of communities, while they may not be regarded as mere parts of any community. What needs to be added to the traditional conditions is that humans do not *share the same qualifying function* with any community. Thus the new condition necessary for sorting out genuine part-whole relations is that genuine parts always have the same qualifying function as the wholes of which they are parts. For one thing to be a part of another, then, it will have to: (1) depend on the other for existence, (2) function in the internal organization of the other, and also (3) have the same qualifying function as the other.

There are cases in which, in ordinary speech, we call one thing part of another only because it satisfies condition two by playing a role in its internal organization or functioning. For instance, it is ordinary to say that a large rock in the corner of the yard is a *part* of the garden. But even the traditional part-whole theory would have had to reject the rock as genuinely a part of the garden since the rock can exist independent of it. Our new concept agrees with this, but gives an additional reason: the rock is physically qualified, while the plants (which really are parts) of the garden are biologically qualified. It is still true that the rock is *included* in the garden, of course, but it is included as a whole within a greater whole, rather than as a *part* of a greater whole. So wherever one thing functions within another but fails any of our rules for being a part of that other, we will call it a *subwhole* of the other. And we will speak of the greater wholes which include subwholes as "encapsulating" them, and the greater wholes as "capsulate wholes." These terms are intended to convey the notion of wholes included in a larger container, or capsule, without actually being parts of the container. And we will now speak of the relation of the sub-wholes to their capsulate whole as "capsulate" relations to distinguish them from part-whole relations.[5]

Our understanding gives results that are unusual relative to the traditional part-whole theory. To illustrate this, take the example of a marble sculpture. The sculpture is an artifact having as its qualifying function the correlation of a cultural foundational function and an aesthetical leading function. How are we to understand the relation of the marble to the work of art as a whole? The marble of which the sculpting is made does not, by itself, possess an active function in any aspect above the physical. Our new criteria require us to say that in this case the marble, as the natural material of the sculpture, is not a part of the work of art but is a subwhole related within a capsulate whole. This allows us to explain the distinctly new whole produced by carving the marble, without having to say either that the marble is *part* of the sculpture (its parts are its head, arms, legs, torso, etc.), or that no new whole has been formed and that it is essentially still just a piece of marble (as Aristotle was forced to say).[6]

Moreover, the relation of the piece of encapsulated marble to the whole sculpture shows another characteristic that is typical between subwholes and their encapsulate whole: no amount of knowledge of the nature of the subwholes existing within an encapsulate whole can ever yield knowledge of the nature of the capsulate whole. This is precisely because the two wholes have different natures owing to the fact that their qualifying functions are different. In this instance it means that knowing all the physics there is to know about marble will never yield any information about the sculpture as a work of art.

Another illustration of part-whole relations may make this clearer. Consider the relation of atoms to a plant in which they exist. Since atoms of every chemical element existed before life arose on earth, and since atoms are not destroyed when the plant is, there is no question that atoms can exist separated from the plant. Moreover, atoms have only a physical qualifying function while the plant exceeds the physical by having a biological qualifying function. The atoms are not, therefore, parts of the plant but stand in a relation of subwhole to a capsulate whole. By contrast, the relation of the plant's cells to the plant as a whole is a different story. The cells function in the internal organization of the plant, and they have the same (biological) leading function as the plant. Therefore their relation to the plant is a genuine part-whole relation.

In every case we can think of, subwholes which are bound together in a capsulate whole retain their own identity since, considered apart from their encapsulation, their qualifying function remains the same. But when functioning within a capsulate whole whose qualifying function exceeds theirs, their own qualifying functions are overridden by that of the capsulate whole. That is, the subwholes exist and function within a whole which has properties and a leading function which none of them possessed when they existed separately. For this reason, subwholes cannot be considered the causes of the capsulate wholes in which they are bound. They are necessary conditions for such wholes, but cannot themselves also be sufficient conditions for them. The additional factor needed to account for capsulate wholes is that they are made possible by a type law. It is the type laws that range across aspects not only to determine how properties of different aspects may be combined in individual things, but also how things with one aspectual qualification can be encapsulated into a larger whole with a different qualification.

Respecting social communities, our definitions of the relations of part to whole and subwhole to encapsulate whole are applied in the same way. One social community is part of another if and only if it cannot exist without the other, functions in the internal organization of the other, and has the same leading function as the other. Otherwise, no matter how much one community may be under the influence (or even the complete control) of another, it is not part of it. Likewise, one community is a subwhole encapsulated within another when: (1) it functions in the internal organization of the other, and (2) has a different leading function which is overridden by the other's, even though (3) it could exist apart from the other. When these definitions are applied to various social communities, the result is very important. For while there are cases in which such communities are actually parts of another, *the major types of social institutions and organizations never are parts of one another.* A corporation, for example, may have within it separately organized divisions or subsidiary companies, which are actually parts of it. And a state may have parts such as provinces, shires, departments, counties, townships, districts, boroughs, and municipalities. The national army and the courts are also parts of the state. But a business can never be a *part* of a state. The two have different leading functions, and therefore different natures and structural purposes. Their internal organizing principle (type law) is also different, so that they are irreducibly different types of social communities.

The same holds true of the relation of family to state. A family has a distinct (ethical) leading function and is structured by a distinct type law. It can exist and function where there is no state. Thus, even when it exists within the territory governed by a particular state, it can never be one of that state's parts. A proof of this is that each member of a family may at the same time be a citizen of a different state, which would be impossible if the family was part of the state. Similarly, a church or synagogue can never be part of a state or of a business or of a family, any more than any of them can be parts of a church or synagogue. All these institutions and organizations stand in whole-whole relations to one another, not part-whole relations.

Neither is there reason to suppose that all the major types of institutions and organizations of society are included in some encapsulate whole as subwholes. What would that encapsulate whole be? The most oft-nominated candidate is the state, but if the state were really all-inclusive, each of the encapsulated subwholes would then have their leading functions overridden by the state's leading function. This means the encapsulated communities would cease to function in the distinctive ways which correspond to their distinctive structural purposes. Instead they would all be absorbed into the purpose of legislating and enforcing public justice, and there would be no communities left to accomplish the purposes of earning a living, producing art, educating the next generation, or expressing faith. The point is simple: either we have distinct communities or we do not. But they cannot retain their distinct structural purposes while at the same time functioning as parts or subwholes of an all-encompassing social community. For this reason the very ideas of a state business, or a state church, or a state school are just as incoherent as the idea of a state family. To the extent that an organization or institution is a church, a school, or a business, it is precisely *not* a state and vice versa. Of course, a state may choose to *support* another community, say, a school, as may a church, labor union, foundation, business, or family. But in every case the support should be afforded in the recognition that a school has a distinct nature from any community supporting it, so that its own internal authority cannot be assimilated to that of the supporting organization.

5. Sphere Sovereignty

These results of our law framework theory lead us to reject any hierarchical view of society as a whole. This is so whether the hierarchy is thought of as having many levels or is simply the difference between the all-encompassing supreme institution and the communities it encompasses. Since the distinctive natures of social communities show how seldom one can be part or subwhole to another, we are led to a structurally pluralistic view of society. This pluralism is the social parallel to the pluralism in our theory of reality: just as there is an irreducible plurality of aspects and no aspect is more real than any other (the cause of any other), so, too, there are irrecducible "spheres" of social life to which the natures of the various communities correspond. These spheres correspond to the aspects which qualify social communities. Using the relations among their qualifying aspects as a guide, our theory says that no social community qualified by one aspect is more real than another community qualfied by another aspect. This means that none includes the others as parts, so there can be no single all-encompassing community in human society. Thus there is no institution which may rightfully claim to have an all-encompassing authority. Instead, there is a plurality of types of communities, each of which enjoys an internal sovereignty in its own social sphere. By "sovereignty" I mean that since each community has its own distinctive structural purpose and internal organization set by its type law, it must also have the authority to make its own rules of operation, and its own decisions about how to fulfill its structural purpose. So "sphere sovereignty,"[7] is the social principle that communities whose structural purpose is qualified by one aspect are to be especially protected from interference from communities qualified by a different aspect.

It should be emphasized right away, however, that this principle is not merely negative. It does not mean only that there are external limits to the authority of each distinctive community which therefore set a "wall of separation" between their spheres of authority. Since the negative limits themselves are set by the internal nature of each community, the principle has the positive aim of allowing each to fulfill its distinctive structural purpose. Thus, sphere sovereignty is not simply a practical piece of advice that says: unless the distinctive character and purposes of communities are recognized, there will be strife between them in any given society. Nor is it a matter of allowing each a niche of noninterference because, say, business has often flourished when that was done. Rather, the sphere limitations of the authority of each type of community are set by the nature of its type, so that over-stepping those limits is harmful to itself as well as other communities.

The idea of sphere sovereignty will now serve as the guiding principle for our general overview of how all the various communities of society should relate to one another. Just as the aspects are distinct, mutually irreducible, and yet inseparable, so, too, are the spheres of social life. The various communities are therefore seen as relating in these ways because they arise out of diverse human needs, abilities, and concerns which are qualified by diverse aspects. For example, we all have concerns about our physical safety, our biological necessities such as food and shelter, and about our sensory perception of the world around us including our avoidance of pain and the enjoyment of pleasure. Often the sciences studying these aspects, which were lower on our list, are called "natural sciences" while we speak of the sciences investigating the aspects higher on our list, such as sociology and economics, as "social sciences." But it is important to notice that the concerns qualified by the aspects studied by social sciences are also "natural"; that is, although the ways we respond to these concerns are our own creations, the concerns themselves are natural to us rather than invented by us. They reflect the way our needs and abilities were designed by God to correspond to the aspects of the created universe.

For example, because of the order of creation all humans inevitably have a natural interest in social matters (in the narrower sense of "social") which results in the development of styles of dress, levels of social status, customs of politeness, etc. They have economic concerns centered on the making of a living, and all express their aesthetical needs or abilities by the creation or enjoyment of art and sport. Likewise, all people are concerned with justice, love, the education of their children, and the exercise of their faith. It is our contention that since these aspects of life are natural, no people can entirely suppress them. Rather they are so pervasive and important to human life that people inevitably form communities to promote and protect them.[8] Nevertheless, it should be clear that the spheres of social sovereignty do not correspond to different groups of people. No one can fail to be concerned with any sphere, whether they are members of a community devoted to its interest or not. And the same people who are members of one such community (say, a state) may also be members of others (e.g., employees of a business, members of a synagogue or church, subscribers to the opera, students of a school, etc.)

In order to make clearer the social overview provided by our principle of sphere sovereignty, it will now be applied to a single issue, that of *the nature and source of authority in society.* This focus will allow us to see how the sphere sovereignty principle answers the questions: By what authority does one person (or group of them) tell others what to do? Where does such authority come from?

There have been many answers given to these questions. One of the most influential answers was Aristotle's theory that the nature of authority lies in rationality and virtue. Those who have the most intelligence and are ethically virtuous should therefore rule the rest. Another enormously influential answer, proposed by Marx, is that the authority to rule resides in economic ownership. This means that those who have the wealth and own the means of producing the necessities of life not only inevitably will, but *should,* rule. Yet another view is that of monarchy, which holds that authority is biologically inherited. On this view, a person rightfully tells others what to do because that person is the nearest of kin to the last person to have that authority. Still another theory is that it is military power which is identical with authority, so that might makes right. And many modern theories follow Rousseau by vesting authority in people's wills, giving the will of the majority or the "general will" the right to rule.

In all these theories the nature of authority is identified with some particular human function: reasoning, acting morally, making money, reproducing, exerting military force, or acts of willing. Each of these is an answer to the question of the *nature* of authority, and each identifies that nature with a particular aspect (or with the human will): authority is fundamentally of a rational, or moral, or economic, or biological, or volitional character. Once this is done, however, the issue of the *source* of authority is also decided. In each case it is seen as originating in a particular function of human nature, which should therefore dominate the whole of human life. For example, the basic nature of authority may be thought to reside in the will of the majority. In that case there may still be other kinds of authorities in society such as the authority of parents in a family, or of a teacher in a school, or of the owner of a business. But these can only exist, ultimately, because it is the majority will to allow them. They must be viewed as subsidiary authorities derived from the fundamental authority.

In the theories of the past, whatever community was supposed to have the kind of authority which is basic to all other kinds of authority was seen as the community which includes the others as its parts. In the history of Western culture the state has most often been accorded that status both in theory and in practice, and this is still true. But no matter which community is assigned this role by a theory, the view of authority it presupposes is reductionist, and the view of society which results is hierarchical and—literally—*totalitarian.* For any community supposed to be the source of all authority is thereby taken to have all other social communities under its authority *in all of their aspects,* and so to be supreme over the totality of human life.

Even individualist theories cannot avoid this totalitarian result once they accept the nature of authority as residing in a particular human function and therefore in a particular institution. For once all authority in the other communities is regarded as derivative from the supreme authority, the other communities themselves cannot help being viewed as *parts* (or at least subwholes) of the supreme community. As we already saw, individualist theories try to avoid totalitarianism by finding some respects in which individuals are exempted from the authority of the supreme institution. But if a particular community is regarded as embodying the kind of authority that is basic to all other kinds, such exemptions become not only hard to find in theory, but impossible to obtain in practice.

The classic statement of the theory that the state is the community with the supreme all-encompassing authority is found in Aristotle's *Politics:*

Every state is a community of some kind, and every community is established with a view to some good; for humans always act in order to obtain that which they think good. But, if all communities aim at some good, the state or political community, which is the highest of all, and which embraces all the rest, aims, and in a greater degree than any other, at the highest good. (*Politics* bk. I, ch. 1)

The schematic drawing in Figure 6 may help represent the hierarchical, and thus totalitarian, overview of society presupposed by the quote, as it applies to modern society.

Now every totalitarian theory of society, identifying the nature and source of authority with some particular aspect of human nature, is utterly at odds with the biblical view that all authority has its source in God. Scripture repeatedly states that all authorities on earth are derivative of God's authority. Thus authority in human life does not have any *one* nature at all. Within creation there is no

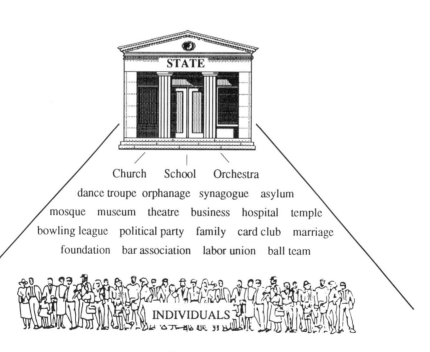

Fig. 6

one supreme kind of authority, because only God has that. Instead, the Scriptures speak of many different kinds of earthly author*ities*. They specifically mention the authority of the husband in a marriage, the parents in a family, the owner in a business, the ruling powers in the state, and the authorities in a synagogue or church. The implication of this for theories of authority seems clear. No single kind of authority is the only kind or the source of all other kinds. Rather, the same nonreductionist view holds for the different aspectual senses of authority as holds for the aspects themselves—and for the same reason: all are created by God, so that the ultimate source of them all is outside creation rather than in any aspect of it. One consequence of this is that it can never be right to suppose that people (or the majority will) are the source or creators of authority. Vote of the majority may be the best way to select those who are to *bear* authority, but it does not create the authority. This is why, on the biblical view, it is never right to defy a genuine authority. We may regard the bearers of authority as unworthy to bear it and seek to replace them with other authority-bearers, but the authority itself may never rightfully be disrespected.

Thus we maintain that our theory of irreducible aspects as distinct social spheres has biblical presuppositions. The only single overarching authority is God's, while within creation there is an irreducible plurality of kinds of authority, each delimited by its own social sphere. The owners of a business, for example, do exercise their authority in virtue of their ownership. But that is because a business is an economically qualified organization and so has an economically qualified authority. The authority of parents in a family, by contrast, does not reside in the fact that they own the home in which the family lives or even in the fact that they economically support the children. It resides in the ethically qualified relation which exists between parent and child in virtue of the way God has created humans. That is, it is an authority qualified by love. So even if the family is not supported by the parents but subsists on welfare, the authority of the parents is normatively intact. On the other hand, a school is a logically qualified organization. By means of education, our concepts of ourselves and the world around us are expanded and enriched. So the authority in a school is an authority based on competence in knowledge; it belongs with those who are expert in the concepts and theories to be taught. The state, too, has its own distinct kind of authority, an authority qualified by justice—more specifically, *public* justice.[9] Its ability to carry out justice must extend to the whole of the public within its territory, of course. Nevertheless, its authority is delimited to but one aspect of that public. At the same time, it is precisely because justice is an aspect of all individuals and communities, the state need not subsume them all as its parts in order to extend its proper authority to all. But if state authority is elevated above all others on the excuse that it is needed for the state to ensure justice to all individuals and communities, totalitarian consequences cannot be avoided—not even by making the state a democracy. Once the state is believed to have an unlimited and overriding authority, it will matter little whether its authority is vested in one person, a governing group, or all the citizens.

The last point is worth dwelling on for a moment because so often democracy is spoken of as though that *form* of government alone is sufficient to guarantee the freedoms we enjoy. It is not. Simply giving everyone a vote does not ensure a single right or freedom. Unless the authority of government is limited in principle, democracy will only guarantee a tyranny of the majority worse than that of a single dictator. (Even with modern surveillance methods it is hard for a dictator to keep track of what everyone is doing, but we are always surrounded by the majority.) What is needed to ensure liberty is the idea of a *limited* state: a state restricted as to what it may make laws about so that there are bounds to its legal competency. And this is precisely the point on which our belief in God guides us. It frees us from reductionist views of human nature and society. It allows us to analyze the true nature of the state as a social institution, and to determine its limits as set by its own nature. Thus on our view the state is not limited merely by what it can get away with or only by the rule that it may not interfere with freedom of religion. Rather, it is limited by its own leading function as set by the law framework of creation. For these reasons it is not too much to say that more rights and freedoms can be preserved where the sphere sovereignty idea prevails even if the state is governed by a king, than where the government is a democracy which operates without any idea of its being restricted to a distinct sphere of authority.[10]

Sometimes people have suggested that totalitarianism can be prevented if we simply limit state authority by saying it must not interfere in the *internal* affairs of other communities. In this way, we would not have to involve ourselves with anything so complicated as a theory of social spheres. Under this guideline, the state would regulate all the external relations among communities, so long as it did not interfere with their internal operations. This proposal is not only mistaken, but preposterous. The internal affairs of a community can never be exempt from the authority of the state where matters of public justice are concerned. It is not true that the state may not prosecute fraud which takes place within a family or church, for instance. Whenever the justitial function of any individual or community impinges on the order of public justice, it falls within the proper purview of the state. By the same token, however, the state may not properly regulate every aspect of external, public life. The internal vs. external distinction is therefore not adequate to prevent a totalitarian state. Only the recognition of the aspectual differences among distinct social spheres can ensure that.

In fact, our law framework theory may now be taken a step further. According to it, we must recognize not only the differences in authorities when they are qualified by different spheres, but also as they are structured differently in communities of distinct types. Even communities which have the same aspectual qualification, and function within the same social sphere, can show variations in the structuring and exercise of the same aspectual kind of authority. Marriage and the family both have the ethical aspect of love as their leading function, but they are not the only communities which are ethically qualified. An orphanage or home for the aged is also led by the ethical norm of love. Yet the authority by which these organizations are governed is not structured or exercised in the same way as is the authority in a marriage or family; even though they have the same ethical leading function they are communities of a different structural type. The delimiting of authorities envisioned by our principle therefore only *begins* by assigning each community to the sphere of operation qualified by its leading function. Variations in types of authorities must also be recognized within the same sphere. Thus while the principle of sphere sovereignty rules out the interference of one social community in the affairs of another where each has a different qualifying sphere, the concept of type laws extends the same mutual noninterference to communities having a distinct type of authority even within the same sphere.

By now it should be clear why our saying that only God has supreme authority, and that all authority ultimately comes from God, is not to be confused with any sort of theocracy. It does not mean that God himself should rule the state, or businesses, or schools, or families. God is the source of authority in our social life through the way he has created humans and the world. On the one hand, this means that there is such a natural need for authority implanted in human nature, that if established authorities are destroyed people inevitably set up new ones. On the other hand, it means that the kinds of authorities people need and recognize correspond to the different spheres of human life. Just as we opposed the notion that the dependency of creation on God was mediated through any one or two of its aspects, so, too, we oppose the idea that God has funneled his authority to all of creation through any one institution such as the church or the state. Each kind of authority that exists in the different spheres of life is directly dependent on God, and none is derived from any another. On our view, then, *there is no single social institution or authority which is supreme over all the rest.* While sphere sovereignty does not oppose a "local" hierarchy of authorities within any community, it denies every idea of a socially "global" authority or a single all-encompassing institution. Each social community is to have its own kind of sovereignty and integrity in its own sphere, and any institution which claims authority over the totality of society usurps a status which belongs only to God.

This principle was clearly recognized by John Calvin in the sixteenth century. By that time there had been centuries of argument (and fighting) over whether the church or the state was the supreme authority in society. Calvin took neither side. Instead, his position was that while some affairs of life fall under the jurisdiction of the state, and others are matters of the church, *most of life* is not be regulated by either one.[11] This idea of distinct and limited spheres of authority for each institution was one of the motivating presuppositions for many of the great changes in the governments of Europe and North America in the two centuries following Calvin. It was also the basis of the doctrine that both individuals and communities have rights relative to the state which are the counterparts to the limits on the authority of governments. It supplied, for example, a justification for the freedom of a family from invasion by the state (the provision that the state must show evidence of crime to a court in order to obtain a search warrant to

enter a private home). Likewise, it is the foundation of the idea
that a government may not rightfully confiscate privately owned
businesses, and it was the presupposition of the Puritan teaching
that government ought not to repress the free expression of ideas
in speech or print.[12] It was also this idea that was reflected (distortedly) in Thomas Jefferson's expression "a wall of separation
between church and state." I say "distortedly" since no two communities can be completely walled off, though the authority of
each can be limited to its own sphere. In fact, the Calvinist background for the ideas expressed in the Declaration of Independence was recognized by George III of England who, upon reading
it, reportedly exclaimed, "The Calvinist churches in the colonies
have gone wild!"

There cannot be a single schema to represent the sphere sovereignty overview of society, because it is incapable of being conveyed in a two-dimensional diagram. To remedy this, I will offer two
drawings. The first, Figure 7, represents an individual's functioning
in the normative aspects that correspond to the social spheres and
qualify the leading functions of various communities.[13]

In this schema the center of the circle represents the individual
person. Every individual has all the aspects to his or her social life
which are designated by the slices of the circle, whether they actively participate in the corresponding communities or not. Outside each slice are named (some of) the communities which are
qualified by that aspect, communities people form to express, promote, and protect the concerns that aspect qualifies.

The second diagram represents a view of several social communities as they range across aspects, from their foundational to their
leading functions, according to their type laws.

As is evident from even this brief sketch, our social theory
wants to take into account all social communities. Just as the law
framework theory attempts to give an account of the nature of everything from an atom to a sculpture, so its application to a theory
of society does not want to leave out any social community whatever. In this respect it contrasts favorably with those theories
which confine themselves only to the relation of the individual to
government, as did Locke and the American founding fathers.
Many modern theories do not do much better, expanding their
scope to include at most the relations of family, government,

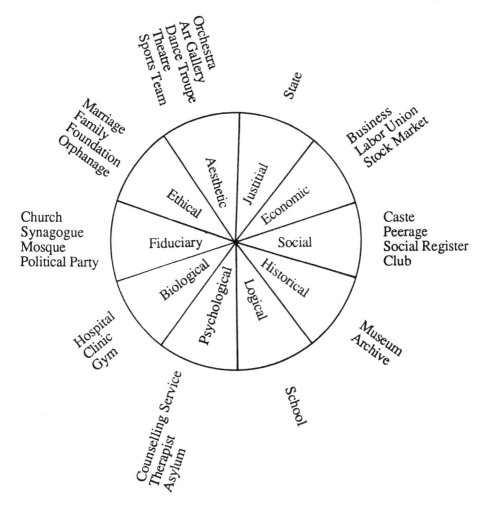

Fig.7

church, and business. As a consequence they invariably miscon-
strue the natures of such organizations as schools, labor unions,
and hospitals, either by subsuming them under the state or regarding them as businesses. Such misunderstandings distort the very
natures of these communities, and do much to harm their effective functioning.

The next chapter will outline a theory of the state which is
guided by both the law framework theory and the principle of

	family	business	state	church or synagogue
fiduciary				L
ethical	L			
justitial			L	
aesthetic				
economic		L		
social				
linguistic				
historical		F	F	F
logical				
sensory				
biotic	F			

F = Foundational function
L = Leading function

sphere sovereignty. In it we will also expand and apply the concept of a type law, so as to arrive at a more detailed account of duties and limits of the state based on a fuller account of its nature. But there is one question concerning the state which is so often raised in connection with the sphere sovereignty idea that I think it should be answered here and now. The question is whether the sphere sovereignty idea of the relations of social communities would not need to be enforced at times, and whether the state would not have to do the enforcing.

The answer to both these questions is "yes." This is only proper since one of the largest benefits of our theory is to be derived from its impact on public justice through legislation. So on our view, guaranteeing the distinctiveness and sphere integrity of all sorts of communities is part of the administration of public justice which is the duty of the state. This does not mean, however, that the state *creates* the sphere boundaries. It only means that it is called upon to observe and enforce them in someting like the way the Supreme Court now attempts to observe and protect constitutional rights in the United States.

This does mean, of course, that the task of enforcing the limits upon the state is entrusted to the state itself. But I see no way around that. And there is risk in entrusting such authority and power to any state no matter how it is conceived. This serves to remind us that the really crucial factor is whether the populace of a given nation—including the officials of government—have their sense of justice and their ideas of social communities guided by ideas of sphere sovereignty and distinct types of communities rather than by some version of the totalitarian idea of society. But even where that is true it will not guarantee the state will never misuse its power. Even though the social and justitial blessings of the sphere sovereignty idea are great, none of its defenders have ever made utopian claims for it. We do not for a moment suppose that even if it were widely believed and rigorously applied by the people and government of a major nation no mistakes would ever be made in its enforcement. We do not believe that, any more than we think that if sphere sovereignty were correctly observed and enforced, all human sin, criminality, poverty, and war would magically disappear. What we do claim is that the biblical principles of our theory are the key to understanding the proper freedoms, rights, and obligations communities have with respect to one an other. Meanwhile, these inter-communal limits, rights, and freedoms are precisely what leave room for delineating the rights and freedoms of individuals in relation to communities, and of individuals in relation to one another.

13

A BIBLICAL THEORY OF THE STATE

1. Introduction

The theory of society sketched in the last chapter may now be brought to bear on political theory, that is, on a theory specifically about the state institution. In referring to this institution, we will not be dealing only with government. A government is the ruling body in a state, as parents are the ruling body in a family or the board of directors is the ruling body in a business. But just as there is more to a family than the parents, and more to a business than the board of directors, there is more to a state than its government. The entire institution of the state includes both government and citizens, and may be defined as: a political community of citizens organized under a government.

Another misunderstanding to avoid is caused by the fact that some states are divided into subdivisions, each of which has its own governing body. As indicated by the definition just offered, however, we will be looking at political communities in their entirety and not merely at their subdivisions. The term 'state' should not, therefore, be thought to refer to any subdivision such as the individual "states" which make up the United States of America. As we will use the term, the entire United States is one political state.

Despite the ever increasing role that government plays in modern life, many who believe in God can find almost no guidance from their faith for their lives as citizens. They can see, of course, that their faith teaches them to demand honesty of state officials, and that it teaches them to obey the law. But these points are more ethical than political, and are so elementary as to supply no guidance for the issues which are difficult for believers to decide upon when they vote as citizens in a democracy. Therefore, we shall now look at how the law framework theory can draw a tighter

connection between our belief in God and some specifically *political* principles which presuppose that belief. We will then
briefly suggest how these principles can be applied to a few selected issues, so as to illustrate their practical consequences. This
does not mean that an entire political theory can be developed
here in one short chapter. As with the previous two chapters, we
can only sketch a blueprint for such a theory. In doing so, we will
concentrate on what the law framework theory has to say about
the distinctive nature of the state.

Dooyeweerd once observed, "Perhaps there is no other . . . community whose character has given rise to such a chaotic diversity
of opinions in modern social philosophy and social science as the
State."[1] He then went on to note that not only in modern theories,
but in the ancient ones as well, the understanding of the nature of
the state has always revolved around the issue of the relation of
"might" to "right." In other words, a central theme in political theory has always been the proper relation between the state's use of
power and the idea of justice. In keeping with the two components
of this central theme, the law framework theory will now be applied to the nature of the state in two parts: one on the power of
the state, and one on justice in the state.

2. The Nature of the State: What It Is

Our theory comes to bear on the nature of the state from several angles. It gives us an overview of society—the sphere sovereignty principle—which frees us from the traditional theories
which ended in some sort of hierarchical totalitarianism. In addition, our theory leads us to look for a community's "foundational
and leading functions" which together "qualify" it so as to give the
aspectual characterization of its nature. Moreover, the relation between the foundational and leading functions of a thing is, on our
theory, made possible by a "type law" which is the structural principle for any thing of that type. And the analysis of any community's type law yields a more specific concept of its nature. This
method can now be applied to the state.

Since the concept of a type law has only been briefly introduced let us expand on it before employing it in relation to the
state. The basic significance of the concept of a type law is that it
denies that any thing—the state included—is infinitely variable or

utterly arbitrary. A type law is our theory's explanation for why it is impossible for us to change something in whatever way we wish and still have it remain the same type of thing. Since we see this as guaranteed by a law of creation, we understand the general internal organization of things of a type as something permanent about that type.[2] Because type laws are interaspectual, they relate the foundational to the leading function in each thing of that type. Interpreting the typical connection of a thing's foundational and leading functions as guaranteed by these laws of creation, we understand the internal parts of it which correspond to those functions as essential to it, and to all other things of the same type.

But here a reminder is in order: while the analysis of a type law can aid us in discerning the parts that are essential to all the members of a type, it does not guarantee that those parts will always be related *exactly* in the way the law shows to be proper. Because type laws are (partly) normative, particular things can conform to their type law in a greater or lesser degree, and thus be better or worse examples of their type. This is true of natural things which are qualified by normative aspects, such as plants and animals, as well as of artifacts. In fact, a thing can be severely deformed before the point is reached at which its variance from its type law is so great that it ceases to be that type of thing altogether. So a type law not only shows us ways a thing of a certain type cannot fail to be (its essential properties and parts), but also how it should be (the right relation of its essential parts). For example, a marriage must include a husband and a wife or there is no marriage, and a family must include parents and children. But the relations between the partners of a marriage or the members of a family may vary so that one marriage or family is very good while another is very bad. Type laws therefore supply an order to creatures which is partly necessary and partly normative; part of what they determine cannot be disobeyed while another part can be. They comprise an interaspectual order that both sets the limits of possibility for a type of things and provides a standard for what they ought to be as things of that type.

In the case of states, then, analyzing their type law will help us to understand both the parts which are inevitable in any state and also how those parts ought to be related. These two must not be confused. That is, the relations it shows to be proper must not be understood as a description of all actual states past and present since any actual state may possess these relations in varying degrees.[3] For example, our finding that the type law for the state requires that it must have some organization of military power will never justify abuses of this power by any actual state. On the contrary, the type is the norm by which the role of the organization of power in any actual state may be judged.

A. State Power

According to our theory of society, the nature of the state-institution is qualified by a correlation between a historical foundational function and a justitial leading function. This means that on the one hand the state is a product of human cultural formation led by historical norms, while on the other its activity in society is led by the norm of justice. Its justitial leading function is the same as what I previously called its "structural purpose," which may be circumscribed as the promotion and achievement of public justice for the entire society living in the territory it governs.

Communities which are historically founded are not only products of cultural formation, but also exert their own sort of cultural-historical influence in society. For each distinct type of community, the cultural influence or power that it wields is of a kind which corresponds to its leading function. For example, a business may be an economic force, a school may exert the power of concepts and ideas, an artistic organization may have aesthetical influence, and a church or political party may have power over the beliefs of a society. The same is true of the state. It, too, exercises an influence or power which corresponds to its leading function. In the case of the state, this is the power of legislation: the state wields the power to enact laws for the accomplishment of its structural purpose, namely, the administration of public justice.

For these reasons, our first approximation of the type law which structurally determines states is that the internal organization of any state must include at least two subdivisions: organs for the enforcement of justice (military and police), and organs for deciding what is just (legislature and courts).

Moreover, this type law shows something important about the proper way these two subdivisions should relate within a state. The organs of force correspond to the state's foundational function, while its organs for establishing and interpreting law correspond to its leading function. Therefore in a properly formed state these two parts of the state should not be identical (as they are in a military dictatorship) nor should the military organ control or direct the establishment and interpretation of law. Rather, the organs of justice should control and direct the organs of the power of enforcement.

This is not to suggest that the state is the only community or social relationship in which justice is a concern, or which may make rules or laws. There needs to be justice in all human relationships and communities—for example, within a school, a business, a marriage, or a family. One of the most important facets of the notion of "sovereignty" in our expression "sphere sovereignty" is that the various types of communities all have the right to make laws or rules to govern their internal operations. But it is only the government—the ruling body in the state—which has the duty and right to legislate and enforce justice for *the public at large*. And it is only the state which does so with the right to use the power of force to back up its laws, as distinguished from other forms of cultural power. This right is conferred by its leading function, in the service of which its power becomes the "rightful" use of force. A family, for example, may seek justice by making rules and may enforce them by means of attitudes of approval and disapproval or punishments connected with family privileges. A business may have its own code, as may a school, a union, or a club. And church law has been highly elaborated. These communities may all impose sanctions up to and including dismissing or ostracizing offending members. But only the state may make laws to establish *public* justice, and impose the sanctions of confiscation of property, loss of liberty, or even death, by means of physical force.[4]

For this reason, we maintain that an important consequence of recognizing the state's type law, as it differs from those of other communities, is that the state is only fully actual where it possesses a monopoly of the power of force in the territory it governs. To the extent it does not possess such a monopoly, its ability to carry out its structural purpose is undercut. In that case, whatever community possesses a competing power is actually a competing government within the same body politic. This can happen in times of civil war, or when a rival political movement arms itself to overthrow the government, or even when an organization usurps the right to achieve its goals by force (such as organized crime).

Thus, while a given society may produce magnificent art or have a strong economy without a strong military force or police protection, it will never have a strong *state* so long as it cannot enforce its own laws or defend its own territory.

Because the state is partly characterized by the possession of the right to use force, some writers in the biblical traditions—such as St Augustine[5]—have suggested that the state has been established in human society only on account of sin. Seeing the state as essentially a restraint on sin, they maintain the state would have no place in a good society where people were not sinful. It is thus an "add on" institution, with no proper role in human affairs as life was originally intended by God. This view has had two important side effects. On the one hand, it has promoted a very narrow view of the proper task of the state, while on the other hand it has fostered a low esteem of the state and politics. This low esteem has, at times, led to the opinion that believers should withdraw from political activity altogether. We must disagree with this as an overly narrow view of the task of the state. As we shall see later in more detail, public justice is a much wider issue than simply the restraint of crime and would be a genuine human need even if there were no sin. In its positive direction the task of the state is to engender peace and harmony among people and among communities. James Skillen has made this same point by comparing the state and the family:

> Biblically speaking, family life was created by God for a positive, loving, nurturing, God-revealing purpose. Part of our identity as God's image is that we are sons and daughters and frequently mothers and fathers. The family did not arise as a technical invention to spank bad children. Punishment and negative discipline are not the *reason* for the family. We recognize of course, that due to sin, parents will have to incorporate punishment into the raising of their children in order to foster healthy families. But spankings and other forms of retribution fit into the deeper, broader, and more original meaning of family life.
>
> Life in political communities is quite different from family life, to be sure. I do not intend to describe civic life as family life writ large. Rather, the analogy is this: the *purpose* for government, the *reason* for political life is not first of all to punish wrongdoing through police officers, trial lawyers, and the military. Rather, the central meaning of political life is to be found in the positive reality of a public community—the healthy interrelationships of people through public legal

means so that commerce, family life, agriculture, industry, science, art, education, and many other things can be carried on all at the same time, all in the same territory, in a harmonious and just fashion.[6]

This helps us to see that even if sin were not a factor, even if people lived in genuine love and harmony with one another, the need for a public order to define justice would still exist. For example, honest differences of opinion could still arise that would need to be settled by impartial experts on justice. No doubt this is why the biblical view of the final destiny of God's people is that they will be citizens of his *kingdom,* which is to be *ruled* by his Messiah. Thus, according to the book of Isaiah, even in that kingdom in which no one will "hurt or harm in all my holy mountain" (11:9), there will still be the need for a ruler who "shall bring forth justice unto truth" and who will "set judgment in the earth" (42:3,4). For these reasons, I think the narrow view is a result of focusing too exclusively on the state's responsibilities in criminal law and national defense to the exclusion of its duties in civil law and international law.

I agree, of course, that the character of state power is completely altered by the fact of sin in human affairs. Were there no sin, people would not have to be compelled to obey laws or court decisions in the ways that are now needed. In this connection it is significant that the book of Isaiah also foresees that in God's final kingdom people will "beat their swords into plowshares and their spears into pruning hooks" and "nation shall not lift up sword against nation" (2:4). But there would still be the need to apply principles of justice to changing human affairs, even if the absence of sin permitted a society in which the power of the state need not be nearly so overtly exercised.[7]

As to the second side effect, there cannot be any doubt as to whether political activity is proper for a believer. From a biblical point of view, what is improper is for believers to abandon the concern for justice and the operation of the state to unbelievers— just as it is improper for us to abandon the doing of science or philosophy to those whose divinity is not God. If our belief in God underlies and directs the whole of life, as Scripture declares, then it must direct political theory and practice as well. And if we allow this direction to be mediated by the development of a biblical theory of reality and society, then it can supply political guidance which is far more specific than simply opposing tyranny, favoring freedom of religion, and calling for government officials to be honest. Such a theoretically developed direction can, in addition, bring to bear an entire overview of society (sphere sovereignty), and offer a specific view of the nature of the state which clarifies its duties and the proper limits of its use of power.

B. Public Justice

According to our law framework theory, there is a distinct aspect of human experience which corresponds to justitial properties possessed by persons, actions, institutions, and rules. There is also a norm which comprises the law side of this justitial aspect. As with the laws and norms of other aspects, we hold that the norm of justice is not merely a human invention, but is part of the law framework which God has built into creation. This norm holds, therefore, for all people at all times, even though its effective application may require the enactment of different legal statutes or the need for varying legal procedures under different circumstances. This justitial aspect of our experience is initially known in the same intuitive way as all the other aspects: we simply encounter it as part of the meaning of our experience of life. The intuition of its norm is what we usually call our "sense of justice," and it is a common intuition among humans everywhere. This norm can be circumscribed as the idea treating others so as to give them their due. This sounds so overly simple that it should be added that the norm has a number of sides to it. It includes such facets as that our treatment of others should be even-handed, should show a proportionality among various dues, and should involve equity in the distribution of dues.

As was the case with other aspects, the intuitive recognition of justitial truths is not confined to those with biblical faith. Many insights about justice have been discovered by those whose faith is in other divinities, so here again we need not look for an *entirely* new understanding of justice. We need not ignore all that has been learned of it in the ancient world, embodied in Roman law, or come down to us through the Anglo-Saxon tradition of common law, for example. Nevertheless, as was also the case with other aspects, the intuitive recognition of justitial truths is inevitably directed and focused by the influence of religious belief. Here, too, this influence is most often transmitted through theories: theories of human nature, of the nature of society, of the nature of the state. And where these theories presuppose a pagan religious belief, the resulting reductionism skews the intuitive sense of justice so as to concentrate it in accordance with whatever aspects are regarded as divine. The result is that some justitial issues are overemphasized while others are not given their due or are missed altogether.

Consider briefly just one example of this. In the United States, the civil law takes for granted that anyone who causes another an injury should compensate the injured party. It is taken for granted because it is considered an obvious requirement of justice that if I cause damage to your person, property, reputation, etc., I should restore your loss. Isn't it amazing, then, that this requirement of justice which seems so obvious for civil cases goes unrecognized for criminal cases? Why should it be that if I *inadvertently* cause you personal injury the law requires me to pay your medical costs and lost work time, but if I *deliberately* cause you the same injury in order to rob you the law does not require me to compensate you?

What lies behind this justitial blindspot is a false view of the state—a view argued against in the last chapter. It is the view which sees the government's authority as originating in the state—in the will of the majority—rather than in the divinely established law framework. Where the authority of the law is viewed as generated by the state itself, it is easy to see all criminal acts as offenses against the state. *So our laws assume the state to be the injured party in criminal actions.* The state receives any fines imposed, any property confiscated, and is considered the party to which any term of imprisonment will count as a debt paid. (We have a common expression that a released convict has "paid his debt to society," where "society" is clearly a synonym for "the state.") This view serves to guarantee that the real injured party, the victim, will remain uncompensated for losses sustained.[8]

By contrast, our theory sees the state as the *bearer,* not the creator, of the authority it wields in enforcing justice. The will of the majority decides who shall be the bearers of that authority, but the authority itself derives from the law framework of creation. The state is thus seen as the institution charged with being the justitial caretaker of its citizens. It must act on their behalf, not on behalf of its own offended majesty. In this way, we see its proper task from a wider angle than does our present criminal code. We see it charged not only with apprehending, punishing, and—if possible—rehabilitating the criminal, but also with providing justice for the real injured party, the victim.

This is but one instance of many legal and political insights our theory can provide. Because of its biblical view of the nature of authority, its differentiation of social spheres, and its analysis of distinctive types of social communities, the law framework theory helps to guide our sense of justice so that it does not get narrowly focused on one particular segment of the justitial spectrum to the neglect of other segments. Perhaps this advantage is best illustrated by comparing the law framework theory to the two most influential constrictive views of justice, individualism and collectivism. We have already seen why both these theories are religiously unacceptable. Each is based on the conviction that the source of authority in social communities is to be located within creation: in individuals possessing a natural right to rule, or in an all-encompassing community.

Against the backdrop of the discussion of these nonbiblical theories in the last chapter, let us now consider each of them specifically with respect to our theory of the nature of the state-institution. Take the individualist view first.

One of the statements of the individualist view which has come to exert a worldwide influence is that offered in the American Declaration of Independence. There Jefferson asserted that "all men are created equal, and are endowed by their Creator with certain inalienable rights" and that "it is to secure these rights that governments are instituted among men." In its historical setting, the American colonists gave these statements as reasons for dismissing George III as king on the ground that he had violated their inalienable rights.[9] This notion of people having rights relative to the state was partly inspired by biblical ideas which came to the colonists from the Reformation through English Puritanism.[10] Nevertheless, to phrase the idea only as that of "rights," which people are supposed to have as qualities indigenous to human nature, is a distortion of the biblical teaching. It leaves out the crucial point that the right to equal justice, which it is encumbent on the state to guarantee to all citizens, is derived from the *norm of justice* which governs creation. The wording of the Declaration ignored the law side of the justitial aspect, and instead attempted to locate the limitations upon the state in the subjective nature of every individual person.[11] So our objection to this way of putting the matter is that rights are left as subjective, rather than normative. We say that a person's having a right is the subjective side of the fact that others have obligations to that person. And these obligations devolve on them because the norm of justice governs all creation. Otherwise, how could the notion of individuals possessing such rights be defended? Unless there is a norm of justice over all creation, how could we know that all people have rights or that all people have the same rights? The only adequate basis for the idea of rights is that they are the result of our being governed by a universal norm. It is because it is universal that the norm governs not only individuals but also communities; it governs the leading function of the state and is the guiding principle to which the state must conform in enacting its statutes.

One of the adverse consequences of locating the basis for rights in the nature of individual persons is seen in a number of recent writers who have maintained that for people to possess a right, they must at least be capable of understanding it and desiring what it guarantees. Otherwise, they have said, it makes no sense to speak of people as actually possessing that right.[12] Others have pointed out that this requires that people's rights develop along with the biological basis of their capabilities.[13] These views are plausible if rights are taken as identical with certain faculties or powers of the human person such as the natural endowments of sight or hearing, for surely no one has the power of sight who cannot see, or the power of hearing who cannot hear. But the result of viewing rights this way is that infants, the severely retarded, the senile, and persons in a coma would therefore have no rights at all. This means, among other things, that it would not be murder to kill them. Or again, a normal adult transported from a primitive culture to a modern state would be unable to understand and desire many of the rights which have come to be recognized in most modern societies and so would not possess these rights according to the individualist theory.[14]

These hypothetical consequences are significantly like ones which have actually occurred in United States history. The framers of the Constitution deliberately avoided extending any political rights to blacks at all, and failed to provide full political rights to women. They seriously debated whether racial differences were sufficient to deny that blacks were to be included among those "endowed by their Creator with certain inalienable rights." But it is only because they thought of justitial rights as inhering in the subjective nature of individuals, that it made any sense to question whether such differences as gender or race were sufficient to deny political rights to women or blacks. By contrast, on the law framework theory the rights of all humans are undeniable since these rights do not originate in each individual's personal capabilities, race, or gender. They are guaranteed by the norms of creation which apply to all people simply because they are human.

There are also other difficulties with the individualist way of viewing rights. One is that unless rights are recognized as the results of aspectual norms, we will be unable to identify them. There is no limit to what people may desire, but those desires can hardly be identical with what they have a right to. Another is that the failure to recognize rights as based on norms will make us more prone to miss the fact that there are different aspectual kinds of rights.

This last point is significantly strengthened when we notice that a crucial element of clarity is missing from any discussion of rights unless we do introduce *aspectual* distinctions. For instance, there needs to be a distinction between moral rights derived from the ethical norm of love and justitial rights derived from norm of justice. It is the latter which sets the limits to state power and produces political rights. It is important not to confuse these two senses of "rights" since they differ in many ways. Unless the different aspectual kinds of norms, obligations, and rights are distinguished, a gross confusion ensues which has induced some writers to argue that an obligation of one kind produces a right of another kind. An example of such a confusion is any argument which concludes that a moral obligation can create a justitial right. Our theory acknowledges that a normative ethical obligation to be loving to others may indeed go hand-in-hand with a corresponding ethical right of others to be treated lovingly. And it acknowledges that the normative obligation to act justly goes hand-in-hand with a corresponding right of others to be treated justly. But this will never yield the conclusion that because one person or community has an *ethical* obligation to another, the other then has a corresponding *justitial* right which should be enforced by public law. Biblical teaching repeatedly makes clear that we have ethical obligations to the poor, for example. But that does not give any particular beggar the legal right to alms from me. It should be clear from the brief sketch of the nature of the state given so far, that the enforcement of moral obligations of love falls outside the proper legal competence of the state. The state is led by norms of justice, not ethics; the accomplishment of public justice is the structural purpose of the state, not the enforcement of non-public morals.

This does not mean that the state has no interest in *public* morality, however. If parents began wholesale evictions of their children from their homes or if 75 percent of the population got drunk every night and could not report to work, the severe disturbance of the public order which would result would certainly have to be dealt with by the state. So while it is not the state's prerogative to rule on all dimensions of human morality (shall businesses be allowed to open on Sunday? Shall people be allowed to engage in prostitution?), the state has a legitimate concern when any issue of moral weight threatens the public order of which it is caretaker. On the other hand, although the state's power is properly limited to the enforcement of justice, not every issue of justice in human life can fall under the purview of the state. The domain of the state is *public* justice. The small-scale injustices that may pass between individuals or within communities cannot and should not all be handled by public law. A parent who continually favors one child over another, for example, not only does something unethical (unloving) but something unjust to the slighted child. No one seriously supposes, however, that so long as the unfavored child is not actually neglected such a breach of justice is part of the state's duty to correct. Rather, its duty extends only to those issues which affect the entire body politic in principle.[15]

This last point was offered to clarify further one of the proper limits on the exercise of state power, but at the same time it also exposes another weakness in the individualistic theory of society and the state. One of the consequences of the individualist view of rights is that if rights are confined to individual persons, no provision is made for public justice and public rights. For if the duties of the state and the limits on its power are set only by the rights of individuals, what happens when there is an injustice which does not violate the rights of any one person? Suppose, for instance, that in the course of manufacturing a product on its own land, a company pollutes a river or the atmosphere which does not belong to any other individual? Or suppose that one company infringes on the rights of another? The individualist theory cannot allow for a legal remedy for such issues without resorting to the fiction that a wronged corporation is an individual person![16] But since this is patently untrue, the conclusion is inevitable: more than persons have rights. Therefore individualism is wrong in saying that rights reside only in individuals. Families, schools, unions, businesses, and the public at large also have rights even though they are not individuals who were "created equal" by God. Unlike individualism, our theory has no problem explaining how this is possible, since the source of rights are norms which govern all creation.

On the collectivist theory, justitial rights must derive from the public at large as organized by the state, rather than from either individuals or from creation norms. Since the collectivist view sees the good of society as a whole as paramount, it has no difficulty with matters of public justice as does the individualist view. But since creation norms are ignored as the basis of justitial rights, the collectivist slant on justice tends to slight both the individual and communities other than the state. Even those socialists who want to allow that rights are not created by the state alone, but derive from society at large, are nevertheless forced in the end to identify society with the state. Try as they will, collectivists cannot escape the consequence of their theory that rights are gifts the state bestows on individuals or communities as it sees fit, and which it can retract or change as it sees fit. This means that the state is, in principle, unlimited in its legal competency. The very idea of justice will then be whatever the state wishes it to be. This allows for a totalitarian state which levels aspectual differences among social spheres, and thus utterly violates the sphere sovereignty of every other social community. Inevitably, this theory is then defended by viewing all other communities as *parts* of the state, which utterly obscures their distinctive type laws and structural purposes.

By contrast, our theory, while agreeing that the state's duty is toward the whole of society, restricts state power to the administration of public justice. Moreover, it finds this restriction not in some supposedly external limit set by another institution (the church, or business, for example) and enforced by the competing power of that other, but in the very nature of the state itself. It is the state's own internal structure which sets its proper limits. And it is the understanding of its nature by its own citizens which is the source of these ideas which then need to be embodied in its constitutional law.

The individualist theory is closer to the biblical view with respect to its desire for a limited state, but by confining legal rights only to individuals, it slights the state's *public* duties. In addition, it has a difficulty with respect to the state's relations to other communities. For it has no way to limit the state's power with respect to them other than accepting the fiction that other communities are individual persons, and declaring the "internal" affairs of each community off-limits to the others (in a way analogous to the way each person's private life is off-limits to strangers). It was in this spirit, for example, that Jefferson wrote of a "wall of separation" between church and state. This idea was also behind the "laissez faire" doctrine that the state should not interfere with business.

Obviously, no two communities in the same society can be completely walled off from one another. Nor is it adequate to say merely that the *internal* affairs of a family, business, or church set the proper limits for the power of the state. This is because "internal" is left too vague by the individualist theory. What is internal to each community cannot be identified with what takes place in the course of its operations, since that could include a blatant felony. Rather, what is "internal" must be defined by the leading function and structural type of each community. Thus, the proper limits on the power of the state are set by its own nature in contrast to the natures of other communities and not just by the external boundaries between one community and another. Unlike the individualist theory, ours does not set up a potentially totalitarian state and then try to find external limits to confine the exercise of its power. As was already pointed out, our theory finds the limits to state power in what the state *is*, rather than only in what it is *not*. So we maintain that the state's duty may require it to exercise its authority in the life of any person or community, so long as that exercise is limited to the administration of public justice.

Therefore, while we can agree with the individualist aim of limiting the state with respect to other communities, we cannot agree with the expression "wall of separation." On the sphere sovereignty principle, it is certainly outside the proper use of state power to require or forbid any particular religious belief, or to regulate the doctrine or worship of any church or synagogue or mosque, etc. Likewise, with respect to the sphere of economics it is outside the proper competency of the state to take over or control private businesses, or to enter into any sort of collusion which would favor one business (or group of them) over others. In a similar way, families should also enjoy a sovereignty in their own social sphere which insulates them from arbitrary interference from the state. A family should enjoy freedom from police invasion or search without a warrant from a court issued on evidence of crime.

At the same time, however, our theory also requires the state to enforce the mutual sphere sovereignty delimitations among all other communities, as well as observe them itself. Thus, while our theory forbids the state from taking over businesses or trying to regulate the entire economy, it may well require child labor laws as an example of the proper role of the state in enforcing sphere boundaries on businesses. Without such laws, businesses once invaded the sphere of family life. They demanded work hours which took young children from their parent's supervision for sixty or more hours per week, precluded any opportunity for the children's education, and even prevented families from worshipping together.

Similarly, we find anti-trust legislation also to be a proper enforcement of justice when it is guided by the sphere sovereignty idea. The individualist contends simply that the state should preserve free competition. But we argue that the state has a broader duty to prevent the non-economic spheres of society from being infringed by the influence of corporations. Especially between 1865 and 1900, this was really a danger in the United States; the large corporations (called "trusts") not only became monopolies in restraint of free trade, but, had they merged, could have formed a totalitarian, business-dominated, state.[17]

In relation to churches and synagogues, the sphere sovereignty principle likewise forbids the state from using its power to favor any one faith, *including our own*. And since the nature of the state has a justitial leading function while the leading function of a church or synagogue is fiduciary, the very concept of a state-church is a contradiction in terms. At the same time, of course, our theory also forbids a church or synagogue to attempt to dictate political policy to the state, or to interfere with the sphere integrity of any other community. But none of these consequences could possibly require the state to be walled off from every religious *belief!* That, as we have seen, is impossible. Every conception of both justice and the state has religious presuppositions, so that every particular state will be conceived of and operated on the basis of either biblical or nonbiblical presuppositions, or some mixture of the two. This is, once again, why it is of the utmost importance that those who believe in God not be discouraged from bringing the social and political consequences of their belief to bear on their political life and on the legislation and operation of their state. This is why it is so important that believers realize how their faith provides for a distinctive theory of justice and the state. Without such a theory, those of biblical faith may be tempted to see the relation of their faith to politics as nothing more than the (unbiblical) program of trying to become a majority so as to force their morals on unbelievers by law.[18]

By contrast, it should be evident by now that the law framework theory is not a *biblical* theory of society and the state in any sense that would distinguish Jews and Christians as a special interest group. It is not an attempt to set a specific agenda for pressuring the government for special treatment for those who believe in God. Rather, it is biblical in the sense of bringing the antireductionist fruits of belief in God to bear on our understanding of justice and the state. As such, the theory requires that government *not* allow justice to be undermined by demands for special favors, but concentrate on the goal of bringing about a maximally just society for all people, whether they believe in God or not.

3. The Nature of the State: What It Is Not

In addition to the individualist and collectivist theories of society which distort the role of the state by skewing the idea of justice, there are other theories specifically about the nature of the state itself which are also objectionable compared to our biblical theory. For the purpose of making our own theory clearer by contrast, I will briefly mention a few of these.

The first of these is the old idea that only one racial or ethnic stock can comprise the citizenry if it is to achieve the necessary political unity to form a state. This idea was popular not only long after striking counterexamples showed it was false, but is occasionally still heard today.[19] We need only recall that a strong state developed in sixteenth-century England when its citizens were ethnically divided into Celts, Saxons, and Normans to see that this is a false requirement. Besides, some of the strongest states in the world today are ethnically quite diverse such as the USA. To be sure, there are extra difficulties to be overcome in fostering political unity where racial or ethnic divisions are strong; "one folk" or "one blood" are not necessary conditions for the existence of such unity. Our contention is that the true nature of political unity is that of a public legal order. Thus racial or ethnic unity not only *is not*, but *ought not* to be regarded as necessary for the unity of a state.

The same is true of the idea that one common language is a requirement for political unity and a strong state. The division of a population by language can be a strong disintegrating factor politically. This was a great problem in the low countries in the past, and resulted in the separation of Belgium from the Netherlands. In more recent times it has threatened the political unity of Canada. Once again, however, it cannot be a necessary condition for political unity if there are strong states which exist without it. And the fact that such states exist is thus evidence supporting our contention about how political unity ought to be viewed. So even though political unity may be easier to achieve in a state whose citizens share a common language, the lack of it does not prevent political unity. Switzerland is perhaps the most notable example of this.

Another idea is that the state needs a common religious basis for its political unity. This is a sore subject of debate in Israel at present, and is an idea advocated by several countries designating themselves "Islamic states." Moreover, the national separation of Pakistan from India in this century was due, in large part, to religious differences. Once again, however, the fact that many states in the world suffer no disintegrating effects by allowing freedom of religion is evidence that unity of religious belief is not a must. In this case, as in the previous cases, it is a confusion about the nature of the state institution (its type law) which leads to seeing the unity of the state as centered in any other social sphere than that of public justice.

Nevertheless, it should be added that the disintegrating forces of ethnic, linguistic, and religious animosity can be easily underestimated by those who have never experienced them. In North America there is a naïveté about religious liberty in particular, because in many localities there is not much religious diversity and because most people falsely assume that all religions are probably very like the ones they are familiar with. When strong diversities of religion—or any of these other factors—arise where they have not previously existed, they can severely test the unity of even the strongest state. This is why it is so important that, as our theory requires, any government be scrupulously even-handed in its treatment of all the diversities it finds in its territory. Differences of culture, custom, language, race, religion, etc., must be recognized and respected because that is required by the norm of justice. The unequal treatment or outright suppression of such differences can never be excused on grounds of political exigency, since they do not affect the real basis of the state's existence.

Another idea of the state which must be rejected by our biblical theory is that of the power-state. This is the blatant adoption of the view which we accused the collectivist theory of society of encouraging, and the individualist theory of failing to guard against adequately. It holds that the state has no limit to its competence in every sphere of life, so that there is no limit, in principle, to state power. Sometimes this view is held quite overtly, as was done by Machiavelli, Hobbes, and Hegel. Often it is disguised to save the appearance of a law-state, as was done by the Fascist and Nazi states of the 1930s. In any case, it is clearly opposed by our sphere sovereignty principle which sees the proper competence of the state limited to the sphere of public justice. It is also at odds with our characterization of the state's type law, which shows that its organs of power should be ruled by its organs of legislation and its judiciary. This means that it is the enforcement of justice which makes the use of power right, not the possession of power which makes right whatever the state wants to do. From a biblical point of view, then, no state is legitimate without this guidance of might by right. No matter how well entrenched its rule, no matter how widely accepted its authority, such a "state" is no more than a band of armed criminals—as Augustine observed.

As we have acknowledged, the individualist theory does want to set limits on the use of state power. One of its severest difficulties in accomplishing this, however, is that the only limit it can propose (which is consistent with the rest of the theory) is to say that the state's power is limited to whatever it takes to protect the rights possessed by individuals. As Jefferson put it, "it is to secure these rights that governments are instituted among men." Earlier I pointed out how this theory left out the important *public* duties of the state. But this criticism has another side as well: when the state does acquire an interest in an issue of a truly *public* nature, there is no way left for individualism to set any *aspectual* limits to its legal competency. Individualism, therefore, not only omits certain duties of the state, it omits an adequate account of the limitations of state power in matters that are properly its duties. This lack of limitation has led to a widespread opinion in the United States that in all matters where there is no clear individual right violated, the majority may do whatever it wants through representative government. Thus government, by vote of the majority, becomes all-sovereign. This genuinely frightening trend is indicated in a number of ways.

Take, for example, the seemingly minor issue of understanding what a driver's license is. There are many reasons why it is proper for the state to register drivers. One is that the license is a form of taxation which helps pay for public roads and other state expenses connected with public safety. Another is that if a driver is reckless or drives while drunk, the state has the duty to protect others by removing such drivers from the road by revoking their licenses. But more and more, such licenses have been viewed as the state's granting *permission* for a person to drive. Since it is not plausible for the individualist theory to claim that we are all born with the natural right to drive a car, driving does not seem to be one of our personal, inborn rights. So since there is no personal driving right to limit the state, its sovereignty over driving may, in principle, be total. Thus driving is regarded as a *privilege* the state grants.[20] This attitude shows a complete lack of appreciation for the sphere sovereignty view that many activities are, in origin, neither rights nor privileges in relation to the state, but are freedoms.[21]

The same point may be made with respect to marriage licenses. On our view, a marriage license should never be seen as obtaining the state's permission to marry, but as a way of registering a marriage with the state so far as its place in the public legal order is concerned. A marriage is essentially an ethical institution, qualified by the norm of love governing the relations between the marriage partners. As such, a marriage is formed by a mutual pledge of exclusive love between the partners; it is not made by the state or by a church or synagogue. A church or synagogue may *bless* a marriage; and a state may *recognize* it; any public ceremony may *declare* it; but only the marriage partners can *make* it.

An even more subtle indication of the failure of individualism to stem the creeping totalitarianism in the public mind of United

States citizens is the use of a seemingly harmless expression which has become current among both politicians and news commentators in recent decades. When speaking of difficulties or scandals within an administration, they have often remarked that it would be better for everyone if the issue were put aside so as not to preoccupy the president's attention. Their way of expressing this point has been to say that we should let the president "get back to the business of running the country." Perhaps such remarks are not intended to be taken literally—not meant to be a job description of the office of president. But there is a real danger that this expression may help obscure some extremely important political concepts, the most fragile of which is that the state is only one of the many social communities of the nation. Of course, it is also true that the president presides over only *one* branch of the federal government, and that the government is but *one* part of the state (albeit the ruling part). These points would no doubt be granted by those who use the expression. But the individualist theory of society is so pervasive an assumption in public opinion, that the implications of its weaknesses are drawn unconsciously by many who could not begin to explain it. In this way many people come to believe that "country" is *en toto* under the control of the government, except where personal rights make them immune. So the danger is that saying the president "runs the country" can serve to entrench this dangerous idea, and to identify the nation with the government in the popular mind.

History shows us the danger of this false identification. In many European countries governments themselves encouraged their citizens to view their *state* as identical with their *country*. To the extent that they succeeded, the people of many nations failed to see their government as but one institution among many in their society. As a result they mistook the pride and power of their government for the honor and dignity of their country. Because of this, governments were enabled to pass off their mutual rivalries as matters of national honor, and thus as supposedly good reasons for war. This identification of the pride of the state with the national honor has been the single greatest cause of European wars over the past three hundred years.[22]

The last view of the nature of the state to be contrasted to our theory is that of the welfare state. On this view, the state is seen primarily as father-provider of the needs of its citizens. The claim of this view is that it is as much the state's duty to provide work, food, clothing, shelter, and health care as it is to provide for protection against crime and invasion.

It is certainly possible that the existence of poverty in a society is a sign of genuine injustice, especially if that society is, on the whole, wealthy. In that case, it would be the duty of the state to correct such injustice. But the injustice involved would have to be a public one since, as we have already noted, it is not the state's duty to correct every injustice. If it is possible for the state to correct public economic injustices without overreaching its own proper responsibilities, then clearly it should do so. But if it begins to violate those limits in the name of economic justice, it can easily become totalitarian. In that case, a greater monster will have been created to combat a lesser one. Thus the state must approach economic injustice with the same respect for the distinctness of other institutions that should characterize all its policies. It must recognize that as a state, it does not generate wealth or health care; the goods and services which need to be justly distributed are produced by farms, businesses, families, hospitals, nursing homes, and orphanages, to name a few. Any policy which would call for the state itself to attempt to create the goods and services which its citizens need, would be self-defeating for its own leading function as well as for the leading functions of the other communities that would get preempted.

There are many ways the state can help to promote justice in the distribution of its citizen's basic needs without overriding the proper roles of other communities. One way is to aid citizens in spreading the cost of such needs over a lifetime through taxation. This is what has been done, for instance, with preparation for retirement needs through social security.[23] This is also the basic idea behind the way the cost of educational services are aided by the state. Rather than have families bear the entire cost of education during the years their children are actually in school, taxation spreads the cost over a lifetime so that all families can have access to schooling for their children. Along this same line, our conception of the nature of the state would see nothing amiss in having taxation help to spread the increasing cost of medical care in a similar way.

But, once again, what is proper in these connections is a far cry from regarding the state itself as the provider or guarantor of the needed goods and services. And it is equally far from seeing it as providing them to *all* its citizens. On the other hand, there is nothing wrong with its promoting and encouraging an equitable and proportional a distribution of basic sustenance needs for the small segments of the citizenry that is utterly indigent, even if this includes making survival needs available at public expense. But even in that case, the state itself should not be the supplier of those needs; that is, there is nothing about such care for the indigent that requires the state to take over the communities which do produce them. Still less is there anything about state support of the destitute to suggest that *everyone* has the right to look to the state to provide for them, irrespective of whether or not they are able to obtain them by their own efforts.

4. Postscript

This sketch of the nature of the state institution has been brief, and is relatively lacking in detail. Also lacking is any attempt to apply its consequences to concrete political and legal matters, since doing that for even a few issues would take another book. In recent years, however, other advocates of the theory have been able to do such work, and there is now a growing body of literature available from the law framework point of view. These authors have been able to point out a significant number of unique insights by which this theory can contribute needed clarification or correction to a host of important issues. In the United States alone, for example, they have been able to expose major injustices embedded in such matters as the ways government related to education, the laws governing how elections are conducted for the House of Representatives, governmental policies concerning poverty and welfare, economic justice, human rights, and environmental concerns, to name but a few. They have also been able to provide additional justification for many elements in our political and legal traditions which are sound, and to point out ways these can be developed further.[24]

Important as all this is, however, it would be a mistake to neglect the fact that our theory also provides positive and corrective insights concerning the other social communities as well as for the state. The natures of these communities have been touched on in this and the previous chapter even more briefly than that of the state. However, a number of authors have also produced excellent work on the law framework view of nonpolitical communities.[25]

My hope is that despite their brevity these chapters have made a start at showing how our view of these communities is distinctive and why, arising as it does from our analysis of their natures as artifacts and from the sphere sovereignty theory of their mutual relations, it derives from methods which presuppose that the whole of creation is directly dependent on God.

AFTERWORD:
FAITH TECTONICS

In the introduction I claimed that a religious belief plays a role in human life analogous to the role played in the earth's geography by its great tectonic plates. The intervening chapters have now presented reasons for believing this to be true for the theories by which we interpret ourselves and our world. We have seen that, at bottom, theories are driven and regulated by whatever idea of divinity has gripped the hearts of their advocates. In that sense a theory is every bit as much an expression of religion as worship is, even though it is a very different type of expression.

We have also seen some important consequences of this discovery for those of us who believe in God. These consequences were spelled out in order to help us invent and/or reinterpret theories so that they are internally regulated by our faith. This was urged in place of the traditional approach of trying to ally our faith with pagan-based theories. We have seen why externally harmonizing such theories with biblical faith merely serves to mask this deeper religious incompatibility.

But at this point it is sometimes objected that there is also another consequence of this discovery which I have—perhaps conveniently—overlooked. It is that this position, if accepted, will only serve to further divide people and set them at odds with one another. For it means that theories are the products of spiritual faith communities working out explanations which differ relative to their religious beliefs. Moreover, the position goes beyond simply uncovering that religious control has in fact occurred. It argues that such control is unavoidable because the role of religious belief is embedded in the very nature of theoretical reasoning. In addition, it acknowledges that because theoretical reasoning is always faith-directed there can be no religiously neutral faculty or procedure by which religious beliefs themselves can be adjudicated. So won't this position result in isolating the "isms" of philosophy and science and encouraging intolerance among them? Won't assigning theories to various faith communities serve to galvanize their advocates into the kind of opposition to one another that will produce a total breakdown in communication? Won't there be rock throwing in place of dialogue?

The answer to such questions is that nothing could be further from the truth. First of all, pointing out the root causes of theory differences does not itself produce intolerance or lack of communication on the part of those who differ, any more than it produces the differences themselves. Intolerance and unwillingness to communicate with those who disagree are the fruits of the sin that infects human nature, not of uncovering the ultimate cause of disagreements. As such, intolerence and its consequences are evils that can and do plague disagreements in philosophy and science as well as in practical life.

The second part of our reply is even more important. It is that uncovering the religious roots of theoretical perspectives actually opens the way to more fruitful communication than is otherwise possible. My reasons for saying this are, first, that if religious control is a fact, then attempts to communicate without an awareness of it will be frustrated by its hidden effects. And second, where the parties to a debate view reason itself as autonomous and neutral, it is hard for each not to see the extent to which the other differs as the extent to which the other is not being rational. The danger, then, is that the other's position will not only be rejected as false, but condemned as irrational. And insofar as rationality is taken as an essential characteristic of being human, it will then be hard to refrain from seeing not only the other position but the other *person* as substandard of even subhuman.

On the other hand, recognizing that all people have religious beliefs which regulate their theorizing can allow thinkers a mutual respect of one another's large-scale theory differences as expressions of their alternative faiths. They may then be able to appreciate why others, starting from their contrary religious beliefs, developed their opposing theories in just the way they did. On this basis they can then explore any points of contact and agreement they may have, as well as gain greater insight into the nature of their genuinely irreconcilable differences. And this may all be done without the temptation of either side to view the other as sub-rational.

In fact, these same benefits may also accrue for differences that occur outside theories. Our focus throughout this book has been on theories exclusively. But we must also acknowledge a corresponding impact of religious belief on practical life—on personal values, attitudes, practices, and lifestyles. We must not allow ourselves to think of this side of life as religiously neutral either. From a biblical viewpoint, in these matters we also either serve the true God or some God-surrogate. So here, too, we must recognize the alternative values and practices of others as the results of their contrary religious convictions, and exhibit the same kind of respect for their differences that our view makes possible for theory differences.

Of course, the mutual respect that I am advocating does not mean letting crime go unrestrained. But that aside, it calls upon us to show love, forbearance, and tolerance with practices and lifestyles that may be at odds with those inspired by biblical belief. In both practical life as in theorizing we must concentrate on the task of recognizing and uprooting what is unbiblical in our own practices and theories, rather than on attacking those of other faith communities. Only then will we be equipped to represent faithfully the consequences of belief in God over the entire spectrum of life for the benefit of all humankind.

This is a painful task. It is always easier to condemn another person than to clean one's own house. But no matter how painful it may be it is far preferable to the only alternative: the compromise of the truth with falsehood which risks losing the proper direction for thought and life altogether.

Notes

2. WHAT IS RELIGION

1. Some scholars doubt whether Buddhism is a religion since Theravada Buddhists do not believe in any gods. But since most Buddhists do believe in gods, I will—for now—include non-Theravada Buddhism as a religion.

2. Paul Tillich, *Systematic Theology* (Chicago: University of Chicago Press, 1951), vol. 1, 11–55. Also see his *The Dynamics of Faith* (New York: Harper & Bros., 1957), 1–40.

3. Tillich, *Dynamics of Faith*, 10, 76–77, 96. But compare also *Systematic Theology*, vol. 1, 211.

4. Tillich, *Dynamics of Faith*, 13.

5. Ibid., 13, 14. Also *Systematic Theology*, vol. 1, 237. It should be mentioned that the latter passage first denies that God is infinite but then speaks of his infinity. I do not know what to make of that, but it does seem that most of what follows continues to view the divine as whatever is infinite in the sense of being both unconditioned and all-inclusive.

6. Tillich, *Dynamics of Faith*, 12.

7. *Introduction to the Study of Religion*, ed. T. W. Hall (San Francisco: Harper & Row, 1978), 16. As far as I know, this definition was first proposed by Josiah Royce who phrased it: "Religion is loyalty to that which the individual finds to be worthful."

8. William Tremmel, *Religion, What Is It?* (New York: Rhinehart and Winston, 1984), 7.

9. Similar difficulties attend other famous attempts to define religious belief. For example, Friedrich Schleiermacher defined it as "the sum of all higher feelings," especially feelings of dependency (*On Religion: Speeches to Its Cultured Despisers* [New York: Harper & Row, 1958], 45). Hegel replied that this would make his dog very religious. Rudolph Otto replaced feelings of dependency with those of awe in the presence of something uncanny or mysterious (*The Idea of the Holy* [New York: Ox-

ford University Press, 1958]). But a tidal wave or earthquake can be experienced as awesome and mysterious without being regarded as holy.

Joachim Wach has suggested religion to be "a response to what is experienced as ultimate reality ... that which conditions all ... which impresses and challenges us" (*The Comparative Study of Religions* [New York: Columbia University Press, 1961], 30). This is much better than most attempts, but falls away at the end: horse races and puzzles can challenge and impress us.

Finally, the "paraphrase" offered by Hans Kung also fails: "a social and individual relationship, vitally realized in a tradition and community, ... with something that transcends or encompasses man and his world" (*Christianity and the World Religions* [Garden City, N.Y.: Doubleday, 1986], xvi). This is too narrow a definition because many pagan religions do not regard the divine as either transcendent or all-encompassing, as will be explained in the next chapter.

10. T. Danzig, *Number: The Language of Science* (Garden City, N.Y.: Doubleday-Anchor, 1954), 42.

11. Likewise, Thales is reported to have held the divine to be "that which has neither beginning nor end" (W. Jeager, *The Theology of the Early Greek Philosophers* [Oxford: Oxford University Press, 1960], 29); while Anaximander said it is whatever is "unborn, imperishable, ... and all-governing one." (See Aristotle's *Physics*, 3.4.203b14.)

12. W. F. Albright has pointed out that the holy, proper name of God which he revealed to Moses (יהוה) means "the one who causes to be." See *From the Stone Age to Christianity* (Garden City, N.Y.: Doubleday, 1957), 15–16.

13. This is the real import of the biblical remark: "The fool has said in his heart 'there is no god'." Contrary to the way Anselm took it, this does not mean that an atheist contradicts himself. Rather it means that anyone who thinks he has no god is self-deceived.

14. "As I have often said, the trust and faith of the heart alone make both God and an idol. If your faith and trust are right, then your God is the true God. On the other hand, if your trust is false and wrong, then you have not the true God. That to which your heart clings and entrusts itself is, I say, really your God" (from the "Larger Catechism" in the *Book of Concord* [Philadelphia: Fortress, 1959], 365). See also the *Lectures on Romans* in the Library of Christian Classics (Philadelphia: Westminster, 1961), vol. 15, 23.

15. See: A. C. Bouquet, *Comparative Religion* (London: Penguin, 1962), 37; H. Dooyeweerd, *A New Critique of Theoretical Thought* (Philadelphia: Presbyterian & Reformed, 1955), vol. 1, 56; N. K. Smith, *The Credibility of Divine Existence* (New York: St. Martin's, 1967), 396; and

William James, *The Varieties of Religious Experience* (New York: Mentor Books, 1958), 42–45.

16. One might claim to believe that nothing at all is nondependent, and so to have no religious belief whatever. My first reason for doubting this is, of course, that Scripture teaches that all people have some religious belief or other. In addition, however, we may notice that the claim that each and every thing depends on something else does not entail that there is nothing whatever self-existent. If each and every thing depended on some other thing, the total array of things would then have to be self-existent since there would be nothing else for it to depend on. This would remain so whether or not the total array is infinite, eternal, or logically necessary. None of these are equivalent to self-existence.

17. Jeager, *Theology of the Early Greek Philosophers*, 10.

18. See Dooyeweerd, *A New Critique*, vol. 2, 316, and B. Malinowski, *Magic, Science, and Religion* (New York: Doubleday, 1948), 19, 20, 76–79. Also Bouquet, *Comparative Religion*, 45, and Nilsson, *A History of Greek Religion* (Oxford: Clarendon, 1967).

19. Nilsson, *History of Greek Religion*, 72.

20. Nicholas Wolterstorff has offered insightful comment on the variability of feelings of confidence vis-à-vis what is seen as objective truth in his comparison of Locke and Calvin. See "The Assurance of Faith" in *Faith and Philosophy* 7, no. 4 (Oct. 1990): 396–417.

21. For example, H. H. Price, "Belief 'In' and Belief 'That'," *Religious Studies* 1, no. 1 (Oct. 1965): 5–27.

22. Biblical writers themselves insist on this point. They maintain that other religious beliefs are ascribing the status that belongs only to God to something other than God (see Is. 42:8, 44:6; Rom. 1:25).

3. TYPES OF RELIGIOUS BELIEF

1. Jeager, *Theology of the Early Greek Philosophers*, 17.

2. W. Heisenberg, *Physics and Philosophy*, 72–73.

3. J. Vander Hoeven, *Karl Marx: The Roots of His Thought* (Amsterdam: Van Gorcum, 1976) 12.

4. J. B. Noss, *Man's Religions* (New York: Macmillan, 1980), 181.

5. W. Herberg, "The Fundamental Outlook of Hebraic Religion," reprinted in *The Ways of Religion*, ed. R. Eastman (New York: Canfield, 1975), 283.

6. Ibid., 284. This point will be developed in more detail in chapter 10.

7. Unless otherwise noted, biblical quotations will be from the Revised Standard Version.

8. A. N. Whitehead, *Adventures of Ideas* (New York: Mentor Books, 1955), 108.

9. A. N Whitehead, *Science and the Modern World* (New York, Free Press, 1967), 92.

4. WHAT IS A THEORY

1. For example: E. Nagel, *The Structure of Science* (New York: Harcourt, Brace & World, 1961), 1–28; K. Popper, *Conjectures and Refutations* (New York: Harper & Row, 1965), 216; J. Kemeny, *A Philosopher Looks at Science* (New York: Van Nostrand Rienhold, 1959), 156ff; R. Giere, *Understanding Scientific Reasoning* (New York: Holt, Reinhart & Watson, 1979), 61, 80, 163; M. Martin, *Concepts of Science in Education* (New York: Scott, Foresman, 1972), 50–58; N. Rescher, *Scientific Explanation* (New York: Free Press, 1970), 8–24; J. J. C. Smart, *Between Philosophy and Science* (New York: Random House, 1968), 53–88; M. Wartofski, *Conceptual Foundations of Scientific Thought* (London: Macmillan, 1968), 35, 240; G. Gale, *Theory of Science* (New York: McGraw-Hill, 1979), 193–235.

2. The main points offered here are a summary of the account Dooyeweerd gives in the *New Critique* (Philadelphia: Presbyterian & Reformed, 1955). See esp. vol. 1, pp. 38ff.

Dooyeweerd uses this account of abstraction as the basis for his "transcendental critique" of theories, because abstraction is (part of) the answer to the transcendental question: "What makes theories possible?" While he acknowledges that this approach owes a debt to Kant, his own development of it (and his subsequent theories) are substantively nonKantian. Dooyeweerd emphasizes that while Kant asked the transcendental question about experience, he never asked it about theories and, as a result, failed to maintain a genuinely transcendental-critical attitude. Thus Kant's attempt fails in just the way Chisholm has accused past transcendental arguments of failing in chapter eight of his *The Foundations of Knowing* (Minneapolis: University of Minnesota Press, 1982), 95–99.

By contrast, Dooyeweerd maintains the transcendental stance by answering the question of the possibility of theories with a description of (rather than a hypothesis about) the activity of high abstraction, which description is subject to confirmation in one's own self-reflection. Thus his account meets the requirements for a successful transcendental argument as Chisholm has stated them. In this connection it is important to notice that Dooyeweerd's account of high abstraction is employed to derive criteria for theories rather than any specific hypotheses.

These criteria are summarized later in this chapter, and their application to the theory of Kant is summarized in note 13.

3. Nagel, *Structure of Science,* 4, 11.

4. Examples of the three ways high abstraction can be involved in theories are as follows: (1) It does not take high abstraction to wonder whether water always puts out fire, but it does to ask how heat is transferred from one object to another. (2) It does not take high abstraction to propose the hypothesis that water will not put out every sort of fire, but it does to frame the theory that heat is transferred by the collision of more rapidly vibrating molecules with molecules vibrating more slowly. (3) It does not take high abstraction to think of the test of throwing water on fires until one is found that is not quenched by water. But it does take high abstraction to conceive of arguments and tests for the molecular theory of heat transfer.

5. Sociology is a more complex example. Some of its theories deal with the social aspects of life, that is, with properties and relations having to do with prestige and status, customs and traditions, styles of dress, etc. Other theories take a range of things (social communities) as their field and deal with one or more aspects of them.

6. G. Ryle, *Dilemmas* (Cambridge: Cambridge University Press, 1956), 13.

7. J. Piaget, *Main Trends in Interdisciplinary Thought* (New York: Harper & Row, 1970), 12–13.

8. If a theory proposed the existence of an entity that could possibly be experienced directly although it has not yet been found, then finding it *would* prove the theory true. For example, the astronomers who theorized that there is a ninth planet in our solar system were proven correct when Pluto was discovered in 1930. The germ theory of disease is another example. Whenever what is proposed by a theory is actually found, the theory ceases to be a guess, and so is no longer a theory. Needless to say, the vast majority of theories in philosophy and the sciences are not ones that propose the existence of entities that are directly discoverable.

9. Michael Polanyi has put this point well in *Personal Knowledge* (New York: Harper & Row, 1962): "All formal rules for scientific procedure must prove ambiguous, for *they will be interpreted quite differently according to the particular conceptions about the nature of things by which the scientist is guided*" (p. 167, emphasis added).

10. "[In cases of theory disputes] it appears that the two sides do not accept the same 'facts' as facts, and still less the same 'evidence' as evidence.... For within two different conceptual frameworks the same range of experience takes the shape of different facts and different evidence" (ibid., 167).

11. *New Critique*, vol. 1, 34–52, 82–85, 545–566; vol. II, 366–380, 429–434, 466–471; vol. III, 1–53, 145.

12. This criterion differs from the usual criticism of eliminative materialism, which is that it denies the existence of beliefs and other propo-

sitional attitudes. Churchland has argued that this criticism begs the question (*A Neuro-Computational Perspective: The Nature of Mind and the Structure of Science* [Cambridge, Mass.: MIT-Bradford, 1989], 111–127). Rather than assume a "folk psychology" which holds beliefs must be nonphysical, my criterion shows why eleminativists must assume their own claim to have nonphysical properties and be governed by nonphysical laws if it is to have meaning that is true rather than false.

13. This is the criterion Dooyeweerd regards as fully transcendental, and which he accuses Kant of having missed. In fact he argues that when it is applied to Kant's own theories, they are disqualified. Dooyeweerd says:

> From the outset Kant derived human knowledge from only two origins: sensitivity and logical thought . . . following the steps of English empiricism, he starts from the dogmatic supposition that the 'datum' in experience is of a purely . . . sensory character. . . .

> In this . . . attitude epistemology simply took for granted that which should be the chief problem of any critique of knowledge, viz. the abstraction of the sensory and logical functions of consciousness from the full systasis . . . of the . . . aspects of human experience. . . . This abstraction is only made in theoretical thought by a process of disjunction and opposition. . . .

> The real datum of human experience precedes every theoretical [abstraction].

> The assumption that certain functions of consciousness, theoretically isolate in the . . . act of cognition are the *data,* was nothing less than the cosmological capital sin. (*New Critique*. vol. II, 431–432).

> The primordial question should be: What do we abstract from the real datum of experience? . . . And only in unbreakable coherence with this primordial question should the second problem be raised: How can the antithesis between the [abstracted aspects] be reconciled by an inter-aspectural . . . synthesis? (ibid, 434).

Of course, this violation of the criterion of self-performative coherence is not true only of Kant but is typical of Western philosophy (Cf. *New Ciritque,* vol. I, 27–162, 297–405; vol. II, 430ff, but esp. 493–575.) We will return to this point again in chapter 8 (esp. in note 1), where it will appear that the issue of how to characterize the datum of experience is crucial in the competing interpretations of physics.

5. THEORIES AND RELIGION: THE ALTERNATIVES

1. S. Kierkegaard, *Fear and Trembling and Sickness Unto Death* (Garden City, N.Y.: Doubleday, 1955), 48.

2. Ibid., 218.

3. S. Kierkegaard, *The Concluding Unscientific Postscript,* reprinted in *Nineteenth-Century Philosophy,* ed. P. Gardiner (New York: Free Press, 1964), 306–307.

4. F. Schleiermacher, *On Religion: Speeches to its Cultured Despisers* (New York: Harper & Brothers, 1958), 46.

5. A. N. Whitehead, *Adventures of Ideas* (New York: Mentor Books, 1955), 165. This has been a prevailing view in Western thought for a long time, and has been shared by thinkers who otherwise differ widely. For example, in his doctoral thesis (Berlin, 1841), Karl Marx quoted David Hume with approval as follows:

> 'Tis certainly a kind of indignity to philosophy, whose sovereign authority ought to be everywhere acknowledged, to oblige her on every occasion to make apologies for her conclusions, and justify herself. . . . This puts one in mind of a king arraigned for high treason against his subjects.

Marx then immediately adds his own comment that "the consciousness of man [is] the supreme divinity. There must be no god on a level with it" (from "Foreword to Thesis: The Difference Between the Natural Philosophy of Democritus and the Natural Philosophy of Epicureus," reprinted in *Marx and Engles on Religion* [Moscow: Foreign Language Publishing House], 14–15.

6. B. Russell, *Why I Am NOT a Christian* (New York: Simon & Schuster, 1957), 32–33.

7. Here again it must be remembered that "sin" is being used in the primarily religious sense explained earlier, and that "grace" is intended to refer to God's gracious attitude of favor toward those who do not deserve it. It is by the grace of God that the human heart is restored to its proper functioning so that it intuitively recognizes his revelation for what it is. In consequence, the recipient of grace experiences it as self-evident that the biblical message is God's word, that it is the truth about God from God. Calvin described the experience this way:

> As to the question, How shall we be persuaded [Scripture] came from God . . .? It is just the same as if it were asked, How shall we learn to distinguish light from darkness, white from black, sweet from bitter? Scripture bears on the face of it as clear evidence of its truth as white and black do of their color, sweet and bitter of their taste. (*Institutes,* I, vii, 2)

8. Thomas Aquinas, *De Trinitate,* exposition 2.3.

9. J. Calvin, *Commentary on the First Book of Moses* (Grand Rapids, Mich.: Eerdmans, 1948), vol. 1, 63.

6. THE IDEA OF RELIGIOUS CONTROL

1. See the insightful remarks of James Barr's article "Literality" in *Faith and Philosophy* 6, no. 4 (Oct. 1989): 412–428.

2. Quoted in C. C. Gillespie, *Genesis and Geology* (New York: Harper & Brothers, 1959), 53.

3. This mistake is not committed by fundamentalists alone; it is the *combination* of this mistake with the encyclopedic assumption which distinguishes fundamentalism. The confusion of God's providence with his acting in creation is common to a wide variety of thinkers. One recent example is found in Stephen Hawking's *A Brief History of Time* (New York: Bantam Books, 1988), 136–141, 174–175. The mistake is also endorsed by Carl Sagan in his introduction to the book.

4. N. H. Ridderbos, *Is There a Conflict Between Genesis 1 and Natural Science?* (Grand Rapids, Mich.: Eerdmans, 1957); also C. Vandewaal, *Search the Scriptures* (St. Catherines, Ontario: Paideia Press, 1978), vol. 1, 53ff. I have defended this reading of Genesis in some detail in an article in the journal of the American Scientific Affiliation. See "Genesis on the Origin of the Human Race," *Perspectives on Science and Christian Faith* 43, no. 1 (March 1991): 2–13.

5. This is the general model that is also followed by scholasticism with the difference that scholastic thinkers do not usually make the encyclopedic assumption. As a result, they more clearly recognize Scripture's religious focus and demand that theories not contradict the doctrines I have called "core" and "secondary" religious beliefs. There have arisen borderline cases, however, in which certain doctrines were interpreted in a way close to the fundamentalist view. The trial of Galileo is a famous example of this and Galileo's reaction was precisely to deny the encyclopedic assumption: "The Bible tells us how to go to heaven, not how the heavens go."

The question of how to distinguish precisely the contents of Scripture which carry the infallibility of revelation which theories may not deny is a difficult hermeneutical issue I cannot hope to settle here. But I do think recognizing the religious focus of Scripture indicates the direction in which such a criterion may be sought. Roughly speaking, we may say that revealed truth includes whatever Scripture teaches (as opposed to merely mentions) concerning: (1) the nature of God and humans, (2) how humans may stand in right relation to God, and (3) whatever else is required for these teachings to be true. As I see it, (3) would include, for example, the factuality of the events involved in the history of the covenant—even if the record of them is not inerrant in every detail.

6. Some critics have objected that it makes no sense to speak of unconscious beliefs since to have a belief one must be aware of its content. This, I think, confuses the dispositional with the manifest sense of "belief." At the end of chapter 2, I took the position that a belief is an acquired disposition to regard a state of affairs as factual and the

statement of it as true; a disposition can exist while remaining unconscious to its possessor.

7. Many well-known discussions of presuppositions by philosophers
and linguists are not revelant here since they deal with it in the sense of
truth conditions instead of belief conditions. For example, B. Russell, "On
Denoting," *Mind* 15 (1905); P. Strawson, "On Referring," *Mind* 59, no.
235 (July 1950), and "Identifying Reference and Truth Values," *Theoria,*
vol. 20, pt. 2 (1964); G. Lakoff, "Linguistics and Natural Logic" in *Semantics of Natural Language,* ed. D. Davidson and G. Harmo (Dordrecht:
Riedel, 1972); J. Katz, *Semantic Theory* (New York: Harper & Row, 1972).

The use of 'presupposition' in these articles as truth conditions is a
technical term that does not correspond to its meaning in ordinary
speech, which is why other thinkers have distinguished the ordinary
meaning by other terms. Isabel Hungerland, for instance, has proposed
"contextual implication" in an article by that title (*Inquiry* 4 [1960]:
211–258). Dierdre Wilson has called the technical meaning "logical presupposition" and the ordinary meaning "nonlogical presupposition"
(*Presuppositions and Non-Truth Conditional Semantics,* [New York: Ac-
ademic Press, 1975] 141 ff). It should be clear that the sense of "presupposition" I am using here is the ordinary, or "nonlogical" meaning.

8. Often actions as well as beliefs are spoken of as having presuppositions. This, too, is an elliptical expression which is, strictly speaking, not
accurate. People presuppose; their actions may be *motivated* by what
they presuppose.

9. A more formal statement of the definition is as follows: A person P
who holds a belief X may be said to presuppose another belief Y in relation to X, provided that:

1. X and Y are not identical;
2. in order to believe X, P would have to believe Y on grounds other than X; and
3. P does not deduce X from Y.

Where there are several possible presuppositions to X, Y is their
disjunction.

It should be noticed that although the "have to" in part 2. of the definition has a logical aspect, it is not strictly logical since its violation does
not result in a formal contradiction. To (believingly) assert X and (believingly) assert $\sim Y$, where Y is a presupposition of X, makes that set of
beliefs what I have called "self-assumptively incoherent" rather than self-
contradictory. The relation is a broadly epistemic one, rather than a narrowly logical one.

P. Strawson has also noticed that more than logical rules alone are involved in this sort of incoherence, though he points it out in a discussion

of presuppositions as truth conditions rather than as belief conditions. See his *Introduction to Logical Theory* (London: Methuen, 1967), 175.

10. N. Wolterstorff has coined this expression for the way particular revealed beliefs can regulate theorizing in *Reason Within the Bounds of Religion* (Grand Rapids, Mich.: Eerdmans, 1976).

It is interesting that in this work Wolterstorff starts from what appears to be a generally scholastic orientation, but significantly amends it in the direction I am advocating here. He says, for example, that theorizing must not only be consistent with religious beliefs but also "comport" with them (p. 72), and that their control should be "internal" to the process of theorizing rather than merely serving as external checkpoints (p. 77). But he does not then define "comport" or give an account of what internal versus external control would be. I therefore regard the radically biblical position advocated here (and to be developed in succeeding chapters) as a further exposition of those two concepts.

7. THEORIES IN MATHEMATICS

1. Quoted by E. Cassirer in *The Philosophy of the Enlightenment.* (Boston: Beacon Press, 1961), 237.

2. Dooyeweerd, *New Critique,* vol. I, 223–261.

3. *Collected Works of John Stuart Mill,* ed. Robson and Macrea. (Toronto: University of Toronto Press, 1973), bk. II, chaps. 5 and 6; and bk. III, chap. 24.

4. B. Russell, *Principles of Mathematics* (New York: W. W. Norton 1938) xi.

5. Ibid., 119:

> ... $1 + 1$ is the number of a [logical] class -w- which is the logical sum of two classes -u- and -v- which have no common term and each have only one term. The chief point to be òbserved is that the logical addition of classes is the fundamental notion, while the arithmetical addition of numbers is wholly subsequent.

Formally, Russell's proposal would read:

$$(\exists u)\,(\exists v)\,(\exists w)\,(\{[(u\epsilon w)\cdot(v\epsilon w)]\cdot(u\neq v)\}\cdot(z)\,\{(z\epsilon w) > [(z = u)\lor(z = v)]\}).$$

It is hard to be sympathetic with his claim that no quantitative meaning is involved in this formula when the symbol ϵ means 'is a member of' which is no different from "is *one* member of." Besides, the existential quantifiers all mean "there exists at least *one* x such that...." In both cases the quantity is unavoidably presupposed by the meaning of the formula, even if the formula's variables range over only logical classes.

6. B. Russell, "The Study of Mathematics," reprinted in *Mysticism and Logic* (Garden City, N.Y.: Doubleday Anchor Books), 65.

7. John Dewey, *Reconstruction in Philosophy* (Boston: Beacon Press, 1964), 156.

8. Ibid., 149.

9. Ibid., 137.

10. For the sake of accuracy, it should be noted that the biological perspective is not the final step of Dewey's theory of reality. That is because he viewed the biological aspect as dependent upon (or included in) the physical. So in the final analysis, it is the physical (or the physico-biotic) aspect of creation which he takes to be the basic nature of reality.

11. Morris Kline, *Mathematical Thought from Ancient to Modern Times* (New York: Oxford University Press, 1972), 32.

12. Ibid., 115.

13. Morris Kline, *Mathematics, The Loss of Certainty* (New York: Oxford University Press, 1980), 236.

14. Ibid., 237.

15. Ibid., 233.

16. Ibid., 6.

17. For the sake of accuracy, it should be acknowledged that for Plato the realm of mathematical entities depended, in turn, upon an even higher realm of entities called Forms. Strictly speaking, then, it is the Forms which are divine in Plato's theory.

It should also be noted that many intuitionists, while declaring the independence of the mathematical from the other aspects of experience, still insist that the truths of math are also somehow dependent on the human mind. This is puzzling because it seems to require both that the truths of math reflect something self-existent and that they be dependent.

One way of reconciling this conflict would be to say, with Kronecker, that God created the natural numbers while all the rest is the work of man. But in commenting on Brouwer's version of intuitionism, Karl Popper has offered another interpretation to reconcile this apparent inconsistency. Popper takes Brouwer's theory to require what Popper calls a "third world" of reality which includes (at least) mathematical and linguistic entities. Like Plato, Popper regards this world as self-existent ("ontologically autonomous"). But unlike Plato, he holds it to be a realm of *possibilities* needing human thought for their actualization. Thus there is a sense in which the third world is dependent on human thought even though it is divine in another sense. Popper's position thus reflects a pagan religious belief. See *Objective Knowledge* (Oxford: Clarendon Press, 1972), esp. 128–190.

18. For example, W. V. O. Quine and Nelson Goodman developed a formal calculus of individuals in order to avoid treating predicates as rep-

resenting really existing universals. See chap. 2 of *The Structure of Appearance* (Indianapolis: Bobbs, Merrill, 1966), 33 ff.

19. For more on the difference belief in God can make to theories in math, see Dooyeweerd's *New Critique,* vol. II, 55–93. This view has been given more detailed development by the following thinkers (among others):

D. H. T. Vollenhoven. *De Wijsbegeerte der Wiskunde van Teistische Standpunt* (Amsterdam: Wed G. Van Soest, 1918).

———. *De Noodzakelijkheid eener Christelijke Logica* (Amsterdam: H. J. Paris, 1932).

———. "Problemen en Richtingen in de Wijsbegeerte der Wiskunde," *Philosophia Reformata* 1 (1936).

———. "Hoofdlijnen der Logica," *Philosophia Reformata* 13 (1948).

D. Strauss. "Number Concept and Number Idea," *Philosophia Reformata* 35, no. 3 (1970) and 35, no. 4 (1971).

———. "Infinity," in *Basic Concepts in Philosophy,* ed. Van Straaten (Oxford: Oxford University Press, 1981).

———. "Are the Natural Sciences Free from Philosophical Presuppositions?" *Philosophia Reformata* 46, no. 1 (1981).

A. Tol. "Counting, Number Concept and Numerosity," in *Hearing and Doing: Philosophical Essays Dedicated to Evan Runner,* ed. Kraay (Toronto: Wedge, 1979).

M. D. Stafleu. "Analysis of Time in Modern Physics," *Philosophia Reformata* 35 (1970).

———. "Metric and Measurement in Physics," *Philosophia Reformata* 37 (1972).

———. "The Mathematical and Technical Opening Up of a Field of Science," *Philosophia Reformata* 43 (1978).

———. *Time and Again: A Systematic Analysis of the Foundations of Physics* (Toronto: Wedge, 1980).

8. THEORIES IN PHYSICS

1. A. Aliotta has made this point well:

When ... [Mach] endeavors to build up a new [picture] of the world on the ruins of the mechanical theory, and substitutes the element of sensation for the material atom, he does but replace mechanical by sensorial mythology. The atom was ... an abstraction; what else is the sensorial element? (*The Idealistic Reaction Against Science* [London: McCaskill, 1914], 65)

This is, of course, the same point on which Dooyeweerd's transcendental critique turns, and which I have called the criterion of self-performative coherency. In note 13 to chapter 4, his critique was applied to the theory of Kant, while here Aliotta applies it to both materialism and phenomenalism.

The point is crucial, for each of the views contrasted in this chapter has differences from the others which stem from alternative conceptions of the character of the datum of experience. And each of these conceptions is dogmatic and in violation of the criterion of self-performative coherency. Moreover, it will appear that in each case the dogmatism is born out of a *religious* conviction about what is self-existent.

In chapter 10 the criterion of self-performative coherency will be developed in more detail to show why it must lead to a recognition of the outright artificiality of the abstractive isolation of *any* aspect.

2. From Mach's *The Conservation of Energy* in J. Blackmore's *Ernst Mach* (Berkeley: University of California Press, 1972), 49.

3. Ibid., 34.

4. Ibid., 74.

5. E. Mach, *The Science of Mechanics* (London: Open Court, 1942), 499.

6. E. Mach, *Knowledge and Error,* (Dordrecht: Reidel, 1975), 354, 358.

7. A. Einstein, *Ideas and Opinions* (New York: Bonanza Books, 1954), 290–291.

8. Ibid., 22.

9. Ibid., 23.

10. *Descartes Selections,* ed. R. Eaton (New York: Scribners, 1953), 178.

11. Einstein, *Ideas and Opinions,* 295.

12. W. Heisenberg, *Physics and Philosophy* (New York: Harper, 1958), 70.

13. Ibid., 71–72.

14. Ibid., 74–75.

15. Ibid., 52.

16. Ibid., 145.

17. Philip Morrison, "The Neutrino," *Scientific American* (Jan. 1956): 61.

18. See R. Gale's *Theory of Science* (New York: McGraw Hill, 1979), 278 ff., and Learned and Eichler, "A Deep-Sea Neutrino Telescope," *Scientific American* (Feb. 1981).

19. Mach, *Knowledge and Error,* 441.

20. For a more detailed treatment of the rationalistic basis for Heisenberg's interpretation of the uncertainty relations, see my article, "A Critique of Descartes and Heisenberg," *Philosophia Reformata* (Nov. 1980): 157–177.

21. Heisenberg, *Physics and Philosophy,* 92. See also 144–146.

22. Ibid., 72–73.

23. For a start of an approach to physics which presupposes belief in God by rejecting the deification of any aspect of creation, see Dooyeweerd's *New Critique*, esp. vol. II, 93–106. This approach has been continued by M. Stafleu in *Time and Again* (Toronto: Wedge, 1980).

9. THEORIES IN PSYCHOLOGY

1. Isaacson, Hutt, and Blum, *Psychology: The Science of Behavior* (New York: Harper & Row, 1965), 6.

2. Ibid., 7.

3. Jean Piaget, *Main Trends in Psychology* (New York: Harper Torchbook, 1973).

4. Ibid., 36.

5. J. Watson, *Behaviorism* (New York: W. W. Norton, 1925), 5.

6. Ibid., 6.

7. E. M. Thorndike, *The Elements of Psychology* (New York: A. G. Seiler, 1913), 2.

8. B. F. Skinner, *Science and Human Behavior* (New York: New York Free Press, 1965), 66.

9. Ibid., 62.

10. B. F. Skinner, *Contingencies of Reinforcement—A Theoretical Analysis* (Englewood Cliffs, N.J.: Appleton-Century-Crofts, 1969), 7.

11. "As a result of this major assumption that there is such a thing as consciousness and that we can analyze it by introspection . . . [there is] no way of experimentally attacking and solving psychological problems and standardizing methods" (Watson, *Behaviorism*, 6).

12.

> To what extent is it helpful to be told 'He drinks because he is thirsty'? If to be thirsty means nothing more than to have a tendency to drink, this is mere redundancy. If it means he drinks because of a state of thirst, an inner causal event is invoked. If this state is purely inferential—if no dimensions are assigned to it which would make direct observation possible—it cannot serve as an explanation. [Even] if it has . . . psychic properties, what role can it play in a science of behavior? (Skinner, *Science and Human Behavior*, 33)

13. "Skinner's Utopia: Panacea or Path to Hell?" *Time* (September 20, 1971): 52.

14. Piaget, *Main Trends in Psychology*, 37.

15. Alfred Adler, *Cooperation Between the Sexes: Writings on Women, Love, Marriage, Sexuality and its Disorders*, ed. Ansbacher and Ansbacher (New York: Doubleday, 1978), 305.

16. Ibid., 307.

17. *The Individual Psychology of Alfred Adler*, ed. Ansbacher and Ansbacher (New York: Basic Books, 1956), 207.

304 NOTES TO PAGES 151–158

18. Adler, *Cooperation Between the Sexes,* 305.

19. Alfred Adler, *Understanding Human Nature* (London: George Allen & Unwin, 1974), 47–48.

20. Adler, *Cooperation Between the Sexes,* 176.

21. Alfred Adler, *The Practice and Theory of Individual Psychology* (London: Routledge & Keagan Paul, 1964), 7–8.

22. Adler, *Cooperation Between the Sexes,* 281.

23. Adler, *Understanding Human Nature,* 27–28.

24. Ibid., 31.

25. Ibid., 26–27.

26. Ibid., 32.

27. Alfred Adler, *Superiority and Social Interest,* ed. Ansbacher and Ansbacher (Evanston, Ill.: Northwestern University Press, 1964), 288.

28. Ibid., 295.

29. Adler, *Cooperation Between the Sexes,* 3–4.

30. Ibid., 136–137.

31. Ibid., 135.

32. Ibid., 270.

33. Ibid., 256.

34. Ibid., 270.

35. Ibid.

36. Adler, *Understanding Human Nature,* 80–81.

37. E. Fromm, *The Crisis of Psychoanalysis* (New York: Holt, Rinehart, Winston, 1970), 47.

38. Ibid., 48.

39. Ibid., 52.

40. Ibid., 117.

41. Ibid., 119.

42. Ibid., 121–123.

43. Ibid., 121.

44. Ibid.

45. D. Hausdorff, *Eric Fromm* (New York: Twayne, 1972), 48.

46. Ibid., 90.

47. Ibid.

48. E. Fromm, *The Heart of Man* (New York: Harper & Row, 1964), 117.

49. Ibid., 117–123.

50. E. Fromm, *The Art of Loving* (New York: Harper & Row, 1956), 61ff.

51. In defense of this crucial turning point in his thought, Fromm gives only a short account of the laws of Western logic to be rejected, and a number of illustrations of statements which supposedly contradict each other but are nonetheless both true. But it would be generous to say

Fromm's case is weak. First he manages to misstate the laws of logic, and then it turns out that not one of his examples is actually of mutually contradictory beliefs. They include, for instance, the Taoist saying: "Gravity is the root of lightness" (*The Art of Loving,* p. 63). In this as in his other examples, Fromm mistakes paradoxical or unusual combinations of terms or qualities for actual contradictions.

52. Fromm, *The Art of Loving,* 64.

53. This remains true despite the many biblical elements in Fromm's thought derived from his Jewish heritage, especially his idea of love as the norm for both the individual and society. Cf. Rabbi Jakob Petchowshi's review of *The Art of Loving,* "Eric Fromm's Midrash on Love," *Commentary* 22 (December 1956): 549.

54. Fromm, *The Art of Loving,* 62.

55. Solomon Asch, *Psychology: A Study of a Science,* ed. S. Koch (New York: McGraw Hill, 1959), vol. 3, 367.

56. J. A. Brown, *Freud and the Post-Freudians* (Baltimore: Penguin, 1961), 15.

57. The classic statement of this point is found in the opening of Calvin's *Institutes* (I, 1 & 2) where he says:

> Our wisdom, in so far as it ought to be deemed true and solid wisdom, consists almost entirely of two parts: the knowledge of God and of ourselves. . . .
> On the other hand, it is evident that man never attains to a true self-knowledge until he has previously contemplated the face of God. . . .

58. See, for example Oscar Cullman, *Immortality of the Soul or Resurrection of the Dead?* (New York: MacMillan, 1958) and the more recent and detailed study in John Cooper, *Body, Soul, and Life Everlasting* (Grand Rapids, Mich.: Eerdmans, 1989).

59. Augustine recognized that the biblical use of the term 'soul' was equivalent to "the life of the body" and did not mean human rationality as it did in Plato and other Greek philosophers (*Retractiones* I, xiii).

60. G. Allport, *The Person in Psychology* (Boston: Beacon Press, 1968), 13–14.

61. Dooyeweerd, *New Critique,* vol. I, p. v.

62. H. Dooyeweerd, *In the Twilight of Western Thought* (Philadelphia: Presbyterian & Reformed, 1960), 179–180.

10. THE NEED FOR A NEW BEGINNING

1. The idea that biblical faith should provide a distinctive perspective for the interpretation of the whole of life, though unpopular, is not new. John Calvin held it in opposition to the prevailing scholasticism of the sixteenth century (see *Institutes* II, 2, 16–18), and it was revived in the

work of Abraham Kuyper (1837–1920). It was Kuyper who directly applied this insight to theories:

> Especially the leading thought which we have formed in that realm of life which holds our chiefest interest exercizes mighty domain upon the whole content of our consciousness, viz. our religious views.... If, then, we make a mistake... how can it fail to communicate itself disasterously to our entire scientific study? (*Encyclopedia of Sacred Theology* [New York: Scribners Sons, 1898], 109–110)

This means theories of philosophy as well as science, according to Kuyper:

> [it follows at the same time that the knowledge of the cosmos as a whole... philosophy... is equally bound to founder upon... sin [in the sense of false religious belief]. (Ibid., 113)

This, Kuyper says, is because such knowledge arises in answer to questions which must include

> questions as to the origin and end of the whole... questions as to absolute [nondependent] being.... (Ibid., 113)

For this reason, biblical faith cannot be confined to providing truth about supernature:

> the Holy Scripture does not only cause us to find justification by faith, but also discloses the foundation of all human life... which must govern all human existence. (*Lectures on Calvinism* [Grand Rapids, Mich.: Eerdmans, 1976], vi. These were the Stone Lectures at Princeton for 1898.)

It is this position which is reflected in his most quoted remark:

> There is not a square inch of our whole human existence of which Christ does not say: Mine! (*Souvereiniteit in Eigen Kring* [Amsterdam: J. H. Kruyt, 1880], 5)

This is the tradition given positive development in the philosophy of Herman Dooyeweerd (1894–1977), whose theories are sketched in the next three chapters. Arthur Holmes has summarized Dooyeweerd's approach as follows:

> Reformed theology (of the Protestant tradition from John Calvin) is dissatisfied with the Thomistic doctrine of nature and grace and stresses instead the sovereignty of God over every operation of human nature and the equally pervasive influence of sin. The problem with natural reason, in this view, is not only man's finiteness but—just as profoundly—his sin. It is a sin to assert the autonomy of philosophical reason... and this sin perverts philosophical understanding. Dooyeweerd, accordingly, draws a sharp line between Christian philosophy, which stems from the regenerate heart in obedience to the sovereign God, and all of the other philosophies. ("Christian Philosophy," *Encyclopedia Britannica*, 1974 edition, vol. 4, 555–556)

2. Each of these two strategies for reduction have been developed along the lines of two main subtypes. A fuller description of these is as follows:

1. Strong Reduction

A. *Meaning Replacement.* The nature of reality is exclusively that of aspect *X,* so that all things have only the *X* kind of properties and are governed by only the *X* kind of laws. This is defended by showing that all the *terms* supposed to have non-*X* meaning can be replaced by *X*-terms without loss of meaning, while not all *X*-terms can be replaced by terms with non-*X* meaning. (Berkeley, Hume, and Ayer used this strategy to defend phenomenalism.)

B. *Factual Identity.* The nature of reality is exclusively that of aspect *X,* so that all things have only the *X* kind of properties and are governed by only the *X* kind of laws. This is defended by arguing that although the *meaning* of non-*X* terms cannot be reduced to that of *X*-terms, their *reference* may be to exclusively *X*-things all the same. The selection of the kind(s) of terms that correspond both extensionally and intensionally to the nature of reality is argued on the basis of their explanatory superiority. The argument tries to show that for anything whatever, the only or best explanation is always one whose primitive terms and laws are of the *X* kind. (J. J. C. Smart defended materialism this way.)

2. Weak Reduction

A. *Causal Dependency.* The nature of reality is basically that of aspect *X* (or of aspects *X* and *Y*). It is the *X*ness of things which make possible the other kinds of properties and laws true of them. So while other kinds are real, and can be proper objects of scientific investigation, there is a one-way causal dependency between the non-*X* aspects and aspect *X.* The non-*X* aspects could not exist without *X,* while *X* could exist without the others. (Aristotle and Descartes both defended theories in which certain aspects were the nature of "substance," and all other aspects were accidental or secondary to substance.)

B. *Epiphenomenalism.* This strategy is much like the causal dependency one, except that the non-*X* aspects are thought to be much less real. They exist, but do not have their own laws and are not proper objects of scientific investigation. All genuine explanation must be exclusively in terms of *X*-properties and laws. (Huxley and Skinner argued that states of consciousness are epiphenomena of bodily processes or behavior.)

These strategies can be combined in various ways in the same theory. A thinker could argue, e.g., that some aspects are to be eliminated by meaning identity while others are to be eliminated by factual identity, and at the same time maintain that still others are either causally dependent or epiphenomenal.

The strategies described here are not the only senses of the term 'reduction' as it is used in philosophy, but are the senses being rejected here as religiously objectionable.

3. As a result, scholastic thinkers have traditionally denied the possibility of a distinctively biblical perspective for philosophy that can delimit a range of acceptable hypotheses. For this reason, Jewish and Christian thinkers have advocated theories which see the basic nature of reality as: Aristotelian form-matter substances (Maimonides, Aquinas), logical substances and physical substances (Leibniz), sensory objects and subjects (Berkeley), and basically physical entities (Gassendi), among others.

4. For this reason it is not scholasticism's splitting of the nature of things from what makes them possible that is being objected to here. That is a step in the right direction, and the theory to be proposed in the next chapter will also do it. Rather it is the way the adaptation scheme leaves some aspect(s) of creation in a semi-divine status which is both objectionable and unnecessary. In this connection it is significant John Deck has shown that even Aquinas could not avoid the consequence of having something about creatures be independent of God, owing to his adherence to Aristotle. See "St. Thomas Aquinas and the Language of Total Dependence," *Dialogue: Canadian Philosophical Review—Revue Canadienne de Philosophie* 6 (1967): 74–88. Some theistic thinkers have gone so far in adapting their theories to the pagan tradition that they see nothing wrong with admitting realities other than God to be as fully divine as he, provided God is the only being said to *control* the world. But our definition of religious belief shows that the central issue here is not simply control; it is *monotheism* that is at stake.

5. Barth, *Church Dogmatics* II, 1, 230.

6. In the passages at 2 Timothy and Titus, the Greek text literally says that God's plan was "before time everlasting."

And while one recent translation has rendered the Revelation text as "let there be no more delay" rather than "there shall be no time," I can find no precedent in the Greek language for using the verb ἐστὶν with χρόνος (rather than χαῖρος) to mean "delay." Besides, the common theme of all these passages strongly suggests God's sovereignty over time. Compare also 1 Corinthians 2:7.

7. Compare also 1 Corinthians 15:24–28 and Colossians 1:17. In the latter passage Christ (in his divine nature) is said to be the one on whom "all things" depend, while the former says that in God's final kingdom he will rule all things except for God himself. It seems quite natural to understand "all things" to have the same extension in each case: Christ rules what depends on him. In that case we have the explicit teaching that nothing about creation is uncreated, only God is.

8. My translation here closely follows the Hebrew text rather than the LXX.

9. It is important to keep in mind that something's being created by God means that it depends on him for its existence, not that there would

be a *time* when it came to be. Even if wisdom is everlasting it (and time itself) is still dependent on God.

10. Some recent writers have made this claim. See, e.g., J. Ross, "Analogy as a Rule of Meaning for Religious Language," *International Philosophical Quarterly* 1, no. 3 (Sept. 1971): 476; and J. McQuarrie, *Principles of Christian Systematic Theology* (Chicago University of Chicago Press, 1951), vol. 1, pt. 2, 235ff.

11. The review of these difficulties follows the splendid discussion by Alvin Plantinga in *Does God Have a Nature?* (Milwaukee: Marquette University Press, 1980), esp. 28ff.

12. *Summa Theologica,* la, q. 3 and la, q. 21, a. 1, ad 4. See also his *Summa Contra Gentiles* I, 38, 45, & 73.

13. Plantinga, *Does God Have a Nature?* 47–61.

14. This is the position which Plantinga advocates at the close of *Does God Have a Nature?* But since he continues to hold that God's own properties and the necessities governing creation must be uncreated, he ends only with the *hope* that there may be some way to construe them as dependent on God and not vice versa (145, 146). In defending God's properties as existing necessarily he even says at one point that surely God "has not *acquired* wisdom" (6), even though that is just what Proverbs seems to say. (Cf. chapter 12 of Augustine's *Confessions* where, on the same grounds, he theorizes that there must be an uncreated wisdom of God in addition to the created wisdom of which Proverbs speaks.)

On the unlikelihood of the prospects for construing God's attributes as uncreated yet dependent on him, see Brian Leftow, "God and Abstract Entities," *Faith and Philosophy* 7, no. 2 (April 1990): 193–217.

15. This is also how 2 Peter 1:4 is to be understood. The "divine nature" which it says believers are enabled to share is the nature created and possessed by the One who is divine. It does not mean that creatures will ever come to be uncreated. Our account therefore regards all the properties God shares with creatures in the same way the Athanasian Creed explains the doctrine of the incarnation. It says the unity of God and Christ is not because God "transforms deity into humanity," but "because God has taken humanity into himself."

16. Scripture does say that God cannot lie (Titus 1:2, Heb. 6:18), but these remarks occur in an explicitly covenantal context meaning that he cannot lie to believers because he has promised not to. It should be borne in mind that at other loci Scripture specifically says that God deceives those who are not believers (Ez. 14:9, 1 Thess. 2:11).

17. William Alston has commented insightfully on the range of possibilities for religious language.

But of course there are various ways in which creaturely terms can be used in speaking of God . . . These ways include:

(1) Straight univocity. Ordinary terms are used in the same ordinary senses of God and human beings.

(2) Modified univocity. Meanings can be defined or otherwise established such that terms can be used with those meanings of both God and human beings.

(3) Special literal meanings. Terms can be given, or otherwise take on, special technical senses in which they apply to God.

(4) Analogy. Terms for creatures can be given analogical extensions so as to be applicable to God.

(5) Metaphor. Terms that apply literally to creatures can be metaphorically applied to God.

(6) Symbol. Ditto for "symbol," in one or another meaning of that term.

The most radical partisans of [God's] otherness, from Dionysius through Aquinas to Tillich, plump for something in the (4) to (6) range and explicitly reject (1). The possibility of (3) has been almost wholly ignored, and (2) has not fared much better. (*Divine Nature and Human Language* [Ithaca, N.Y.: Cornell University Press, 1989], 65)

As I understand Alston's breakdown, my proposal corresponds to his (2).

18. *Martin Luther,* ed. John Dillenberger (New York: Doubleday Anchor, 1961), 196.

19. Calvin repeats the same point several times over in the *Institutes* (e.g., I, xiii, 21; I, xvii, 13). Nevertheless, I must hesitate to attribute to him exactly the theory I am proposing because he also says things that are inconsistent with it. For example, he says that we know "not only what God is in himself, but in what character he is pleased to manifest himself" (III, ii, 6). And in other places he speaks as if God accommodated only the language of revelation (I, xvii, 13). This is not my proposal at all, since I deny that—aside from figurative language—what Scripture attributes to God is not literally true of him. My proposal is that God accommodated *himself* so that our language can really describe him.

20. J. Calvin, *Commentary on the First Book of Moses Called Genesis,* (Grand Rapids, Mich.: Baker Book House, 1979) vol. 1, 60. It is significant that Calvin frequently insists God's transcendence means he is not subject to the laws which govern creation. For example: "Not that God should be [regarded as] subject to the law, unless insofar as he is a law unto himself" (*De Aeternal Praedestinatione,* C.R. 36, 36); and "We do not imagine God to be arbitrary [*exlex*]. He is a law to himself. The will of God is . . . the law of all laws" (*Institutes,* III, xiii, 2), Again "It is perverse to measure [the] Divine by the standard of human justice." (*Institutes,* III, xxiv, 17). Dooyeweerd has remarked that with this position Calvin "cut off at the root the interference of speculative metaphysics in the affairs of the Christian religion" by refusing to "elevate human reason to the throne of God" (*New Critique,* I, 93).

Karl Barth has also defended the same point by saying that the idea of God in classical theology

> is made up of a series of . . . attributes which are . . . primarily attributes of the human mind, in which the latter sees its own characteristics . . . transcended in the absolute . . . [But in this way] I never come upon an absolute being confronting and transcendent to me, but only again and again upon my own being. And proving the existence of a being whom I have conjured up by means of my own self-transcendence, I shall again and again succeed only in proving my own existence. (*Church Dogmatics,* vol. III, pt. 1, 360)

In this way, Calvin, Dooyeweerd, and Barth are all in agreement with Pascal's remark that the God of the philosophers is not the biblical creator—the God of Abraham, Isaac, and Jacob.

21. For a more detailed treatment of yet other objections, see my "Religious Language: A New Look at an Old Problem" in *Rationality in the Calvinian Tradition* (Lanham, Md.: University Press of America, 1983), 385–407; and "Divine Accommodation: An Alternative Theory of Religious Language" in the *Tydskrif vir Christelike Wetenscap.* (Bloemfontein: 2de Kwartaal, 1988), 94–127.

22. E.g., Gregory of Nyssa (*Adu Eun.* orat. 12), Hilary (*De Trin.* 1, 19, iv, 2), Thomas Aquinas (*Summa Contra Gentiles* I, 30), and John Calvin (*Institutes* I, vii, 4 & 5; I, xiii, 1; I xiv, 1).

23. E.g., see Plantinga, *Does God Have a Nature?* 95ff.

24. There is another fault with the criticisms which take the form of asking "Could God do *X?*" where *X* is some patent absurdity. This is that the "could" in the question must mean (minimally) "is it logically possible that?" Thus the question amounts to asking whether it is logically possible that God do something logically impossible.

If such a question is asked of the acts God performs in his accommodation to us, acts which take place within creation, then the answer is that these must all conform to laws of creation to be recognized and known by us as acts at all. But if the question is asked of God's bringing into existence or sustaining of creatures other than himself, then one of its presuppositions is that the laws of logic hold for God and his creating. But that begs the issue. If God has brought into existence all the laws of creation, then those laws cannot have governed his creation of them. God does not create within the limits of what is possible, but has created the laws which determine what is possible within creation. *God created laws of possibility in every aspectual sense that holds for creatures, including logical possibility, and it is these which set the limits of what we can conceive.*

On the other hand, the question could be intended to ask whether in some transcendental (aspectually unspecifiable) sense of "could" God might have made the laws of possibility other than what they are. In that

case, of course, the answer is "yes." There are no limits we can know
which hold for the being of God or his creating, precisely because all the
limits—along with the beings to which they apply—depend on God for
their existence. So even this answer must be given with the recognition
that the laws he has in fact set over creation do now govern us and what
we can conceive.

As a result, we can have no conception of what a creation governed by
other laws would be like. Thus every suggested absurdity this may be accused of generating will fail to be a genuine example of what creation
would be like if the laws were different just because we can conceive of
that suggested absurdity.

For the same reasons, God's self-existence is not to be identified with
his being logically necessary. The logical necessity of anything is a consequence of its being governed by logical laws, which are not themselves
divine and so do not govern the being of God. This is why *whatever can
be proven would thereby not be God.* Nor is God to be thought of as existing in all possible worlds. There is no absolute, uncreated environment
of logical possibility in which God exists. Logical possibility is a constituent part of the law-side of creation and—aside from God's accommodation to it—is only rightly applied to existing creatures as limits upon
what they may do, or cause, or undergo.

As an extension of the last point, we contend that the mere logical possibility of a concept is not sufficient to show the real possibility of what
is conceived. Real possibility is always determined by the co-sovereignty
of all the aspectual kinds of possibility. (Real possibility corresponds with
the idea of a "type law" to be introduced in the radically biblical theory
of reality sketched in the succeeding chapters.)

For a closely reasoned defense of these points, see the important articles of James Ross, "God, Creator of Kinds and Possibilities: *Requiescant
universalia ante res*" in *Rationality, Religious Belief, & Moral Commit-
ment* (Ithaca, N.Y.: Cornell University Press, 1986), 315ff; and "The Crash
of Modal Metaphysics," *Review of Metaphysics* 43, no. 2 (Dec. 1989).

25. It might also be objected here that our criteria of coherency will
themselves fail to be religiously neutral if our central thesis is correct.
Doesn't that then undermine their force with respect to those who do
not believe in God? Doesn't it require that they somehow beg the question against reduction theories?

The answer is that they are, indeed, not religiously neutral. But the
sense in which they are affected by religious belief is that they are among
the states of affairs made *more likely to be noticed* if one starts from belief in God and the nondivinity of any aspect of creation. But since the
criteria are not themselves *hypotheses* whose entire plausibility depends
on adopting a particular perspective, I do not think their force is under-

mined any more than the force of logical rules is undermined by the fact that thinkers have differing philosophical explanations of their status.

26. The same criticism applies equally to all the rest of the host of Plato's abstractions. Whether it is entire aspects which are proclaimed self-existent, or single perfections, it is precisely their ability to exist independently of all else that cannot be conceived.

Far from being the obvious or "natural" way to think of abstractions, the belief in their self-existence is a learned faith at odds with biblical faith.

27. In this connection I have often recalled the candor of Paul Ziff's remarks in a lecture he gave in 1962 at the University of Pennsylvania. Speaking of why he is a materialist Ziff said, "If you ask me why I'm a materialist I'm not sure what to say. It's not because of the arguments. I guess I'd just have to say *the world looks irresistibly physical to me.*"

11. A THEORY OF REALITY

1. The law framework theory presented here is a summary of the theory first developed by Herman Dooyeweerd in his *Wijsbegeerte de Wetsidee* (Amsterdam, 1935), and later expanded in the *New Critique,* especially in volume III.

2. Despite the openness of this list to revision, I find it to have been convincingly defended by Dooyeweerd. See *New Critique,* vol. II, 79–163.

3. T. Dantzig, *Number: The Language of Science* (Garden City, N.Y.: Doubleday, 1954), 2–3.

4. See Dooyeweerd, *New Critique,* vol. II, 93–106; and M. D. Stafleu, *Time and Again* (Toronto: Wedge, 1980), 80ff.

5. The exact order of preconditionality is as open to revision as are the members of the list and some advocates of the law framework theory have proposed alternatives. The theory being sketched here would need modification were the list or its order different, but it would not be affected in its essentials. Whatever aspects are taken as genuine would still be regarded as directly dependent on God, equally real, and mutually irreducible.

6. Some of the consequences of this part of the law framework theory have been developed with respect to a theory of universals by Hendrick Hart, *Understanding Our World* (Lantham, Md.: University Press of America, 1984).

7. Two observations seem in order here: (A) Recent research suggests that certain animals may also have limited logical or linguistic active functions. See "Conversations with a Gorilla," Francine Patterson, *National Geographic* (October 1978). (B) There is good reason to suppose

that single-celled organisms should not be classified as either plants or animals. See Uko Zylstra's "Dooyeweerd's Concept of Classification in Biology," in *Life is Religion*, ed. H. Vander Goot (St. Catherines, Ontario: Paideia Press: 1981), 239–248.

8. The fact that humans have an active function in every aspect is not, however, their only difference from other creatures. As was mentioned in chapter 9, the identity of each human is centered in the self which Scripture calls the heart or soul, which is the root of all human aspectual functions and the seat of consciousness and can survive the death of the body (Prov. 4:23; Ps. 22:26).

Our theory infers from these points that the heart has a "prefunctional" side which is not exhausted by its temporal functions under aspectual laws. This has two important consequences: (1) it allows for genuine human freedom in thought and action relative to the laws of each aspect. Humans are limited by what is possible and impossible under aspectual laws, but are not determined by them; (2) the essentially religious character of the human heart is not identical with its function in the fiduciary aspect of trust or faith, the heart's religious character lies in its innate pre-functional disposition to understand itself (and everything else) in the light of whatever it believes to be divine.

9. Our ordinary use of the term 'cause' often fails to correspond to the way it is used in science and philosophy. We normally speak of one event causing another even though it is not both a necessary and sufficient condition for the other, which is what is usually sought in science.

Andre Troost has given a good example of how events qualified by different aspects are ordinarily spoken of as causes of each other, but are not causes in the sense of being both necessary and sufficient conditions. Suppose a violinist cuts her finger at dinner. In the ordinary sense of "cause," we could say that the (physical) cut caused her (sensory) pain, which caused her to (aesthetically) ruin a concert, which caused her to be (legally) fired, which caused some (unethical) swearing on her part. But in each case, the preceeding event was only a sufficient precondition for its successor, lacking any necessary connection to it. Each of these preconditions could have occurred without the ensuing result.

10. Despite this emphasis it would be inaccurate to call this a *theory* of naive realism. "Naive experience" is experience as we have it prior to breaking it up by high abstraction and so is not a theory at all. The upshot of our critique is to show that theories of reality must leave naive experience intact or be guilty of serious incoherency. Philosophy must explain naive experience, not explain it away.

11. This point was supported earlier by our "experiment in thought" argument (in connection with self-performative coherency), but it can also be supported by an analysis of the fundamental concepts in each aspect. Dooyeweerd has shown in detail how these concepts exhibit ele-

ments of meaning drawn from all the other aspects. See *New Critique,* vol. II, 55–180; also the monograph *De Analogische grondbegrippen der vakwetenschappen en hun betrekking tot de structuur van de menselijken ervaringshorizon* (Amsterdam: Noord-Hollandsche Uigevers Maatscappij, 1954) (unpublished translation by Robert Knudsen).

12. Dooyeweerd, *New Critique,* vol. III, 53–253.

13. What I have here termed "type laws," Dooyeweerd called "individuality structures" which he described as making possible "the typical arrangement of the... aspects within a structural whole." I have altered the expression because "individuality structure" has been so often misunderstood to refer to the factual organization of particular individuals, rather than to the *laws* which make *types* of individuals possible.

14. Speaking of a thing as the "individual structural assemblage of all its properties" is not intended to slight the fact that things are constructed of parts. Rather, it reflects the lesson of modern philosophy that the continued analysis of parts ends in the analysis of properties. Our difference from the ways that lesson has been carried out in nonbiblically based theories is that while they have insisted on looking for the one or two property kinds which make all others possible or into which all others are resolvable, we contend that no aspect plays either role.

15. This point corresponds to the one made in note 24 in chapter 10. It is the type laws in conjunction with aspectual laws that determine what things are really possible, and no merely aspectual possibility can do that alone—not even logical possibility as has so often been assumed (e.g., Leibniz, "Meditations on Knowledge, Truth, and Ideas" and "On the Method of Distinguishing Real from Imaginary Phenomena"). The mere absence of logical contradiction from a concept does not show it corresponds to a real entity or state of affairs. For example, a square circle can be defined as an enclosed plane figure with four equal sides and four equal interior angles whose circumference is at every point equidistant from its center. There is no strictly logical incoherence in such a definition; its incoherence lies in the spatial incompatibilities it asserts, which cannot be discovered by logic alone. Or consider Leibniz's conclusion that there is no real limit to velocity because there is no logical limit to conceiving an increase over any speed whatever. The lack of a logically conceptual limit does not prevent there being a real *physical* limit to velocity as has been shown by relativity physics.

Thus the fact that it is possible for us to form the concept of a talking rock does not mean such things really are possible. To say the concept is logically possible means only that it can be thought without contradiction; but while the concept is possible, the thing is not. Again, see the two articles cited earlier by James Ross, "God the Creator of Kinds and Possibilities" and "The Crash of Modal Metaphysics."

It should be noted, however, that while arguing against the (Platonistic) idea that logical possibility is self-existent and equivalent to real possibility, Ross sometimes does so from the (Aristotelian) idea that possibility depends on the natures of real beings. In "The Crash of Modal Metaphysics," for example, he says that possibilities are the "logical auras" of the natures of real beings (264). By contrast, the law framework theory holds that both real beings and the aspectual laws determining what is possible for them exist in mutual correlation. Neither causes the other, but both depend on God.

12. A BIBLICAL THEORY OF SOCIETY

1. This is a continuation of the point made in chapter 10 about the difference between the biblical idea of perfection and the idea of perfection derived from ancient Greek philosophy. There our reason for rejecting the traditional doctrine of God's perfections was that the idea it employed is clearly the pagan Greek idea and not the biblical one.

2. The best known objectivist theories, like those of Plato and Aristotle, have tried to get around this difficulty by regarding the nature of anything capable of violating a norm as strongly dualistic. In that way the ability to act contrary to a norm is explained by saying that the normative order is intrinsic to one side of the duality but disobeyed by the other side. The problem with this is that the two sides of the duality are then mutually contrary as to their distinct natures so that it is impossible to explain how they could combine into a union, let alone into an individual unity. Cf. Dooyeweerd's criticism in the *New Critique,* vol. III, 10–18.

3. I say "usually" because the theory of Thomas Hobbes is a notable exception. Hobbes started with an individualist position, but then argued that the best state people can make is one that allows no limits to its authority, leaving citizens no rights save self-preservation. Needless to say, his argument for this is unconvincing.

4. Some Thomist thinkers have referred to what I am calling a "hierarchical" view of society as the "subsidiary" view. See, e.g., Yves Simon, *Philosophy of Democracy* (Chicago: University of Chicago Press, 1951), and his *A General Theory of Authority* (Notre Dame, Ind.: University of Notre Dame Press, 1962). As will soon become apparent, our theory rejects the hierarchical view with the exception of those auxiliary communities formed expressly to support and serve another—e.g., an organization formed to raise money for a school or an orchestra.

5. Dooyeweerd also calls whole-whole relations "enkaptic relations" (*New Critique,* vol. III, 627–784). I think it confusing, however, to use the same term for both whole-whole relations in which neither is a subwhole to the other as well as for relations in which one is a subwhole to

the other. So I have introduced the expression 'whole-whole' for the first and retained 'encapsulate' only for the second.

6. Aristotle, *Metaphysics* bk. Z, 1043a.

7. This concept was first given systematic elaboration in social theory by Abraham Kuyper, who coined the term 'sphere sovereignty'. See his Stone Lectures given at Princeton, titled *Calvinism* (Grand Rapids, Mich.: Eerdmans, 1976). In this connection it is important to notice that while the sphere sovereignty theory explains the natures of social communities in terms of their qualifying aspects, this is not to be confused with the notion that once a community is formed it has proprietary rights over the aspect qualifying its leading function. Businesses do not have sole say in economic matters any more than it is only the state which is concerned with justice or only schools that may educate. The social spheres are constantly participated in by all people and all communities.

8. Dooyeweerd points out that the failure to develop differentiated communities corresponding to the distinct social concerns of life is the hallmark of primitive societies. In them there is usually a single community, such as an extended family or tribe, which is the sole curator of all social interests. He gives an account of how the lack of differentiation has been overcome in history, and of how the process is controlled by religious belief. See *New Critique*, vol. II, 68–72 and 192ff (esp. 298–330).

9. Though the state is qualified by its justitial leading function, it is further limited by having *public* justice, rather than every sort of justice, as its structural purpose. Its duty of enforcement does not, therefore, extend to such things as countermanding parents' ideas of the proper bedtime for their children, or a church's rules about who may participate in its sacraments, etc., even if those ideas really are unjust. This will become clearer when the type law for the state is explicated in the next chapter.

10. Dooyeweerd offers and extensive critique of a number of major social theories to establish this point. See the *New Critique*, vol. III, 198–261.

11. See Calvin's remarks in the *Institutes* III, ix, 6.

12. The classic case for freedom of speech and press was made by the Calvinist John Milton in his essay "Areopagitica" (1644).

13. In most societies the linguistic aspect lacks any community specifically devoted to it, so I have not included the linguistic aspect as a segment of the diagram. The only exception I know to this is the Bureau Française which attempts to regulate the French language.

13. A BIBLICAL THEORY OF THE STATE

1. Dooyeweerd, *New Critique*, vol. III, 380.

2. Cf. Calvin's remarkable comment in the *Institutes,* II, 2, 16.

3. The historical process by which states arose and assumed differing forms is another side to their variation. That side is accounted for by Dooyeweerd's analysis of the historical "opening process" of social communities alluded to in an earlier note. See the *New Critique,* vol. II, 181–192, 335–365.

4. This contrast is drawn, of course, with the treatment of adults in mind. Parents are often obliged to use force to restrain young children as when a toddler is put in a playpen or a child is punished. However, the state has a duty to protect children from abuses of parental force.

5. Augustine, *The City of God,* bk. 19, 12–17. Dooyeweerd himself also held this view in *The Christian Idea of the State* (Nutley, N.J.: Craig Press, 1968), 40. There he specifically sides with Augustine against Aquinas who held (as I do) that it is only the state's need for military power which is the result of sin. In the *New Critique,* vol. III, 423, however, he has altered his view and agrees with Aquinas.

6. James Skillen, "The Bible, Politics, and Democracy," paper delivered in a conference sponsored by the Centre for Religion and Society of the Rockford Institute, Wheaton, Ill., November 1985, p. 6.

7. We often overlook the fact that the exercise of force need not be violent or threaten violence. The erection of a toll gate or the placing of a temporary barrier across a street are also forms of force. So is the padlocking of a confiscated property or the attachment of wages. Cf. N. K. Smith, "The Moral Sanction of Force," *The Credibility of Divine Existence* (New York: St. Martin's Press, 1967), 214ff.

8. This is not to suggest that the state can *never* be the injured party. In such cases as treason, theft of state property, or tax evasion, it clearly is.

9. It is fascinating to notice how the individualism of the Declaration gives way to a collectivism of majority rule in the American Constitution. For where the Declaration speaks of "*inalienable* rights," the rights mentioned in the Constitution are all *amendments* which can be repealed by vote of the Congress or the states. Thus, there is not a single inalienable right guaranteed by the Constitution.

10. Jefferson had originally proposed the wording: "We hold these truths to be sacred and undeniable." Franklin thought that sounded too religious and talked him into substituting the more rationalistic phrase: "We hold these truths to be self-evident."

Nevertheless, there had been a strong connection made between the self-evidency and religious truth among the Puritans who, (prior to Locke) had also connected biblical teaching to the idea of limited government. It was a combination of Locke's theory with the older Puritan heritage that was advocated by the colonists. See Staughton Lynd, *Intellectual Origins of American Radicalism* (New York: Pantheon, 1968), 20, 24–31.

11. Jefferson does refer to the "Laws of Nature and Nature's God" in the opening paragraph. However, he does not specifically connect this allusion to his point about individual rights, but only to the "separate but equal station" to which the United States is entitled among nations. Many subsequent discussions of rights follow his lead in failing to connect rights to norms.

12. For example: Mary Warren, "On the Moral and Legal Status of Abortion," *Monist* 57, no. 1 (Jan. 1973): 55; and Michael Tooley, "Abortion and Infanticide," *Philosophy and Public Affairs* 2 (1971).

13. Thomas Hayes, "A Biological View," *Commonweal* 85 (March 1967): 677–678.

14. It is interesting in this connection that other writers have tried to avoid these consequences by basing rights on the ability of a being to *feel* rather than to *think*. Thus they have taken the position that animals also have rights.

On the law framework account of a right, this basis for rights is still too tied to the subjective condition of the beings in question, and thus still too limited. On our view, not only animals, but the whole of inanimate creation has rights. This is because humans have justitial (and ethical) obligations not only to other humans, but to the whole of creation. We have been charged with caring for, and improving on, creation because it has been entrusted to our care by God its owner.

15. It is a source of great confusion that most discussions of what is called "ethics" fail to distinguish adequately between the ethical aspect and the justitial aspect. Frequently the issues of justice which are not of a *public* character, and are therefore not matters about which the state should enact laws, are called "ethical" issues even though they are about obligations of justice rather than love.

16. According to the individualist tradition of the United States only individual persons had rights, so the law was forced to invent the fiction that corporations are persons in order to give them legal standing before the courts. The inadequacy of that view has come to be recognized in this country, especially since the work of Hohfeld. Courts cannot adequately provide legal remedies on the assumption that only individuals have rights as is shown by cases such as class actions and others involving non-Hohfeldian parties. See Cover, Fiss, and Resnik, *Procedure* (New York: Westbury, 1988).

17. See the comments of Bob Goudzwaard in *Capitalism and Progress* (Grand Rapids, Mich.: Eerdmans, 1979), 110–113.

18. James Skillen has put this part of the theory very well in his article "Going Beyond Liberalism to Christian Social Philosophy" in *Christian Scholar's Review* 19, no. 3 (March 1990). Skillen emphasizes that the law framework theory's insistence on government even-handedness toward all is not a concession to relativism. Instead, it is a point of *justice* whose

biblical basis is this: God is longsuffering and patient until the final judgment.... [This is] a testimony not to God's relativistic nonchalance about
sin but rather his mercy and grace. If God is patient ... then we, too, must
be the same....

If government restrains itself from forcing all citizens to confess one faith,
or forcing all parents to send their children to a single school system, or
forcing all friendships to meet the same sexual behavior patterns, it does
not thereby act as a relativist.... Government fulfills its duties before God
when it seeks to advance public justice which includes full protection of
the confessional rights of those non-political, non-governmental institutions
and relationships which must be free to obey or disobey God's laws in their
own realms.

19. In November 1986, Japanese Prime Minister, Yasuhiro Nakasone,
commented publicly that the United States was suffering a national decline because it was allowing its population to be diluted with a mixture
of races.

20. For example, the course materials provided by the state of
Pennsylvania for the driver's education course I took explicitly made
this claim.

21. On the sphere sovereignty view, it is the duty of the state to protect such freedoms. Thus, while we do not have a *right* to marry or do
business (no one violates our rights who refuses to marry us or do business with us), we have the *right to be free* to marry or to do business.

22. Cf. the remarks of Otto Von Bismarck justifying his editing of the
Ems telegram in order to incite the Franco-Prussian war (*Bismarck. The
Man and the Statesman: Being the Reminiscences of Otto, Prince of Bismarck,* trans. A. J. Butler, [New York: Harper & Row, 1899], vol. II,
97–101).

23. The current problems with the U.S. social security system are not
the fault of the idea itself, but have come about because the social security fund was raided to help pay for World War II. Had the fund remained
untouched, as was originally promised, there would now be no crisis
over how it can meet future payouts.

24. On the issue of government's role in education, see R. McCarthy et
al., *Society, State, and Schools* (Grand Rapids, Mich.: Eerdmans, 1981),
and McCarthy, Skillen and Harper, *Disestablishment a Second Time:
Genuine Pluralism for America's Schools* (Grand Rapids, Mich.: Christian University Press and Eerdmans, 1982).

On the issue of how elections are conducted for the House, see *Justice
for Representation,* a position paper of the Association for Public Justice,
Washington, D.C., by James Skillen, the Association's Research Director.
The APJ is devoted to educating people to the connection between biblical faith and politics via the law framework theory.

On the issue of poverty and welfare, see *Thine is the Kingdom* (Grand Rapids, Mich.: Eerdmans, 1984), esp. pp. 90–113.

On economic justice more generally, see Bob Goudzwaard, *Capitalism and Progress,* trans. and ed. Josina Zylstra (Toronto and Grand Rapids, Mich.: Wedgewood and Eerdmans, 1979), and Alan Storkey, *Transforming Economics: A Christian Way to Employment* (London: SPCK, 1986).

On environmental issues, see *Tending the Garden,* ed. Wesley Grandberg-Michaelson (Grand Rapids, Mich.: Eerdmans, 1987).

On human rights issues, see Johan Van Der Vyver, *Seven Lectures on Human Rights* (Capetown: Juta, 1976), and Max Stackhouse, *Creeds, Society, and Human Rights: A Study in Three Cultures* (Grand Rapids, Mich.: Eerdmans, 1984).

25. For example, James Olthuis's excellent works on marriage and family: *I Pledge You My Troth* (New York: Harper & Row, 1975) and *Keeping Our Troth* (San Francisco, Harper & Row, 1986).

INDEX